BYRON AND THE HONOURABLE AUGUSTA LEIGH

BYRON
AND THE HONOURABLE
AUGUSTA LEIGH

JOHN S. CHAPMAN

NEW HAVEN AND LONDON
YALE UNIVERSITY PRESS
1975

Designed by Sally Sullivan
and set in Granjon type.
Printed in the United States of America by
Vail-Ballou Press, Inc., Binghamton, N.Y.

Published in Great Britain, Europe, and Africa by
Yale University Press, Ltd., London.
Distributed in Latin America by Kaiman & Polon,
Inc., New York City; in India by UBS Publishers'
Distributors Pvt., Ltd., Delhi; in Japan by
John Weatherhill, Inc., Tokyo.

*To that amiable
and most gracious lady
Mae*

CONTENTS

PREFACE

This study is not another biography of Byron but an attempt to examine narrowly the evidence both for and against his supposed incest with his half sister, the Honourable Mrs. Augusta Leigh. In a way it is a kind of detective story. Much of the evidence would not be admissible in a court of law, but enough remains to allow tentative conclusions or perhaps to render less persuasive some interpretations others have offered. (See below, note 7 on pages 245-47.)

For the benefit of readers unfamiliar with details of Byron's life or the milieu, social, intellectual, and moral, in which he lived, there is a section of antecedent action, a who was who, and a calendar of principal dates. And because people have a quite reasonable interest in denouements there is a sequel.

Most of the material from which this work is drawn consists of secondary sources. As the notes will indicate, Thomas Moore's *Life and Letters of Lord Byron,* Prothero's *The Works of Lord Byron,* and John Murray's *Lord Byron's Correspondence* have constituted the chief sources from which Byron's own record of events has been taken. Professor Marchand's volume, *"Alas! The Love of Women!",* the third in his definitive edition of Byron's letters, did not become available in time for consideration. But probably the most significant of Byron's own statements have already appeared in full.

Correspondents who have been most helpful and generous of

their information include the Reverend Derek D. Billings, present Vicar of Bottisham, who supplied a true copy of Medora's baptismal record; Mr. Paul Sykes, lately Librarian of the City of Nottingham Public Libraries, and hence custodian of the various collections at Newstead; Dr. Vera Cacciatora, Curator of the Keats-Shelle Museum at Rome; Mr. Ian G. I. Fraser of the British Council at Athens; Leggatt's and Christie's, both of which London firms assigned staff members to reply to queries.

Miss Frieda Wilkins, Archivist of the City of Nottingham Public Libraries, most generously provided transportation and allowed access to the storage rooms at Newstead Abbey. Especially to Lt. Col. and Mrs. R. Geoffrey Byron I wish to recognize my obligations for repeated courtesies, warm hospitality under rather trying conditions, and free opportunity to examine seals and paintings in their collection.

To a friend of many years, Professor J. Lon Tinkle of Southern Methodist University, warm thanks are due for his original reading and appraisal of this work, and particularly for his gracious assistance in placing the book. For their hard work at the purely mechanical task of getting all this typed up, my thanks are due to my secretary, Mrs. Marguerite Ray, to Mr. and Mrs. Frederick D. Hamilton, and especially to Mrs. Frances Beresford Bearden, who made the final draft. In spite of all these obligations, this would probably never have become a book without the devoted editorship of Mrs. Ellen Graham.

WHO WAS WHO
IN BYRON'S ENGLAND

ANNESLEY, LADY CATHERINE: The sister of Lady Frances Webster, a member of the house party at Aston in October 1813.
Byron seems to have found her physically rather attractive
but, he suspected, "méchante."

BESSBOROUGH, LADY: Mother of Lady Caroline Lamb, sister of
"the beautiful Duchess" of Devonshire, and sometime mistress of Granville. To Byron she was preeminently "Lady
Blarney."

BURDETT, SIR FRANCIS: A baronet and Radical Whig, who was
M.P. for Westminster. He married one of the daughters of
Thomas Coutts, a very wealthy banker. Though he and
Byron shared somewhat similar political views they seem not
to have been close associates, except inasmuch as Hobhouse,
who was much attached to Sir Francis, brought them together. Burdett served as Byron's representative in business
affairs related to the Noel estate.

BYRON, ADA: Byron's daughter by Lady Byron. In later years she
married Lord King, who became the first Earl of Lovelace,
and their son in turn assembled the material that was published as *Astarte*.

BYRON, CAPTAIN GEORGE ANSON: A first cousin of the poet and
subsequently seventh Lord Byron. His title of "Captain"
derived from the Navy. On earlier acquaintance the poet

apparently approved of his heir, but Captain Byron's behavior during the separation gained the pronounced distaste
of his cousin.

BYRON, ADMIRAL JOHN: Brother of the fifth, "the wicked Lord"
Byron, and notable for rather consistently bad luck at sea.
Through a series of his descendants the title has come down
to the present and eleventh Lord Byron.

BYRON, CAPTAIN JOHN: Byron's father, known as "Mad Jack," a
son of the Admiral.

CARLISLE, EARL OF: A Tory minister and great favorite of George
III. He married a cousin of Captain John Byron and was
appointed Byron's guardian. Augusta spent much of her
youth in his household and remained on very intimate terms
with his daughters, who eventually became the Duchess of
Rutland, Lady Cawdor, and Lady Gertrude Sloane.

CAROLINE, PRINCESS: Wife of the Prince of Wales, who subsequently became George IV (q.v.). But Princess Caroline, in
a celebrated trial, was so much maligned (or else so much
of the truth about her appeared) that she did not accede as
Queen.

CHARLEMONT, LADY: Wife of one of the Irish peers, a Whig bluestocking, and evidently a very beautiful one. Tom Moore
was a familiar in her household and probably was responsible for Byron's introduction to her.

CHARLOTTE, PRINCESS: Daughter of the Prince of Wales and Princess Caroline. Her mother seems to have encouraged her in
what were for the time and her position escapades. As Heiress Presumptive after her father, Princess Charlotte unavoid-
ably attracted major political interest and her activities acquired national importance.

CHARLOTTE, QUEEN: Wife of George III.

CHICHESTER, COUNTESS OF: Daughter of the Marquess and Marchioness of Carmarthen and therefore half sister to Augusta

on the maternal side, since it was her mother who eloped with and eventually married Captain John Byron.

COWPER, EMILY, COUNTESS: Daughter of Lord and Lady Melbourne. She was a patroness of Almack's, the exclusive club, and was at the top of London fashion. Following the death of her first husband, she became the wife of the famous Lord Palmerston.

DALLAS, ROBERT CHARLES: A distant relative and toady of the poet. A minor Grub Street type, he was the beneficiary of many of Byron's copyrights and rushed out a "Life" within a year or so of his benefactor's death, much to the irritation of quite a number of the poet's friends.

DAVIES, SCROPE BERDMORE: A friend of Byron at Cambridge. He became a Fellow of the University, but his passion for gambling kept him in London much of the time and eventually led to his ruin.

ELPHINSTONE, MISS MERCER: The daughter of Admiral Lord Keith. She was something of a savante as well as being attractive and very rich. Though much sought in marriage she remained single until 1817, when she married the Comte de Flahaut. It is probable that she and Byron engaged in a little mild flirtation.

FORBES, LADY ADELAIDE: Daughter of Lord Granard. For a brief time Byron considered her as matrimonial prospect, chiefly at the urging of Tom Moore, but Lady Adelaide's sister, Lady Rancliffe, took a rather unfavorable view, and Byron withdrew.

GEORGE IV: Eldest son of George III. As such he naturally acquired the title Prince of Wales. He was intermittently Prince Regent, during the various incapacities of his father.

GLENBERVIE, SYLVESTER DOUGLAS, EARL OF: Glenbervie was one of the upper echelon of civil servants who never quite made it to minister, but really kept the machinery of government in motion. Considerably older than Byron, he seems to have encountered the poet at rare intervals, but Glenbervie was something of a gossip and has left some interesting recollections of his long life.

HANSON, JOHN: Byron's solicitor. During the poet's youth he served somewhat *in loco parentis* and in spite of his exceptionally poor performance the poet continued to respect him.

HEATHCOTE, LADY: Wife of Sir Gilbert Heathcote and a Whig hostess of about the second rank.

HOBHOUSE, JOHN CAM: Later Lord Broughton, one of Byron's closest friends from university days, companion during the first year of his pilgrimage to the East, a Horatio to the poet's Hamlet.

HODGSON, THE REVEREND FRANCIS: A friend of Byron from school and university. The friendship was a close and lasting one, not altogether to the detriment of the minister.

HOLDERNESS, LADY: Mother of the Marchioness of Carmarthen and therefore Augusta's grandmother.

JERSEY, LADY: One of the patronesses of Almack's and a supreme leader of Whig society. She took an early interest in Byron and remained one of his consistent supporters throughout the trouble.

KINNAIRD, DOUGLAS: A friend from Cambridge who served Byron as banker and in the poet's later years took over the management of all his affairs. They were also closely associated at Drury Lane.

LAMB, GEORGE: Son of Lady Melbourne and brother of William. He married Caroline St. Jules, the "other Caro," who seems to have been as much a tribulation to the family as Lady Caroline.

LAMB, WILLIAM: Subsequently Viscount Melbourne and prime minister in the early years of Queen Victoria. His only distinction during the period of interest here was that he was the husband of Lady Caroline.

LEEDS, DUKE OF: Half brother on the maternal side to Augusta. There is little evidence to suggest he played any part in any of the main events of this story.

MELBOURNE, LADY: Byron's great friend and confidante. In her late fifties when they met, she was still a charming and attractive woman.

MILBANKE, ANNA ISABELLA: The lady who became Lady Byron. Known also as Annabella and to Byron as "Bell," she was singularly unsuited to become the wife of the poet.

MILBANKE, SIR RALPH AND LADY: Parents of Anna Isabella, their only child. Sir Ralph was the brother of Lady Melbourne, but was a rather dull and stupefying type. Lady Milbanke, from whose family came the Noel name and fortune, was particularly active in promoting the separation.

MOORE, THOMAS: Irish poet, probably best known as author of *Lalla Rookh*. After a rather poor beginning, he eventually became Byron's closest literary friend and subsequently literary executor and biographer.

OSSULSTONE, LADY: Born Corisande de Gramont, brought to England in early childhood to escape the Terror. In society she ranked clearly in the second echelon.

OXFORD, LADY: A celebrated beauty who was beginning to fade a little by the time of Byron's attachment. She was an intimate of Caroline, Princess of Wales, and seems to have played a considerable role in the more surreptitious political maneuvers of the period.

RANCLIFFE, LADY: One of the secondary leaders of Whig society. The Rancliffes were particularly associated with Tom Moore, through whom Byron became acquainted with them.

RUTLAND, DUKE OF: Courtier and great favorite of the Regent.

The Duchess, daughter of Lord Carlisle, may have been
Augusta's hostess when she came up to London in June 1813.

SHELLEY, LADY FRANCES: Wife of the baronet and sportsman, Sir
John Shelley, a distant relative of the poet. Lady Frances and
Sir John appear to have been Tories and were on excellent
terms with the Duke of Wellington—there was even a trace
of scandal—and with the Duke of Rutland.

SLOANE, LADY GERTRUDE: One of the daughters of the Earl of
Carlisle, guardian of Byron. Lady Caroline Lamb referred
to her as Lady Gertrude Stanley, and it is not certain which
form is correct. Her husband, William Sloane Stanley, was
a member of the landed gentry.

VILLIERS, MRS. THERESA: Wife of a minor functionary who was
dismissed from his post about the time Colonel Leigh retired. Theresa and Augusta apparently had been friends for
a good many years.

WEBSTER, LADY FRANCES: Wife of James Wedderburn Webster
and sister of Lady Catherine Annesley. Lady Frances was
Byron's hostess at the house party at Aston in the autumn
of 1813.

WEBSTER, JAMES WEDDERBURN: A friend of Byron from the university. Webster served for a time in the 10th Hussars and
fancied himself a great beau.

WALES, PRINCE AND PRINCESS OF. See George IV and Princess
Caroline.

WILMOT, ROBERT JOHN: One of Byron's cousins. Upon his wife's
inheritance of a considerable fortune, he added her family
name of Horton. In later years he was an M.P. and eventually succeeded to a baronetcy.

WILMOT, MRS.: There are in fact two Mrs. Wilmots, and there
arises a certain confusion when Byron refers to the name.
One of them was wife of Robert John (above), while the

second was a minor writer and a member of the Southey coterie. In 1819 this one married Lord Dacre and it seems Byron was thinking of her when he wrote "she is a Swan."

A BYRONIC CALENDAR

The Years 1788–1812

22 Jan. 1788	Birth of George Gordon Byron.
1789	Mrs. Byron leaves Captain John Byron and establishes herself with her son at Aberdeen.
2 August 1791	Death of Captain John Byron. Lord Carlisle is appointed guardian of George Gordon Byron.
1790–1798	Residence and schooling at Aberdeen.
21 May 1798	Death of the fifth Lord Byron. George Gordon Byron becomes the sixth lord.
August 1798	Removal to Nottingham.
1801–1805	Education at Harrow. Infatuation with Mary Chaworth during 1803.
1805	Mary Chaworth marries John Musters.
1805–1807	At Cambridge. Publication of *Hours of Idleness, Poems on Various Occasions.*
1807	Marriage of the Honourable Augusta Byron and Colonel George Leigh.
1809	Colonel Leigh is dismissed from his position in the household of the Prince of Wales and resigns his commission.
March 1809	Publication of *English Bards and Scotch Reviewers;* final and complete rupture of relations between Byron and Lord Carlisle.

1809–1811   Extended travels in the eastern Mediterranean
             area.

July 1811   Byron returns from the East and takes up
             residence at Newstead Abbey.

March 1812   Publication of the first two cantos of *Childe
             Harold;* instant fame; beginning of the af-
             fair with Lady Caroline Lamb.

Sept.–Dec. 1812   Rupture of relations with Lady Caroline and
             commencement of liaison with Lady Oxford.

The Year 1813

June   Lady Oxford and family prepare for depar-
             ture to the Continent.

26–27 June   Augusta Leigh arrives in London.

27 June   Party at Lady Davy's.

30 June   Byron attends a party, evidently not in Au-
             gusta's company.

1 July   Byron takes Augusta to gathering at Al-
             mack's.

2 July   Proceedings against Claughton in Chancery
             Court. During portions of the next several
             days there are sittings with Thomas Phillips
             for a portrait.

5–6 July   Party at Lady Heathcote's at which Lady
             Caroline Lamb injures herself.

8–10(?) July The exact date is uncertain. Byron attends a
             bachelor dinner at Frere's.

8 July   Byron writes Moore that Augusta's presence
             in London is a "great comfort."

13 July   Byron writes Moore that he is interested in
             Lady Adelaide Forbes. The precise date of

	Augusta's departure from London is not established but it may be as early as 12 July.
22–25 July	Byron leaves London and goes "into the country." The dates are not completely certain but seem the most probable ones (see chapter 10). Revision and additions to *The Giaour* take place throughout this time, as presumably do further sittings with Phillips and proceedings in Chancery.
3–5 August	Byron makes a quick trip into the country and returns to London with Augusta; plans for both of them to emigrate.
12 August	Byron writes that he is "near London." It is possible this date corresponds with a time at which he takes or sends Augusta to some country house.
12 Aug.–10 Sept.	Byron is in London almost continuously.
11–14 Sept.	Byron is at Cambridge during a part of the time.
16–26 Sept.	Byron is a guest of the Wedderburn Websters at Aston.
26 Sept.–2 Oct.	Byron avoids the running of the St. Leger at Doncaster and returns to London.
3 Oct.–15 Nov.	Continuation of the house party with the Websters, with 10–14 days intervening when the party moves to Newstead Abbey; romance with Lady Frances Webster.
16 Nov.	Byron returns to his lodgings in London and begins his journal on the following day.
15 Dec.	Augusta comes up to London for several days.
ca. 26–30 Dec.	Byron spends several days at Six Mile Bottom.

The Year 1814

14 Jan.–5 Feb.	Byron and Augusta are at Newstead Abbey.
20 Jan.	Publication of *The Corsair* and acknowledgment of "Lines to a Lady Weeping."
8 Feb.	Hobhouse returns to London and hears Byron's "confessions."
5–7 April	Byron goes to Six Mile Bottom; birth of Medora? (see chapter 9).
15 April	Reputed date of the birth of Medora Leigh.
20 April	Byron resumes the social life he has largely forsaken.
25 April	The date of the well-known "ape" letter to Lady Melbourne.
20 July–4 Aug.	Seaside holiday at Hastings with Augusta, her children, and other guests.
August	Byron and Augusta engage in several efforts to find a wife for him.
9 Sept.	Byron addresses a proposal of marriage to Miss Anna Isabella Milbanke and receives a rather ready acceptance.

The Year 1815

January	Marriage with Miss Milbanke and "treacle-moon."
February	Lord and Lady Byron install themselves at 13 Piccadilly.
20 Feb.	Augusta receives an appointment as Woman of the Bedchamber to Queen Charlotte.
April–June	Augusta spends several weeks at 13 Piccadilly.

August–Sept.   At Lady Byron's request Augusta again comes to London to be with her during the final months of pregnancy. She becomes a regular part of the household and remains with them throughout.

10 Dec.   Birth of Ada Augusta Byron, Lady Byron's only child, later to become the Countess of Lovelace.

The Year 1816

5 Jan.   Lady Byron leaves London to return to her parents.

Jan.–March   Completion of measures for permanent separation.

24 April   Byron leaves London en route to Italy.

The Years of the Deaths

November 1823   Throughout the interval Byron has lived in Italy and employed himself in various amours as well as a considerable literary output. At this time he leaves for Greece to assist in its liberation.

15 Feb. 1824   Byron has a convulsion, followed by a slow recovery.

19 April 1824   Death of Byron.

16 July 1824   Burial in the vault at Hucknall, near Newstead.

29 April 1849   Death of Medora.

3 May 1850   Death of Colonel George Leigh.

12 Oct. 1851   Death of Augusta.

27 Nov. 1852   Death of Ada, Countess of Lovelace.
         1868   Death of Lady Byron.

Note: The specific dates in 1813 have to be inferred or derived from dates of letters. It is probable that the error is not greater than one day in most instances. One of the major areas of uncertainty is the date in July when Byron had been "into the country."

≥ 1 ≤

THE PROBLEM

The sixth Lord Byron has now been dead for a hundred and fifty years; and one may well ask why, after so long a time, his unbeatified bones may not rest in peace. Certainly his position as a man of letters and as a poet is secure, and perhaps that should be enough. With any ordinary man it would be, but Byron was no ordinary man. He was the raw material of legends and they have flourished.

To biographers the most fascinating of these has been the story of his supposed incest with his half sister, the Honourable Mrs. Augusta Leigh. Rumors of incest began as early as January 1814,[1] apparently instigated by Lady Caroline Lamb, with whom the poet had formed a liaison early in 1812 and from whom he had been trying to dissociate himself since November 1812.[2] Both Lady Caroline's mother, the Countess of Bessborough, and her mother-in-law, Lady Melbourne, had viewed with great anxiety the Caroline–Byron affair and each had implored the poet to break away.[3] Lady Caroline by no means had acquiesced.

The rumors attracted little credence and gradually died away, but when Lady Byron refused to reveal her grounds for demanding a permanent separation from her husband in 1816, the silence on her side provided a basis for charges not fit to be mentioned.[4] Lady Caroline, who had consistently maintained her interest in the poet, began to produce "revelations" that consorted well with Lady Byron's silence. To all who would listen she offered the simple logic of putting two and two together: if Lady Byron was too magnanimous to specify her charges, they must have been very horrible; Byron and Augusta had been together frequently since June of 1813; in the interval between his last documented and unabashedly public liaison with Lady Oxford (November 1812 to June 1813) and his marriage (January 1815) the poet had had no known mistress. Ergo, he must have engaged in illicit relations with Augusta. Lady Caroline's speculation and deduction began to acquire an appearance of reasonable probability.

One may well ask, why all the bother? After all Augusta was only a half sister, so that the relationship—if it occurred—could have been no more than demi-incest. In terms of human genetics it varied but slightly from the successive first-cousin marriages common among the British aristocracy of the time and almost a regular practice among royalty. Moreover, though incest constitutes a somewhat unusual form of sexual aberration, one may question its importance as an issue. It seems likely that the real interest for biographers has lain in the fact that during the period in question, about a year and a half following June 1813, there exists and persists an element of mystery: Byron was clearly involved in some affair of considerable consequence and everyone, ever since Lady Caroline, has wanted to know what he was about.

It is fair to report that the usual verdict of biographers over the past fifty years has been that incest was pretty well established. This was not true of the first biographical accounts that appeared in the years soon after Byron's death. Thomas Moore, who of course knew the poet very well and had kept up a correspondence with him for many years, does not allude to the question at all, though he hardly could have avoided knowledge of the gossip and the charges. Medwin, Trelawney, Dallas, and Hodgson in their memorabilia likewise make no reference to the subject. Of these Hodgson certainly knew the nature of the reports, from letters Augusta sent him regularly throughout the last four months preceding Byron's exile; and Dallas may very well have known of them.

During the next thirty years Lady Byron entrusted to successive confidantes her conviction that Byron had had relations with Augusta. Either of her own motion or partly stimulated by her lawyers, she set herself to gather every shred of evidence and opinion that might remotely support the proposition.[5] In spite of her repeated confidences, however, the story remained largely in limbo until 1869 when Harriet Beecher Stowe, having served as recipient of the confidential revelation, found herself far too well aware of a good story and a literary scoop to contain it any longer and published the general outline of Lady Byron's case in the *Atlantic Monthly*.[6] The article naturally provoked extensive and heated discussion, but succeeding biographers, such as Jeaffreson, continued to discredit the allegations.

So affairs rested until 1909 when the grandson of Lord and Lady Byron, Lord Lovelace, fabricated out of his grandmother's enormous collection of scraps of notes a book he called *Astarte*, which presented in exhaustive detail most of the evidence Lady Byron had collected. Since this edition of *Astarte* was privately printed and its circulation sharply limited and controlled, it produced not even a biographical ripple. In 1921, however, Lord Lovelace's widow, the Dowager Countess, brought out a revised and enlarged edition and provided subsequent biographers access to a very considerable amount of hitherto suppressed information.

The biographers who followed have divided in their conclusions about the probability of incest; [7] but it is common to most of their studies that the evidence for or against an incestuous affair with Augusta has appeared in the course of a full-length biography, which demands a sequential and narrative form. Detailed consideration of evidence, on the other hand, calls for a different ordering, particularly if one piece of evidence of an earlier date has to stand against another piece several months—or years—later. Since the focus of this book is upon evidence, it will frequently violate the temporal sequence.

The action centers upon four principals: Byron, Augusta Leigh, her husband (and first cousin) Colonel George Leigh, and Lady Caroline Lamb. Lady Caroline Lamb appears as a principal because throughout the period of this study she never relinquished the idea that by some technique she could reestablish her hold on Byron. In effect, he had jilted her and she had vowed revenge.[8] As for Colonel Leigh, most of the biographies of Byron have had little to say about him; yet as the husband of Augusta, cuckolded by Byron or by someone else, or as the real parent of the child Medora, he deserves some degree of appraisal. His actions and reactions may be as informative as those of any of the other principals.

Nearly all pertinent events and a good many of the pertinent statements occur between June 1813 and July 1814, but some closely related material of subsequent years requires juxtaposition to establish meaning or consequence. The approach is perhaps microscopic, but the task is to solve a problem, if possible, rather than to paint a portrait.

One may begin with the simple statement that by August and September 1813 both Augusta and Byron considered themselves in near catastrophic trouble. It is not of moment if their perception of trouble may have been exaggerated. But it is of very great importance if their trouble was joint and shared, or if each had succeeded in attracting disaster separately and independently of the other. The law of parsimony, generally so valuable in scientific thinking, does not necessarily apply equally well to human affairs, particularly if the humans involved were so adept at attracting misfortune as Byron and his sister. One of the possibilities requiring consideration, therefore, is that each may have engaged in an independent liaison. If their indiscretions were not joint, it will be necessary to search for a possible accomplice for each. But even if that search should prove to be successful, it would not completely exclude the possibility that on a midsummer's night in 1813 they forgot their sibship. Other material necessarily will become pertinent either to increase or decrease that possibility.

Much of the evidence lies in Byron's letters to regular correspondents—Thomas Moore, his publisher John Murray, and Lady Melbourne. But Lady Melbourne wrote some letters and a few of them survive. Byron's oldest and most intimate friend Hobhouse kept a diary—though rather irregularly. Lady Caroline Lamb left few letters, but a good many gossipy memoirs record her actions and behavior. And, of course, some of Augusta's correspondence survives. For the rest, evidence comes from an occasional reference or comment scattered through recollections of many types of diarists and writers of letters. Some of the material is contradictory; some statements seem to deny specific events. A necessary function, therefore, is to test the reliability of each witness. If a statement appears to be false, did the individual who made it lie; and if he lied, did he lie maliciously and systematically? When two persons rendered conflicting reports, which is the more accurate? Is there independent support for any statement—that is, support by some uninvolved person? Is there any possibility that some of the surviving evidence may be spurious, or that some evidence may have been altered or destroyed?

Investigative reportage demands not only evaluation of evidence and sources but discovery as well. Have others overlooked a clue? Did Byron allow some hint to appear or, more likely, did he lay a palpably misleading trail? Did some of his correspondents, or even a mere acquaintance in correspondence with someone else, let fall a sentence that would be highly illuminating in another setting? One further assumes that so special a person as a genius and a poet has comprehensible and even familiar motives. If Byron performed some apparently irrelevant act at a certain time, was it really irrelevant, or did he act from a specific motive? In this volume there is a lot of turning over of rocks.

It may occasion surprise that Lady Byron appears so briefly in these pages. The reason is simple: most of the events occurred before she began to take any but the most peripheral part in the action. Which is as well, for I find her an extraordinarily unappealing type.

❧ 2 ❧

THE SETTING

The social structure and intellectual ambience of Regency England constitute elements that affected Byron's rise to fame as well as his rapid decline and fall. At the top of society, of course, were the royal family and, very near them, the rich older aristocracy who among themselves tended to regard the House of Hanover as foreign upstarts, but who did not permit their distaste to inhibit their pursuit of patronage. Just beneath the old aristocracy was a new breed of nobles, most of whom had acquired titles and riches in consequence of royal favor in immediately preceding reigns. In terms of personal prestige and, often, of political power the equals of the new nobles were the old landed gentry, mostly untitled but intricately allied by blood and marriage to the great barons. In large measure it was this group who dominated the House of Commons: acres rather than people determined the composition of Parliament.

Beneath all these a slowly developing middle class was trying to claw its way to political power. Among them were clever debaters and pamphleteers ambitious for places in the Commons, civil servants of the upper levels who hoped to become ministers, quite a few lawyers of eminence who would settle for a knighthood but hoped for a peerage, and an occasional physician. Even a rare banker, become enormously rich like Thomas Coutts, exerted a degree of power, since nearly all the royal princes and quite a few of the aristocracy were deep in debt.[1] But the vast majority of Englishmen constituted a faceless lower class, whose function was to serve the rest of society, as domestics, as tenants, as conveniences.

Such, in brief, was the social structure. As for the intellectual milieu, the American Revolution and the French Revolution were forty and twenty-five years past, but their germinal concepts were very much alive and at large among the English intelligentsia.[2] The Irish question was acute and generated alignments as much in Parliament as in pamphlets and conversation.[3] Byron's frequent allusions to Methodism [4] indicate how far the Established Church was failing to meet the needs of the people, whatever it might do to preserve the status quo.

In many ways the general atmosphere was similar to that of the present epoch. The traditional status of women underwent reexamination; and if the resultant system of ideas was not quite as definite as Women's Liberation a resemblance is nonetheless evident. Individual freedom was a shibboleth, and the ladies of the period applied it as readily to their domestic status as to public activities. They did not hesitate to intervene in politics, although not at the most direct level, nor did they any longer acknowledge that letters were the province of men alone.

That most volatile of indicators, taste, was undergoing a sharp change from the neo-Gothic of Horace Walpole to a brand of Orientalism possibly best exemplified by the Pavilion at Brighton, construction of which began in 1784. How much this change in style accelerated as a result of Napoleon's Egyptian adventure, how much it owed to English inability to exploit the colonies that had become the United States of America, and how much came about from the vast commerical success of the East India Company is uncertain. At any rate between the realm of India and well-known Europe lay a territory and a series of countries and customs that had been closed to travel for a long time. All that was exotic, exciting, and mysterious had its origins somewhere in what had been the Ottoman Empire. It was as chic to be Turkish as it is now to be African.

In yet another respect the Regency resembled our current period. As mysticism and occultism flourish at the moment, the English of Byron's period were turning from the Established Church to find some kind of satisfaction in other forms of religion—or in none at all. German mysticism had its effect, although it was never fully congenial to the English mode. Few went so far as Lady Hester Stanhope in adopting Moslem life, but there was a ready audience for "the different." For many of the more serious-minded upper middlebrows and lower highbrows, Methodism and other evangelical sects appeared to offer the desired variety of religious experience.

All these newly rationalized and popularized concepts permeated the structure of English higher society and produced significant effects in morality, religion, and politics. Byron, as a sensitive man and as an intellectual, could not avoid the spirit of his time; indeed he became a living symbol of it. Like many another powerful personality he was part creature, part creator. His "orientalities," the sensuousness of his poetry, his scorn for the established, his genuine interest in reform, all accorded perfectly with a very brief epoch. Such a diet is a bit rich for the generality and leads quickly to satiety and then to revulsion. When that happens, the Victorians take over, and the hero of the Romantics becomes the outcast of their successors.[5]

The Moral Milieu

It would be a mistake to suppose that the bacchanalia of the aristocrats reflected the manners of the entire society. The middle class of London contained a considerable number of Scots who had learned that habits of industry and sobriety—not excluding immorality if it was inexpensive—would contribute significantly to their rise to fame and fortune in the capital. The Protestant ethic serves very well the purposes of a rising middle class, and though the wild days of the Regency lasted a few more years, the Victorian mode was incipient. In spirit and in conduct, the titled gentlemen of 1810—Byron included—belonged to l'ancien régime.

Moreover, the mode and manners of the capital were not necessarily those of the country. While in London a select circle that considered itself avant garde was running out of time, in the country the landed gentry and the old aristocracy were leading rather humdrum lives with no more exciting interludes than clandestine romances with local barmaids or tenants' daughters. Such an aristocrat as Augusta's grandmother Lady Holderness heralded the approaching epoch as she read Scriptures and led family prayers, at least when the grandchildren were at home.[6] Lady Frances Webster's hesitations and agonizing over Byron probably had somewhat the same origins, while Miss Anna Isabella Milbanke, only a few years younger than Byron, manifested all the premonitory virtues and vices of the Victorian era.

The Political Milieu

Political parties of necessity are constantly on the alert for effective recruits. By the time of Byron's explosive eminence, in

1812, the Whig party was in sore need of new blood. Their function, as Loyal Opposition, had consisted of increasing the ministerial and parliamentary power vis-à-vis the monarch. The party
had used the Prince of Wales against George III, and then the
Princess of Wales against the Prince when the Prince became
Regent.[7] But the Princess represented an alignment *faute de
mieux,* and the Prince as Regent acted very much in the pattern
of George III. The addition of a sharp, satiric pen, when a party
is out of office, is always to be desired.

More than this, the current leaders of the great Whig families
of former years were exhibiting lassitude and decadence. In past
time a Harley, Osborne, or Godolphin had held the highest ministerial posts, had acquired wealth and titles, may even have
ruled the rulers of England for short spans. Two or three generations distant from the high tide of the family fortune, their
descendants, now respectively Lords Oxford and Jersey and the
Duke of Leeds, devoted themselves to the pursuit of pleasure
and were largely ineffective in Regency politics. By family connection, his own convictions, and his ability, Byron recom-
mended himself to an opposition coalition that included these
and other peers, a variety of Scots and Irish noblemen, and a few
true reformers such as Sheridan, Tooke, and Burdett.

But if one of the curious effects of inherited position was an
enervation of the male line, this did not necessarily apply to their
wives. As the male grip slackened, the ladies took over, and with
the exception of Lord Holland the effective political activists of
the time were Ladies Holland, Jersey, Oxford, and Melbourne.[8]
They constituted themselves the Advanced Thinkers of the
Regency, and it is entirely possible their easy virtue arose as
much from political as from libidinous urge. After all, one
way to make a man join a party is to get him to fall in love with
a member in good standing. Certainly both of Byron's *amies* as

well as the various ladies he considered for marriage were partisans.

At any rate, Miss Mercer Elphinstone, for example, was so committed politically that the Prince Regent sought to deny her (as well as Sir Francis Burdett and others of similar liberal views) access to the Princess of Wales.[9] Byron acknowledges in one of his letters that he does not perform his senatorial duties except as a result of the urging of Lady Oxford.[10] Lady Caroline Lamb, along with her husband's sister-in-law, "the other Caro," took effective part in the Honourable George Lamb's campaign for election from Westminster and threatened the merchants with boycott if they failed to vote correctly.[11] The fact that the ladies in politics of that period were in no way accountable for their violent positions—by way of either duel or official responsibility—favored their intransigence. But it was a *time* of violent politics. As John Wilson Croker wrote, "Party is in England stronger than love, avarice, or ambition; it is often compounded of them, but it is stronger than any of them individually."[12]

Samuel Chew is at least partly right in his argument that Byron's rise to fame and his precipitous fall possessed a political element.[13] Unfortunately, the cost of partisan support is conformity to the party. One measure of a man's actions is their political consequences. Byron was not the man to accept party constraints—or any other kind of constraints. He acknowledged the authorship of "Lines to a Lady Weeping"; he openly admired Napoleon and criticized English military leaders at a time when such attitudes bordered on treason;[14] he allowed a public scandal to develop around his separation from Lady Byron. By 1816 he had become a political liability; and in that year all the ladies cut him,[15] all except Lady Jersey and Miss Elphinstone, the first of whom felt so strong socially that she thought she could get by with anything, the other of whom was labeled a confirmed Foxite, excessively dangerous in her views.

The Religious Milieu

Just as Byron was unsatisfactory as a political partisan, his attitudes toward religion denied him a base with any group. Several biographers have pointed out the Calvinistic elements in his early training.[16] Many of his associates were at least nominally Anglican, while his closest literary friend, Tom Moore, was Roman Catholic. Byron was basically a skeptic, a Protestant in a very nondenominational sense of the word. In the social ambience of his life, the attitude of avowed skepticism was no advantage. In political fields, it rendered him suspect. Regardless of one's private opinions and moral attitude, in public one professed some kind of belief.

At least a part of Byron's fall resulted by reason of a general opinion that his attitudes and writings were subversive of religion, which every right-thinking person regarded as a good thing, however little he might be constrained by its tenets. Indeed some of the most violent attacks against Byron's poetry stem from the reviewers' estimates of its effects on morals and religion.[17] Byron, I think, prided himself on his intellectual honesty. When Miss Milbanke inquired about his belief in the Nicene Creed, he did not avoid the question, nor admit belief—as she interpreted his answer—but replied very exactly that he did not disbelieve it.[18] At another time he implied that he believed all religions in part, a statement almost equal to saying that he accepted none of them. His fall from the position he had achieved in 1812–14 thus had a religious as well as a political basis. In every respect, at the intellectual level he was an enemy of society, and his private life, which had become all too public, furnished a pretext for the expulsion of a dangerous man.

❧ 3 ❧

THE RULES OF
COMFORTABLE ADULTERY

It is evident from the memoirs, journals, and biographies of the period that promiscuity was standard practice among the nobility of England of the Regency. The royal family in this respect set a mode which the aristocrats of England found eminently congenial and agreeable to follow.[1]

In many ways the development of some kind of unacknowledged extramarital system was a necessity for the upper classes. Most marriages at these social levels were solely *de convenance.* Some peer needed money and very reasonably undertook to marry a girl who was due to inherit a fortune, if she didn't have one already. Titles, landholdings, political advancement, and wealth were the principal objects of matrimony.[2] So far as the man and woman were concerned it was largely a matter of their not being totally antipathetic. The second concern—sometimes primary —was to insure the birth of an heir.

It is obvious that some sort of ameliorative system had to be invented. Divorce, very difficult to obtain and always associated with scandal,[3] was permitted only for adultery with discovery in flagrante, and then only if the consort could not be subjected to a countersuit. But since rank and political power were so closely allied at the time, public scandal had to be avoided. Gossip within the group was expected and enjoyable, but for one's private affairs to reach the commonalty was unthinkable.

In consequence of these varied restrictions, the invention of a set of rules of the game was requisite. First, the arrangement had to be extramarital. This restriction was all but explicit: it signified that widows and single ladies were out of bounds. The game of love was restricted to married ladies living with their husbands.

This restriction was, at bottom, civilized and humane. In the absence of effective contraceptive devices, amorous activities would normally result in a significant number of births—and the presumption under these circumstances, the shadow of the doubt, belonged to the baby. It was legitimate by law, if only in the face of a remote chance of paternity by the mother's husband.

The second rule was that the husband had to be acquiescent or indifferent, since any other attitude might give rise to public scandal. To fair-minded people, this stricture appeared perfectly reasonable since the gentleman himself was probably already engaged in an amour with some other noble's wife. Thus it was possible for Lord Y's illegitimate son to inherit the title of Lord Z, while Lord Z's bastard might inherit from Lord Y. If nothing else, the system allowed extensive interchange of genes among the more vigorous families of the aristocracy. In some cases it assured an unfortunate peer of a son to succeed to his title.

The third rule was that these attachments should be of relatively restricted duration. Prolonged attachments took on a domestic quality and after a time were bound to elicit remark, which could result in all kinds of unpleasantnesses, such as duels. The perfect exemplar of this point of view was Lady Oxford, whose successive affairs with Sir Francis Burdett and Lord Archibald Hamilton and perhaps others earned her family the title of the Harleian Miscellany.[4]

For the monogamously inclined there existed outside of the social circles in which a gentleman and his wife moved a demi-monde that has been fully described and annotated by Harriette Wilson. This assured a man a constant, reliable, and devoted woman, who required little more than his regular attention and a comfortable mode of life. In a few instances these arrangements proved so agreeable that they culminated in marriage.[5]

The significant flaws in the system arose from two peculiarities of human conduct. The first was that one or both of the participants in the extramarital affair might become inordinately enamored. The second was that the horn-bearing husband might become annoyed. Byron's several affairs of 1812–1814 reveal the human fallibility that threatened and eventually wrecked the system. William Lamb was apparently entirely acquiescent and complaisant with respect to Byron and Lady Caroline.[6] But Lady Caroline broke the rules by becoming infatuated and behaving in a wholly unacceptable fashion. On the other hand, the affair with Lady Oxford was quite idyllic until Byron's continuing presence became somewhat embarrassing to Lord Oxford.[7] The non-affair with Lady Frances Webster reveals an additional weakness inherent in the arrangement. Lady Frances was not quite ready to enter the system, while Webster—whatever his own activities, and they were extensive—was unwilling to accept the role he so steadily assigned to other husbands.[8]

The English system was entirely English and pertains only to the upper class. Barmaids and servants who became pregnant were treated with kindness and some money and there was no further concern[9]—and this could extend so far as to a literary type like Claire Clairmont.[10] On the other hand, the system had differences from those prevalent on the Continent. The long affair with Teresa Guiccioli was apparently in the Italian tradition and contained large elements of domesticity.[11] In England it would surely have produced a scandal, almost certainly a divorce; in Italy it resulted only in ennui on Byron's part.

❧ 4 ❦

THE BARON HIMSELF

Birth and Youth

The infant who was to receive the name George Gordon Byron entered the world in a caul. This relatively uncommon obstetrical event clearly was an omen, as any old wife could tell one, though no two of them might agree on what it signified. But when the caul was opened and the child appeared the beneficent promise of the caul met an instant contradiction: the infant's right foot was deformed. In terms of eighteenth-century belief the child was "marked." From available descriptions the foot exhibited characteristic clubbing. The heel is drawn upward by congenital shortening of the tendon of Achilles, while the foot as a whole is turned inward.

It seems that in Byron's case the deformity was a relatively mild one and in later years he apparently almost concealed its existence, in part by developing a peculiar, gliding gait, in part by some kind of built-up boot.[1] A foot of this type is relatively unstable, and muscular development of the thigh and foot on the affected side lags behind that on the sound side. At Byron's death it was noted that the right leg was smaller and less muscular than the left.[2]

For a sensitive and bright child the physical handicap itself may be less than the psychological damage that comes of the recognition that one is "different," or even that his body is less than perfect. Far worse is the notice such a deformity attracts. While Byron experienced little inhibition in ordinary physical activities during his early life and boyhood, what other boys said must have been pretty hard to take. Both his mother and Mary Chaworth, one of his first loves, seem to have made remarks that were no less than devastating.[3]

It is almost a medical truism that if one congenital anomaly exists there may well be others. In Byron's case there is evidence from ordinary observation that another and rather exceptional one could also be recognized. His half sister, Augusta Leigh, repeatedly refers to his "little eye," and her observation has been abundantly confirmed.[4] The significance of the small eye and its possible relation to the deformed foot are examined in detail in the Appendix.

Other circumstances surrounding Byron's birth were scarcely more auspicious than the "marking." His mother, the former Miss Gordon of Gight, an heiress in a minor way, had become infatuated with Captain John Byron, whose main interest in the Scottish lady centered on her inheritance. Captain Byron, known to his friends as "Mad Jack," had earlier eloped with the Marchioness of Carmarthen and, after a scandalous divorce by the Marquess, had married her. By this marriage there was one surviving child, Augusta. Soon after Augusta's birth, her mother died, and Captain Byron looked about for further marital means of support. Miss Gordon was the unlucky lady—unlucky because the Captain rather promptly plundered her of her small fortune and by the time George Gordon Byron was born appeared only intermittently to see if he could obtain further sustenance from his wife's remaining funds.

Mrs. Byron placed the last residual of her capital beyond her reach, since she knew she would surely yield to the Captain's blandishments if any considerable sum were available, and returned with her infant son to Scotland where she could live less expensively than in London. Accounts of Mrs. Byron vary somewhat: in some descriptions she appears as a termagant, in others as a usually kindly mother with bouts of flaring temper followed by excessive demonstrations of affection.[5] At best, one could not describe her as a calm and stable person, nor can one expect equanimity in a child subjected to this kind of instability in his sole parent.

Perhaps it was because of his uncertainty about his mother's attitude that George so readily formed strong attachments to various young cousins whom he saw from time to time. Certainly he seems as a very small boy to have formed an intense affection for his cousin Mary Duff. Augusta also was permitted on occasion to visit her stepmother—if Mrs. Byron's relationship to her deserves such a title. By his own retrospective account, it seems as if Byron had a large reserve of affection ("flames before most people begin to burn") [6] available for almost anyone who neither domineered over him nor raged at him.

Except for what he regarded as his precocious capacity for affection, Byron seemed not significantly different from other boys of eight and nine as he went along to school in Aberdeen. One story has it that at about this time a servant girl, in whose charge he was, crept into bed with him one night and initiated him into some of the mysteries of sexual activity.[7] The only significance of any of this is to confirm his own account that he was generally precocious.

When George was ten years old he became the sixth Baron

Byron, with all the encumbrances and honors pertaining to the title. Unfortunately for him and his mother, the title brought with it no significant improvement in their financial status, but led them to move to Nottingham, though not into Newstead Abbey, the support of which they could not afford. About this time also Mrs. Byron abandoned one rather hopeless practitioner who had been endeavoring to correct her son's deformity and placed the boy in the care of what passed for experts in the city of London. These gentlemen managed to inflict a good bit of pain, perhaps to impair the boy's physical activity as a result of the devices they prescribed, but to change the condition not at all.[8]

There are no other records as to Byron's growth and development, but certainly by the time he was fifteen he had achieved sufficient physical and sexual maturity to feel excessively strong attachment to Mary Chaworth.[9] If one assumes a relatively normal and equal development, he would have been sexually competent by this time, and if that is true, he would have attained close to his maximum height. Certainly there appears to be a partial correlation between rapid early and midgrowth, early puberty, and intellect. Thus, it is quite likely—though not recorded—that up to about fourteen years of age Byron was somewhat larger than other boys of the same years. That he was in intellect rather more advanced than his peers is indicated by the fact that his first love was a girl some four years older than he and, according to the biographers, not entirely indifferent to his infatuation.[10]

During the years at Harrow, Byron apparently made every effort to keep up with or to surpass the other boys. He was an excellent swimmer, and he played cricket well enough, in spite of his handicap, to make the Harrow team.[11] Very early in youth he had begun to ride, and though accounts differ as to his riding skill it apparently was not poor.[12] Certainly he rode as well as one could who had a weak and underdeveloped right leg.

The picture up to this point is that of a healthy, physically active, possibly even overactive boy. It is a probable inference that he was more advanced physically, sexually, and intellectually than boys in the same form. And though his record as a student was spotty, Dr. Drury, the Master of Harrow, had recognized in him exceptional capacity.[13] Byron already wrote rhymes, and, though he seemed never to study, he apparently was already reading omnivorously and retaining extremely well great chunks of everything he read.

Young Manhood

This was the character of the person who at the age of eighteen went up to Cambridge. He was Lord Byron, and very conscious of it. More than this, he was acutely competitive at the physical level. If at Cambridge the prize was not for athletic but for sexual prowess and alcoholic consumption, he was ready to match himself against anyone. While in residence he led about as dissolute and extravagant a life as most young men who are cut loose for the first time and who have a deal of energy. Ostensibly and among his fellows, he was as rowdy and bawdy as the best. Beyond a question, however, during all this period he read extensively if erratically, and he continued to versify. This period also was the time of his infatuation with Edleston, a young chorister.[14] Clearly in Freudian terms it was a homosexual state, but there is no evidence upon which to base a clear conclusion as to overt activity. Quite possibly it may have been at the conscious level a protector-dependent relationship such as occurs fairly commonly among young men and such as would be particularly reassuring to the protector who happened to have a serious and obvious physical defect.

During the autumn preceding his entry to Cambridge, Byron's weight had reached 202 pounds, according to Marchand.[15] Since he would have been at this age within about a half-inch of his mature height of five feet eight and one-half inches, he must have been enormously fat. Byron himself told Trelawney that at one time his weight had reached 14 stone (196 pounds),[16] and the figure corresponds well enough. Weight gain of this type sometimes occurs during a major growth period and is (in theory) a part of the general response of the body to growth hormone. Otherwise, it may only be guessed that he attacked food with the same energy and drive that he directed toward everything else.

It was probably soon after this time that he began the weight reduction that was thereafter to be a regular feature of his life. Certainly by the time he had left Cambridge he was considerably lighter, though by no means wraithlike. As he reached his twenty-first birthday, Byron should have been essentially as he was to remain for the next few years. According to his own description he was five feet eight and a half inches in height,[17] and as he told Trelawney he tried to keep his weight around 11 stone (154 pounds). At his stated height, the weight would have been about right for a well-formed and reasonably muscular man.

That he was physically active and muscularly well-coordinated there appears to be little doubt. He boxed and fenced, swam and rode a great deal, and to judge from his ability to swim powerfully it is probable his arms and shoulders were somewhat heavy for the rest of his body. Certainly if his statement is true that his arms were rather long for his height, his legs also may have been relatively long and his trunk shorter and more compact. All his portraits reinforce this impression through suggestion of a neck both thick and round. In short, but for his bad foot, he would have been distinctly an athletic type, perhaps on the order of a college quarterback of the 1920s.

His hair was wavy, light to medium brown, and carefully tended. According to one of the ladies his eyes varied from grey to violet, depending on his mood,[18] but Medwin much later stated that they were "greyish-brown." By all his contemporaries he was regarded as remarkably handsome. His portraits show a deep cleft in the chin and quite small ears. In one of them, that of 1814, there is the impression that his left ear may have been somewhat misshapen and pointed toward the back, though this may be a fault in the painting. Add to all this very white teeth, of which he was justly proud and of which he took very good care,[19] a voice stated to have been soft and vibrant, and hands and feet small for his size, and one has a fairly complete physical picture of Lord Byron from 1808 to 1815, the Byron of pictures and the Byron of the ladies.

It is not inappropriate to comment on his relative stature. During Byron's life the average height of Englishmen was about five feet five or six inches. Army regulations in this epoch forbade the recruiting of men under five feet four.[20] For his time, therefore, he was well above average height for Englishmen generally. It probably would not be true that he much passed, if he exceeded at all, the average height of men of his rank, who undoubtedly received far better and more ample nurture than the average Englishman. Nor was excessive weight unusual among all ranks, but especially among the privileged classes. The royal princes set a pattern of corpulence that the dandies alone attempted to avoid.[21]

The Problem of Sexuality

Emphasis upon Byron's physical strength and athletic constitution in the preceding pages has laid a predicate for consideration of what seems to be a rather excessive libido. The two conditions appear to be frequently closely associated in human constitution—

unusual physical (and perhaps mental) vigor and a strong sexual drive. Without resort to humoral concepts of physiology, it seems fairly clear that whatever is meant by vigor (and there are no measurements for this subtle but real quality) extends throughout the organization of a human being. Precocity and rapid growth are only two features of the endowment, which probably has a very complex genetic origin.

This kind of make-up provides something of a problem for a schoolboy, particularly if he happens to be sufficiently handsome. The English public school of the nineteenth century allowed students relatively little outside association and kept boys in continuous and intimate contact. The arguments for Byron's homosexuality during his years at Harrow have appeared elsewhere in detail.[22] Whether or not he formed overt relationships with any of the other younger students is at best a guess, though certainly not an improbable or unreasonable suspicion.

With respect to later homosexual activity the record remains rather murky. In an extensive analysis of this question, Knight concludes that certainly during the poet's Grand Tour of the East he was overtly active as a homosexual, suggests that his affair of the summer of 1813 that so agitated Lady Melbourne was a relapse into homosexuality, and postulates that in his last few months in Greece Byron reverted once again to a homosexual relationship with a young Greek boy of whom he seems to have been very fond.[23]

In contrast there is the incident, when Byron was fifteen, of a visit at his mother's urgent solicitation to Lord Grey de Ruthyn who held the lease of Newstead Abbey. What happened on that occasion he never divulged, stating only that it was unfit to mention.[24] Very probably Grey made overtures; the experience, whatever it was, so much agitated and angered Byron that he would never again have anything to do with that gentleman.

Certainly there seems little doubt that throughout the greater part of his adult life the poet was basically heterosexual. The list of girls and women who aroused his interest is much too long to permit recapitulation. If one accepts all the evidence, what seems most likely is that Byron experienced the same evolution and maturation of sexual direction that Freud described. If such a conclusion approaches accuracy, relapses or reversions to homosexual activity, such as that Knight suggested with the Greek boy, were largely opportunistic and not characteristic of the mature man.

Of more interest is Byron's recognition of a powerful sexual urge and his sometimes strenuous efforts to keep it under control. While dieting unquestionably served the primary purpose of maintaining an acceptable thinness, the poet recognized quite clearly that if restriction of food was severe enough it sufficed to "cool his passions." [25]

A Calvinistic or Other Code

One of the paradoxes of Byron was what several writers have referred to as a basically Calvinistic attitude toward life.[26] Certainly when he was a young boy he must have undergone some degree of exposure to doctrines of Calvin. Unquestionably Harrow brought with it familiarity with the Church of England. Seemingly the inoculations did not take too well. And yet every biographer has had to reckon with the fact that the poet had principles and a kind of code to which he adhered about as consistently as any man.

Was the code Christian, out of Calvinism, as Knight has argued, or was it of a different origin? Any reply to the question is a matter of subjective interpretation, and it may be that the system by which Byron measured himself and his world was syncretic to the degree that its attribution is impossible. That he possessed a code rests unchallenged: it is impossible to produce rational satire in the absence of standards. For satire is in essence an attack on the world, on actions, customs, and attitudes. And there is no reason at all to attack and no impulse to prompt an attack unless the events and attitudes fail to meet some kind of standard the writer has created for himself and his kind.

Lady Byron remarked of the poet that he suffered from the handicap of a classical education.[27] The phrase is pregnant with implication, both with respect to Byron's view of the world and with regard to her appraisal of her husband. In Lady Byron's terms, the phrase may signify that Byron was not Christian, that he was more an antique Roman than a Scot, more Horatian than Calvinistic. That her words are pejorative there is little doubt: perhaps she was taking aim at skepticism. Since she failed to elaborate and since her concern in context was with conformity to her own concept of sexual mores, an equally probable interpretation is that he enjoyed altogether too much a variety of activity. Possibly she meant only that his education had rendered her efforts to "redeem" him quite ineffectual.

To this substructure one may well add a system of ideas derived from the French Revolution. These included concepts of social justice and the dignity of man, which in Byron's scheme of things in no way contradicted his view of himself as nobleman. Seemingly from this set of affirmations arose his admiration for Washington and Bolivar and his ambition in some manner to emulate them.[28] To one with a classical education, the distance from the republics of Rome and Greece to those of America was small indeed; the virtues of the heroes of either place were almost identical.

While the body of his works and the records of his actions permit almost limitless selection of illustrations to support any hypothesis, Byron's words and deeds permit a summary. In his relations within his circle of chosen men, there exists no instance of pettiness, cowardice, falsehood, or dishonor. The flaws of his character appear primarily in his associations with women. Miss Mayne, whose sympathies lay with Lady Caroline and Lady Byron, called attention to this imbalance long ago, and it remains today a valid description.[29]

A dichotomy of behavior of this type may, in Byron's case, have had two origins, one pretty certainly derivative from the other. The proximate source is, of course, the English public school, which for generations has instructed boys in the rules of a masculine society. But the code of the schoolboy derives implicitly and explicitly from education in the much older code of the Greek and Roman heroic ages. In either system woman appears only intermittently as a bewildering and disturbing element, a species of being who does not know or understand the rules and probably would not conform to them if she did.

One has only to contrast the steadiness of Byron's friendships with men (for example, Hobhouse, Kinnaird, Davies, Hodgson) and the tempestuousness of his relations with ladies to perceive how inadequate was his code to cope with a mixed society. Undeniably there are elements of homosexuality in the ancient codes as in the Harrovian, if one views them with Freudian bifocals. These latent or sublimated features, however, do not establish the existence of overt homosexuality: they may only result in a variety of contemptuous disregard for *das ewige Weiblichheit*.

The Prince of Cats

Between 1812 and 1814, Byron experienced an unexampled literary and personal success. Whether or not he was beautiful, as Lady Caroline Lamb said,[30] he was a very handsome man apparently. His poems enjoyed both critical and popular acclaim.

Lord Byron. This portrait, of uncertain provenance but resembling the Phillips portraits, is in the possession of John S. Chapman.

He was, on the record, an extremely eligible bachelor, the bearer of an ancient and noble—if not honored—name. His associates included the major men of letters of the epoch and the principal political leaders of the Whig party. But one would have to list among his liabilities a deformed foot, a state of approaching bankruptcy, and a sharp and critical intelligence well able to express itself in sometimes biting satire.

This was the period of his amours with Lady Caroline and Lady Oxford, of bachelor dinners with wits and dandies, of drinking bouts with men like Sheridan, and of parties at the Princess of Wales'. About this time the Princess of Wales wrote, "Lord Byron was of the party on Sunday; and he was really the hero of the party, for he was in very high spirits, free like a bird in the air." And again she wrote that she had at dinner "Lord Byron and the dear Gell, and Craven and Lady Oxford, Mr. Beauclerc and Lord Henry [Fitzgerald], and we were very merry I assure you. It was daylight before we parted." [31]

Byron, sponsored by men like Lord Holland, became a member of the best clubs, though it isn't clear how he paid his dues. Directed by his own tastes he foregathered also with pugilistic types, boxed when he felt like it, and practiced with pistols or with his fencing master at intervals. To all appearances he was healthy, full of animal life, and ready for anything.

In 1813 Byron, then twenty-five years old, had had the usual experiences of an Englishman of upper class, first in Harrow and then in Cambridge. To this he had added a series of adventures in the East, adventures about which there is relatively little information. Whatever they were, his Eastern experiences would not have constituted very suitable preparation for a mixed society at the top of the British social scale. Long before this, however, he had come to regard himself as shy (a family trait, he said).[32]

In addition to his temperamental unfitness for his role in London society, Byron had acute intelligence. By this time, in addition to Greek, Latin, and French, which he had acquired at school, he added a fairly usable vocabulary of Turkish and possibly a smattering of other Eastern dialects. He read and retained voraciously, possessed as he seemed to be of almost photographic memory. During his undergraduate days he had begun to ask the hard questions that most bright undergraduates ask. Unlike many of them, he continued the questioning—and a search for answers.

The life of the higher social ranks into which he had entered was one of sensuous hedonism. To what extent his earlier Calvinistic indoctrination may have created conflict is uncertain. Even if Calvinism had nothing to do with it, Byron's intelligence and his special variety of ambition created in his heart a kind of fighting. On the one hand were fun and flattery, on the other his complete awareness of the triviality and aimlessness of that kind of existence.[33] The people he knew were not stupid—merely, they had no purpose.

Although it has attracted little attention, Byron was ambitious in his way. One doesn't write without some expectation of being published. In Byron's instance the advantage he hoped to derive was not financial, for until 1816 he regularly assigned his claims to friends. What he sought was fame, but fame of a different order from that of literature. Yet, his early attempts in the House of Lords soon convinced him that his path to glory did not follow a political route.[34]

Byron's great ambition was to become a man of action, a leader of an oppressed people to whom he might bring freedom. Temporarily thwarted or forgotten in the hedonism of the moment or the charm of some lady, the theme recurs again and again in his letters, his journal, and his poems. Even as Augusta approached London in June 1813 to see a man and a half brother

whom she had not seen in several years, Byron was beginning
The Giaour, which, whatever else it may be, is a puerile version
of the same purpose that was to take him, against his will and
contrary to his better judgment, to Greece.

ᢒ 5 ᢒ

THE HONOURABLE AUGUSTA LEIGH

According to the rules of the Church of England of her time, Augusta Byron was a bastard—not that there was anything very exceptional about that, for many of the noble houses of England had origins of uncertain paternity and quite a few of the heirs to titles were only nominally the sons of preceding lords. Miss Mayne in her biography of Byron refers to the marriage of Augusta's mother to Captain John Byron as "adulterous." [1] But Miss Mayne did not approve of Augusta and tended to look with disapproval at just about everything associated with her. At least, there was a marriage.

The facts were simple and not notably different from what is almost routine today, but were scandalous in the late eighteenth century. Lady Amelia D'Arcy, Baroness Conyers in her own right, daughter of the Earl of Holderness, had first married the Marquess of Carmarthen. Having provided the Marquess with a son and a daughter, and probably somewhat ennuyée in a marriage of political and economic sanctions only, the Marchioness chanced to meet Captain Byron, who evidently was something of a dasher. Unlike her friends, instead of settling down into quiet and well-bred adultery, she ran away with him to France. The

Marquess divorced her, Mad Jack married her, and shortly begat upon her a daughter who was duly christened Mary Augusta. Not long after the birth Lady Amelia died.

Upon the death of her daughter, Lady Holderness took over the rearing of Augusta, along with that of her other two grandchildren. The grandson was due to inherit his father's title and become Marquess of Carmarthen and then Duke of Leeds. The Carmarthen granddaughter was to marry very handsomely and become the Countess of Chichester.

Life as a Poor Relation

The story of the star-crossed Byron granddaughter concerns us here. Lady Holderness, dowager and grandmother, was both elderly and pious. She held, with some appearance of good judgment, that neither Mad Jack nor the Marquess was apt to provide a very good milieu for the rearing of young ladies. The training and care she gave her grandchildren were both devout [2] and —in the spirit of another time—almost Victorian. Perhaps the unsavory life of the Lady Amelia lent Lady Holderness an even firmer hand with the children: it was not wholly resolved even a hundred years later that bad blood wouldn't tell.

While the Holderness part of her rearing was essentially religious, at least at an obvious level, Augusta at times went for extended visits with some of her other kin, among them Mrs. Byron, by official record her stepmother, though perhaps neither Augusta nor Mrs. Byron quite acknowledged that relationship. During these visits, the young girl for the first time encountered her half brother, who was four years younger than she and who in addition was crippled. The boy was difficult and his mother vehement. Augusta, during the time she was a guest in the Byron menage, was cheerful and sympathetic with the little boy. No doubt she was also affectionate;[3] but if his journals and diaries reflect his earlier years, Byron was considerably more attached to his cousin Mary Duff, and later to another cousin, Margaret Parker, and in adolescence to Mary Chaworth, than he was at any time to Augusta.

It appears also that by the time Byron was sent to boarding school, Augusta returned to her grandmother and to whatever schooling she may have received. Thereafter they saw little or nothing of each other. In the years that followed, Byron inherited the title, lived the life of a schoolboy at Harrow and that of rake at Cambridge, and then departed on his pilgrimage to the East.

Of these years in Augusta's life there is almost no record at all. At various times she lived in the household of the Earl of Carlisle and at such times was reared with his daughters.[4] Augusta seems to have been rather happy in this dependent relationship and to have jested and charmed her way admirably with these kin of her father. If she felt her position as an orphaned poor relation, none of her surviving letters gives a hint of it.

Love and Marriage

In 1804, apparently as a result of a letter she wrote to him, Byron replied that love was a pretty poor thing, but if she had to be in love, go ahead—or comments to that effect.[5] Augusta indeed had fallen in love with a first cousin, Colonel George Leigh, of the Tenth Hussars, who was several years older than she. There is no record of the courtship—or the pursuit—but marriage did not occur until 1807. Possibly Leigh's financial situation simply did not permit an earlier marriage or possibly he may have regarded marriage as something a cavalry officer in a crack outfit succumbed to when he no longer found the young girls ready and willing. That it was not a marriage of necessity is indicated by the fact that their first child, Georgiana Augusta, was born 4 November 1808.[6]

In 1809, Leigh resigned his commission as lieutenant colonel of the Tenth and was dismissed from some type of post that dealt with the horses and the hounds of the Prince of Wales. The Prince deeded to him a house he had been occupying at Six Mile Bottom, convenient to the courses at Newmarket, and cut him adrift.[7] Since the Colonel really knew nothing at all except horses and army, he was essentially a man without a function at the relatively early age of thirty-two. Obviously, on account of birth and station he could not go to work, and lacking anything else to do he resigned himself to a life of racing, shooting, and gambling.

And uxoriousness. Augusta Charlotte was entered in Augusta's Bible as being born on 9 February 1811. And George Henry John appears on the list as having been born on 3 June 1812. (There appears here some conflict of information. Both Marchand and Mayne state that Augusta had three daughters by 1812,[8] and Byron's letters of 1812–1813 always refer to his "nieces"[9] without mention at all of a nephew.)

In the section on Colonel Leigh appears further description of the financial woes of the family at Six Mile Bottom. As early as August 1811 they were in considerable difficulty, but as Byron wrote to Augusta he could do nothing to help.[10] Though he was famous, his own situation was little less straitened than that of the Leighs, and he had to reply to Augusta that much as he wished, he could send no money because of his own "impecuniosity."[11]

There seems to have been relatively little correspondence between Byron and Augusta during the next several months. The poet was pretty thoroughly occupied with his life as a lion in London, to say nothing of Lady Caroline Lamb's importunities and his Olympian interlude with Lady Oxford. Byron's judg-

ment of the situation at Six Mile Bottom, however, was simple:
Leigh was "very helpless." [12] He should try to do something—
anything. But perhaps this was unduly harsh. Leigh may have
understood completely that any hope of appointment from various royal dukes was fatuous. Whatever his difficulty with the
Prince of Wales, it seems to have been sufficient to cut him off
permanently from any of the sinecures which normally fell to
retired officers of intermediate grade.

1813 Expedition to London

In late June 1813 Augusta apparently decided that if anything
could be done to alleviate their situation she would have to do it
herself. In her thinking, the only reasonable place to seek financial solace was in London, and there she betook herself. Her arrival was not entirely opportune, for Byron wrote with a trace of
annoyance to Lady Melbourne that Augusta's visit precluded a
final leave-taking of Lady Oxford. On the same date, 27 June, he
wrote Augusta setting a time and place to meet her in the city.
The dateline could have been in error, for under the same date he
sent a note to Lady Davy requesting that he might bring his
sister to dinner that evening.[13]

It is almost certain the note to Augusta was directed to a London address. In another place, evidence will indicate that she had
received an invitation from either Lady Gertrude Sloane or the
Duchess of Rutland, both daughters of the Earl of Carlisle. Of
one thing we may be sure—she could not have sustained the expense of a good hotel, and certainly would not have chosen a
shabby one. As for Byron's digs, she could hardly have stayed
there if she had had to, since Byron later wrote of his apartment
at the Albany that it was much more commodious, thirty by
forty feet, than the place he had occupied in Bennet Street.[14]

It was suggested above that Augusta had probably decided to take affairs into her own hands, since Leigh had demonstrated either inability or unwillingness to take any effectual steps. This construction of her visit seems the most probable. Surely there was no reason for her to have had any other purpose, except one. There is a possibility, nowhere expressed, that she was on the point of leaving her husband. She was still young; and for six years she had experienced only poverty and humiliation, child-bearing and child-rearing, and isolation in the country from the people she had known when she was a young girl. Clearly, life at Six Mile Bottom would not be the sort of thing a lively young woman nearing thirty could take without an occasional interlude.[15] But there is no indication whatever, either in earlier or in later correspondence, that at this period she was seriously considering a break with Leigh. Since she knew Byron had been considering the sale of Newstead, she may have anticipated that he would have some available money.

Augusta as a person remains somewhat ill-defined. Mayne refers to her as "voluptuous," without giving the source of her report.[16] Retrospectively in 1817 Lady Byron wrote of having met Augusta in London in that summer of 1813, "one night at Lady Glenbervie's"; and apparently she found Augusta good company, for she wrote, "The peculiar charm of A's society is a refined species of comic wit."[17] This speaks rather well for the spirit of a woman whose recent experiences had been those of Six Mile Bottom.

For the rest of Augusta's character there is much surmise and little solid information. Marchand refers to her as 'amoral as a rabbit,"[18] a view seemingly heavily tinctured with Lady Byron's firm opinion that she suffered from a species of "moral idiotcy";[19] but except for the premised affair with Byron, he offers no substantiation. Certainly there is nothing to suggest promiscuity of any significant degree. During much of her life up to 1814, about the only available men except for the Colonel would have been grooms and farmhands. One has to consider that she may have had a brief interlude with some gentleman in London, quite aside from Byron, but the evidence for that possibility is yet to be developed. If she was unfaithful to Leigh at all, presumably it was on only one occasion, the one concerned with the pregnancy that resulted in Medora.

With respect to Augusta's temperament, it seems as if Lady Byron's summary was fairly accurate. One can suppose from Byron's nickname for her, "Goose," that she was given to chatter, voluble and perhaps disconnected, but very probably amusing. Her letters, except for very brief ones, do not betoken an acutely analytical intelligence, but seem to imply a warm and somewhat emotional woman. Her other characteristics emerge from the account of her life.

Augusta's accomplishments were relatively limited. Having been reared somewhat disconnectedly first in one aristocratic household and then another, she had learned French—fairly extensively, but not very grammatically. If she had learned to play any musical instrument, there is no record of it, nor does it appear that she painted or sketched. If she had learned fancy needlework—regarded as a proper accomplishment of young ladies—by the time of this account her skills may have been converted to patching and darning. For after Leigh's resignation, their life was that of impoverished gentry who owned only the land their house stood on. She appears to have read books—but mostly those Byron picked out and sent to her. If she was no paragon of learning it must be said in her defense that the birth of seven children in twelve years is not conducive to the dedicated pursuit of the arts and sciences. Byron's steadfast devotion—whatever its nature—rather certainly establishes the fact that she was no fool, though

*The Honourable Augusta Leigh, sketched by Sir George Hayter. Repro-
duced by permission of the Trustees of the British Museum.*

her intelligence surely must have been intuitive rather than rational.

Thus it seems that Augusta was a likeable and lively woman, humorous, maybe sometimes witty: her friends enjoyed her company. That she preserved this personality in the face of her hardships and the disappointment of her expectations of life says a lot for the strength of her character. Furthermore she possessed sufficient courage and independence to undertake to salvage the fortunes of her menage when her husband proved himself unequal to the task. One can hardly avoid the suspicion that the proponents of Lord Lovelace's thesis have found it necessary to paint her as both immoral and stupid: they can account for Byron readily enough, but Augusta's character has required considerable manipulation to fit into the pattern. In producing the transformation, for which Lady Byron is basically responsible, Lovelace's adherents have necessarily ignored Byron's repeated encomiums.[20]

For Augusta's physical appearance we are dependent upon two pieces of portraiture. One of these, now at Newstead Abbey, is a rather poor miniature, limited of course to the head and shoulders, of a young woman with triangular face, abundant dark hair, and quite heavy brows. The other, clearly established as a portrait of Augusta, is Sir George Hayter's pencil, pen, and India ink sketch, showing a lady of classically handsome and serene aspect.

❧ 6 ❧

LIEUTENANT COLONEL
GEORGE LEIGH

In the many biographical treatments of Byron and Augusta, the person and personality of her husband, Colonel George Leigh, have received little notice. Most biographers have been content to dismiss the Colonel with a brief note of scorn or condemnation. Yet as the putative bearer of horns and third member of a triangle, however short the duration of that triangle, he deserves a certain amount of consideration, or at least of interest. Who was this man, and what attitudes did Byron and Augusta, as well as some other acquaintances, bear toward him? And what was his own attitude toward Byron and toward the rumors that spread about London in 1816 and subsequently?

George Leigh was the son of Lieutenant General Charles Leigh and his wife Frances Byron, daughter of Foul-Weather Jack, the unfortunate admiral.[1] After quite irregular and incomplete schooling he joined the Tenth Royal Hussars (Uhlans), the Prince of Wales' Own, as a cornet in 1792.[2] While this does not clearly establish his age, it would be reasonable to infer that at the time he was about fifteen years old. A subsequent letter of the Prince appears to set the year of his birth around 1777.

The Gilded Youth

The Tenth Hussars were a crack outfit, of which the Prince of Wales was honorary colonel. Under usual peacetime conditions they would have been a regiment of light cavalry devoted to elaborate parade duty and ceremonial exercises. In effect, as royal families viewed the military at the time, they constituted a set of living toys subject to whims and caprices transmitted as military orders of the titular commander. It signifies a little of the éclat of the regiment that George Brummell was an officer after he left Eton and Oxford.[3]

The motto of the regiment was appropriate to its special relation to the royal family, *Ich dien,* "I serve." The uniform was suitably ostentatious, consisting of frogged jacket, Hessian boots, shako hat with cockade, and over all a pelisse of sheepskin. One writer indeed speaks of the uniform as an "adornment."[4] At the turn of the century the regiment was stationed at Brighton, a chosen resort of the Prince of Wales. Their more public activities consisted of parading, hunting, steeplechasing, and dancing. Among the officers at that time was Leigh, who is described as part of a "Watteau-like group" of great elegance.[5]

It may well be asked how a not very significant or important young man came to high rank, which Leigh eventually achieved, in an outfit of this type. The answer lies in the attitude of the Prince of Wales toward Leigh's father. In 1798, for example, the Prince of Wales wrote his brother the Duke of York, who was commander-in-chief of the armies at the time: "Lt. General Leigh is with me and I am desirous of retaining him with me unless you should have any orders for him."[6] The preferment of General Leigh makes it very clear that he was a successful courtier: colonel, 1782; major general, 1793; lieutenant general, 1798. He was in addition one of the Grooms of the Bedchamber and subsequently in 1812 became Lieutenant Governor of the Isle of Wight. None of the promotions, it may be remarked, resulted from military activities, unless some of the much earlier ones. And, as the Prince indicates in a letter below, General Leigh was so much a favorite that the Prince's regard for him carried over to his son.

The Warrior

As for the military career of Colonel George Leigh, it was not altogether undistinguished. His promotion, from cornet in 1792 to lieutenant colonel by 1800 and to effective command of the regiment by 1804, was rapid and unquestionably was owing entirely to the favor of the Prince. However, the Tenth Hussars embarked for Spain in October 1807, to serve under General Sir John Moore, who was in great difficulty at La Coruña. The function of the regiment was to cover Moore's retreat and serve as rear guard. As the retreat drew near Mayorza, Paget sent Leigh with two squadrons to dislodge a threatening French force. The attack was completely successful and resulted in the capture of 90 enemy troops. Again the regiment attacked the French at Benavente and drove them off Moore's retreating columns, with a loss of 200 to the enemy and 50 killed and wounded among the Tenth.[7]

The weather was terrible and the conditions of retreat were incredibly severe. It is reported that during this period Captain Darby and 17 men of the Tenth perished from cold and exhaustion. In such a retreat, the function of a light cavalry unit is to serve as a screen and as skirmishers, with no time for rest of man or horse. The retreat in this series of moves culminated in the battle of La Coruña, in which the French were held off long enough for Moore to embark the remnants of his force. The Tenth, the last to leave, destroyed its horses, embarked, and reached England in the first week of February 1808.[8] As for Leigh's part in the disastrous action, a military historian (*Memoirs of the Tenth Hussars*) writes: "He had many opportunities of distinguishing himself. He was awarded the gold medal for Sahagan and Benevente, and was promoted to a brevet colonelcy."[9] It is not at all a bad record for a playboy, a favorite, and a field officer in his thirties.

The bloody, dirty, and exhausting job was a total contrast with all his previous military experience. In 1796, for example, Leigh's duty seemed mainly to consist of acting as courier for private correspondence among members of the royal family. He carried notes back and forth between the Queen and the Prince, and between the Prince and his numerous brothers. One gains an insight into the internal politics of the army as well as into the nature of promotion from the following letter from the Prince of Wales to the Duke of York in 1799. There was apparently dissension among officers of the Tenth and the Prince felt the need of intervention. He decided to follow regulations:

> . . . and to oblige George Leigh, though much against his inclination, to purchase the Lt. Colcy., which has restored good humor and unanimity in the Corps. . . . George Leigh is only apprehensive that he should appear in your eyes to have acted inconsistently, and it is therefore that I charge him with the delivery of this letter himself, to assure you that it was not till I took it upon myself to promise that I would write to you and explain the circumstance of its being in consequence of the application of the officers that I could induce him to assent to the purchase money being lodged by his father.[10]

This letter makes it clear that both purchase and favoritism played a considerable part in promotion—and indeed the Duke of York a little later was forced into temporary retirement by his flagrant traffic in commissions.[11] Nevertheless, the Prince of Wales' communication establishes not only that Leigh in this instance behaved with admirable tact and judgment, even with honor, but that he was highly regarded by his fellow officers. Or, as the Duke, happy to hear of improved morale, replied to Leigh's sponsor:

> As for George Leigh I think it would have been impossible for him to allow anybody to purchase over him, and I beg that you will assure him that I do not see any inconsistency in his conduct, and that this diffidence of himself does him credit.[12]

Behind the correspondence lies the fact that the Duke of Clarence was attempting to gain preferment for an officer named Cottin, that the Tenth had become surly and rebellious at the prospect of Cottin's coming in as their effective commandant, and that the only satisfactory solution seemed to be to advance the senior major of the Tenth. As for Cottin, by 1803 he was senior major of the Royal Spelthorn Legion, a not very prestigious outfit, and it was reported he could not afford to buy himself a horse.

The Courtier

It is obvious that neither George Leigh nor his father had money to spare. Further to assist the son of his old friend, the Prince appointed Leigh to some kind of "Household" position in January 1800, a post that carried with it an additional stipend. In his special capacity Leigh had the job of managing the Prince's horses and hounds, as well as being a kind of personal manager of transport. He had not held his new place long before he attracted unfavorable comment. General Samuel Hulse writes to Robert Gray on 24 March 1800:

> Col. Leigh came here on Thursday last to dinner with a commission to give a large sum of money for a horse which Sr. F. Pool would not part with. He also told me he was to farm the hounds at £12[00] to 1500 a year; surely these sums could be disposed of to the credit of H. R. Highness and not for the amusement of George Leigh.[13]

The meaning of the letter is unclear. If the animals involved belonged in name to the regiment, Leigh was behaving in an appropriate manner. If he was acting as equerry, the sums in fact were being dispensed with the knowledge and approval of the Prince and for his benefit. Hulse arouses the suspicion, however, that Leigh may have been using equerry funds for his own concerns and interests, possibly without the assent of H.R.H. Almost as probably, Hulse's letter may signify his concern and envy at the emergence of a new favorite.

The correspondence of the Prince of Wales from this date until 1804 indicates that Leigh was leading a pleasant and reasonably active life as courier among the royal family. That his position was not an exalted one may be inferred from the rather sour comment by Robert Raikes that Leigh "had a long run of favoritism . . . but his confidences were limited to the turf, and his influence never extended beyond the stable."[14] However, one does not particularly need to presume that Leigh aspired to any higher position in the Prince's confidence, or that he had any capacity for more intricate problems. He was, in effect, regimental commander for all ordinary activities and carried administrative and command responsibility. That this was not an utterly empty position is indicated by a letter from Major Henry Seymour to the Prince of Wales, a fine example of a subordinate proceeding out of channels:

> When I reflect upon your Royal Highness's most gracious
> interference in the very unpleasant misunderstanding which
> existed last winter between Colonel Leigh and me, as well
> as upon the communication which you were pleased to make
> me in consequence of it, pointing out that a repetition of
> similar conduct on the part of a Commanding Officer must
> inevitably subvert the discipline of the Regiment, I conceive
> it to be as much my duty to your Royal Highness (tho' it is
> not without infinite pain and regret that I do so) to lay be-
> fore you my present very uncomfortable situation, as it is due
> to myself for the sake of my own character to do away with
> the charge and insinuations which Colonel Leigh has made
> and thrown out against me. . . . I must first disclaim in the
> most solemn manner having ever encouraged anything like
> a party or faction in the Regiment. . . . I believe no such
> thing ever has existed, and that there never was more har-
> mony and union amongst the officers generally, or warmer
> sentiments of dutiful attachment towards your Royal High-
> ness, and zeal for the interests of the Regiment. Colonel
> Leigh has however avowed publicly that *I am at the head of*
> *a party against him and that he is resolved no means shall be*
> *left untried by him to ruin me,* and this declaration was made
> by him at a time when I supposed that a good and proper
> understanding existed between us. In addition to this Colonel
> Leigh's conduct which your Royal Highness witnessed last
> winter has been repeated toward me in a variety of instances.
> He has reprimanded me with severity one day for doing that
> which on the day before he had ordered me to do; and when
> I waited upon him at his room in obedience to his positive

orders, the last time he arrived at Guilford, he told me in the hearing of his Dragoon, *that he would not speak to me except in the presence of a third person.* If I have acted in a manner to justify Colonel Leigh in such behavior your Royal Highness as Colonel of the Regiment ought to be made acquainted with the circumstances of my misconduct. . . .[15]

What this difficulty was all about is not clear. Nothing in the Prince's published correspondence gives any further clue, and it is not apparent whether Seymour obtained the audience he requested. In any case, neither the letter nor the possible audience affected Leigh's standing with the Prince, for all through 1805 the Colonel remained on trusted terms as courier between H.R.H. and members of his family. Indeed in August of that year, Leigh became first lieutenant colonel of the Tenth in title as well as in command.

Meanwhile, Colonel Leigh's age, rank, and perquisites apparently led him to consider marriage. At least they were sufficient to lead a young lady to regard him as marriageable. Byron wrote to Augusta, March 1804, "When you see my Cousin and future Brother George Leigh, tell him that I already consider him as my Friend, for whomever is beloved by you, my amiable Sister, will be equally dear to me." In October 1804, Byron again wrote Augusta to make fun of her affection as "utter nonsense." "Can't you drive this Cousin of ours out of your pretty little head?" [16]

Colonel Leigh's position continued solid into 1806, for Thomas Tyrwhitt wrote Colonel McMahon, private secretary to the Prince of Wales, in August of that year to ask, "Is George Leigh to be tucked up?",[17] referring to a report that he was soon to marry. And in 1807 the marriage with Augusta Byron, his first cousin, took place. Elwin says that he was Augusta's choice and that in fact she waited three years for him.[18] Byron in one of his letters remarks, ". . . she *would* have him." [19] There may be question if the poet's reference is to Augusta.

As marriages went, or as the upper classes evaluated them, this one should not have been too promising. To it Leigh brought only his position and his preferment by the Prince. In terms of family connection, since he was a first cousin on the Byron side, expectations were slender and the only hope or prospect lay in whatever the Colonel's father might leave. As for Augusta she brought distinctly better family connections, in the sense that she was the daughter of a baroness, but in the hard, fiscal sense her only contribution was an income of £350 per year settled on her by the Countess of Holderness.[20] Clearly the situation called for good judgment, skillful management, and a tight budget, about none of which either Augusta or the Colonel had any knowledge.

Colonel and Mrs. Leigh took up residence at Six Mile Bottom, a short distance from Newmarket, where the Prince's interest in racing brought him frequently and where he kept both racing stables and stud farm. Though Leigh already had some kind of responsibility for horses and hounds, it would appear that at this time the Prince largely turned over to him the management of his racing stable. Elwin writes that thereafter Leigh associated "with wealthy racing men, like Lord Darlington, Sir Harry Featherstonehaugh, and Lord Frederick Bentinck," living much beyond his means.[21]

The Prince continued his interest in the Leighs. In 1807 Augusta wrote Colonel McMahon, H.R.H.'s private secretary and factotum, to thank him for the present of a beautiful clock he had sent to Six Mile Bottom, perhaps as a wedding gift. She further thanked McMahon for all the comfort and advice he had given Leigh, "in many moments of distress and perplexity," an indication perhaps that Leigh was beginning to encounter financial problems.[22]

And in 1808, on behalf of General Leigh the Prince wrote the Duke of York, ". . . a few lines to beg your interference in favour of my old servant and most respectable friend, in whose wellfare [sic] I am most particularly interested, to obtain for him the government of Hull that is now vacant . . . to which his services as a soldier so well entitle him." [23] It is not evident anywhere that the General had been assisting George Leigh, but it seems a reasonable presumption and a probable inference that the Prince in assisting the father may have been trying in some degree to ameliorate George Leigh's difficulties.

The Fall from Grace

By 1809, however, something quite serious had occurred that materially affected George Leigh's position with the Prince. In February, the Prince wrote Colonel McMahon:

I forgot when you was with me this morning to desire you to direct Bricknall to call upon Lt. Col. Leigh to ask his pleasure as to the form of settlement to be drawn up for putting him in possession of the premises of the Six Mile Bottom, which I *have given* him. Whatever may be the ungrateful return I have met with from this man, for now two and thirty years unremitting protection and kindness, still in consideration of his family [Augusta and child?] and the sincere regard I shall ever feel for my old friend, his father, who is the most honourable of men, you will acquaint Genl. Hulse and though in the option that was *propos'd to Lt. Col. Leigh, at my desire through Lord Paget, he has chosen to dismiss himself from my family,* yet that I mean not to withdraw his salary from him, but to continue it as a *pension.* The Gen'l. will therefore have it transferred to that list and acquaint him accordingly. I know you too well, my dear friend, not to be certain what your feelings must be upon such unexampled conduct.[24]

This letter signifies that Leigh had in some fashion incurred a choice of either resigning or being discharged from the Prince of Wales' household. No note or other correspondence indicates what caused his contemptuous dismissal. In view of General Hulse's earlier comment in regard to Leigh's use of funds "for his own pleasure," as well as the Prince's letter to McMahon, the impression is very strong that Leigh may have been caught with his fingers in the till.[25] Or Hulse, envious, may have begun as far back as 1804 a campaign that culminated in this event. During this epoch, while it may have been permissible for a member of the household of the royal family to make a reasonable profit on all transactions, and in the army for civilians at higher levels to shave a percentage off purchases, there were probably agreed-upon limits. It is evident that Leigh was in financial difficulty; it is equally evident from the Prince's letter that the Prince recognized his straits and in preference to scandal simply paid the Colonel off with a pension and a gift of the house at Six Mile Bottom. In effect Leigh was without a job—discharged both from the army and from his position in the Household.

The Racing Tout

He seems to have been in 1809 about thirty-two years old. The only things he knew anything about were horses and the army.

As a courtier he had destroyed himself. Furthermore, at the time and place and under the conditions of his termination, he would not and could not have known what to do with himself. It was accepted that men at a certain level of "good family" had as possible careers only the Church, the military, and government. If these were closed, there was literally nothing such a man could do except to become a scrounger. But scrounging was not acceptable either—at least in its open and acknowledged state—whereas gambling debts, and other kinds, were so common among the better classes, including the royal household and the households of the royal princes, that they were almost a sign of good birth. George Leigh turned to following the races, undoubtedly betting, and perhaps trading horses. All the biographers make it clear that from this time forward financial affairs at Six Mile Bottom varied from bad to terrible. Augusta wrote Byron in 1811, almost immediately upon his return from the East, asking for help.[26] Byron was financially in no better condition than the Leighs, and at that time he could send no money. By this time the Leighs had had their third child, and had no means of support other than Leigh's pension, if it was being paid, and Augusta's small income. Marchand puts the situation succinctly, if not very charitably. "Augusta's affairs had gone from bad to worse. Herself extremely inept at handling money, she was soon brought heavily into debt by her irresponsible husband, who followed the races from one track to another and was seldom home except for the Newmarket events."[27] The fact, of course, was that Augusta had very little money to handle, and that George Leigh was trying to gain whatever he could in the only area in which he had any knowledge at all. This does not gainsay the fact that neither had much judgment or any experience in business affairs. Further, each faced the social pressure that demanded certain life styles of members of "good families." Their problem was, simply stated: they could not undertake to earn money and they had to live far above their income.

Whether the family really had any income other than Augusta's legacy remains quite uncertain. Though Leigh was supposed at the time of his resignation to have received a continuation of his salary in the form of a pension, arrangements of this kind were notoriously unreliable, and, as later incidents suggest, it is quite possible that the Colonel received nothing until about 1830. How far Leigh himself proceeded in efforts to acquire some type of stipend never emerges. Perhaps he had exhausted all the avenues open to him. At any rate it was at this point that Augusta came to town and that Byron wrote Lady Melbourne: "Poor soul! She likes her husband. I think her thanking you for your abetment of her abominable marriage (*seven years* after the event!!) is the only instance of similar gratitude upon record. However, now she is married, I hope she will remain so." [28]

The letter seems to dispel any suspicion that Augusta was on the point of separation and to confirm that her fundamental reason for coming to London was to find some kind of sinecure that would a little alleviate their troubles. What emerges also is that Augusta "liked" George Leigh—in short, that with all his failings he was an agreeable and pleasant man, most of the time.

≫ 7 ≪

LADY CAROLINE LAMB

The marriage of Lady Henrietta Spencer and Frederick Ponsonby, third Earl of Bessborough, was a social event of the first magnitude. The bride was the sister of "the beautiful Duchess" of Devonshire and the Earl was rich. Unlike most other marriages of the time, this one resulted in few children and only one daughter, Caroline. Lady Bessborough, described in *In Whig Society* as "brilliant and fascinating,"[1] apparently had led a somewhat riotous life as a young woman, such that Lady Melbourne wrote to her, on the marriage of Lady Caroline to her son William, that she hoped the daughter would turn out better than the mother.[2] It was the same Lady Bessborough to whom Byron refers as "Lady Blarney."

Lady Caroline Ponsonby married William Lamb, second and reportedly illegitimate son of Lord and Lady Melbourne, on 6 June 1805. When the news of the approaching marriage became general, Lord Carlisle didn't believe the rumor and thought it was a joke.[3] William Lamb wrote his fiancée, however, that "Ly. Jersey was particularly gracious, and Ly. Eliz.th Villiers [sister-in-law of Lady Jersey] begg'd we would tell you how very happy she was at it. . . . Ld. and Ly. Melbourne supped and both were kind and happy. . . ."[4] They could hardly be otherwise, for the marriage served to cement a political alliance between the Melbournes and the Duke of Devonshire. The chief reaction, Lamb wrote Lady Caroline, was surprise.

The surprise apparently arose from the fact that Lamb was a very retiring and studious man, while Lady Caroline already had achieved something of a reputation for instability and exuberance. Later rumor has it that Lamb may have been a homosexual, but no definite support for the assertion exists. Certainly he was not social; perhaps the best definition of him was that he was a very intelligent recluse.[5] In later years, after Caroline's death, as Lord Melbourne he became Queen Victoria's favorite Prime Minister.

As for Lady Caroline, as described by Lady Morgan, "She was tall and slight in her figure, her countenance was grave, her eyes dark, large, bright, her complexion fair. Her voice was soft, low, caressing, at once a beauty and a charm. . . . Her main topic of conversation was herself, but her approach was at once elegant and eloquent." "She had a restless craving after excitement."[6]

Minto saw them about three months after the wedding. "A daughter of Lady Bessborough's is a lively and rather pretty a girl; they say she is very clever," while Lamb was a "remarkably pleasant, clear, and well-informed young man."[7] Marriage changed the pursuits of neither: Lamb remained bookish, while Lady Caroline roamed at large. Harriette Wilson, certainly not a reliable reporter, passed along from her French maid an account of an illness of Lady Caroline's young son. Lady Caroline "hired a stout young doctor to attend on him." The doctor kept much to his bedchamber, and Lady Caroline called on him there late at night. Someone found on his bed one morning a silk stocking "very like Her Ladyship's."[8] This domestic interlude aside, Lady Caroline spent her time migrating from one house party to another, attending soirées in London, and now and then engaging in more or less pointless amours.

Only five years or less after the marriage, Lady Caroline's conduct had so disturbed her mother-in-law that Lady Melbourne
sent her the following admonition:

> I only write a few lines for the purpose of preventing yr.
> coming to me loaded with falsehood and flattery under the
> impression it will have any effect. . . . I see you have no
> shame or compunction for your past conduct. . . . Yr. be-
> havior last night was so disgraceful in its appearance and so
> disgusting in its motives that it is impossible it should ever
> be effaced from my mind.[9]

The letter seems to refer to an unseemly interest Lady Caroline
had shown in Sir Godfrey Webster, and suggests that Harriette
Wilson's maid may not have lied after all. Whatever the situation, Lady Caroline replied blandly that she was wholly innocent
and even prudish till William Lamb taught her many things she
had never heard of.[10] Wherever she learned her accomplishments
she apparently practiced them rather indiscriminately. For in a
much later letter to Byron, Lady Melbourne writes:

> . . . she always told me you continually sd. that she had ex-
> posed herself so much before she was acquainted with you,
> tht. her character could not suffer, as it was already gone.
> . . . what you sd. was perfectly true and in my opinion ex-
> culpates you entirely.[11]

If Lady Caroline had truly been pretty promiscuous, the advent
of Byron at least had the effect for a time of concentrating all
her energy and affection in a single direction. He became an
obsession; the more he retreated the more she pursued. Her
grandmother wrote Lady Bessborough in November 1812, after
one of her more garish indiscretions, "She is I hear at Panshanger
[Lord Cowper's country seat]. . . . Dear child, it is grievous to
me how she trifles with her own and her husband's happiness." [12]

Of the liaison that developed between Byron and Lady Caroline, little need be said: it is familiar to all who have read the standard biographies. Mayne and Marchand make Byron out as something of a cad; Elwin is somewhat kinder and recognizes that Lady Caroline made herself a nuisance. In present-day terms Lady Caroline was aggressively possessive and Byron was not amenable. Both Lady Caroline's mother-in-law, Lady Melbourne, for whom the poet had the greatest respect and affection, and her mother, Lady Bessborough, had strongly urged him to break off the relationship.[13] Byron complied, or tried to comply. Lady Caroline would have none of it; in her view Byron was jilting her. The more he tried to pull away, the more fiercely she pursued him; her fury was that of a woman who considered herself scorned.

Byron's affair with Lady Caroline had begun in 1812, when he suddenly found himself famous. Since in her calmer moments Lady Caroline considered herself something of a bluestocking and patroness of the arts, she found it relatively easy to meet Byron within a short time of his rise to fame. Having once met him, she became obsessed with the idea that he and she had some kind of fate thrust upon them,[14] perhaps her way of expressing her determination that he was to become her sole property. As for Byron, it should be remembered that he had encountered very few ladies of upper caste before this time and, flattered as he may have been by the adulation poured upon him, he had essentially no experience upon which to draw.

Certainly Lady Caroline did not conform to the Mediterranean style of beauty that the poet idealized. She represented more nearly his concept of an etherealized version of English women. "Her eyes, indeed, were dark, her complexion was fair, her figure slight, her hair fawn-flaxen shot with gold." [15] That she was intelligent went unquestioned, that her rapid change of mood was completely fascinating no one could deny, and that her husband

seemed not to care what she did seemed obvious. Given en-
dowments of this type, Lady Caroline found no difficulty in com-
mandeering any man she happened to choose—and she chose
Byron.

Their affair proved to be tempestuous, not only by reason of the
characters of the two principals, but almost surely exacerbated—so
far as Lady Caroline was concerned—by the opposition of Lady
Melbourne, who hoped to put an end to the affair before it became a public scandal. It is interesting that Byron proved so
readily amenable to the interruption, and one suspects more than
a wish to please Lady Melbourne. Perhaps a liaison with Lady
Caroline was altogether too strenuous: like many another seduc-
tive lady, she did not know when to ease off a little. Her affection was too voracious for a man who had other concerns and
for whom there were other and less demanding *amies* at hand.

There are a few important points in the relationship of Byron
and Lady Caroline that deserve stronger emphasis than is usually
accorded. William and Caroline Lamb lived in Melbourne House
with Lord and Lady Melbourne. Although it was one of the great
houses of London, there was unavoidable proximity. On one
known occasion Lady Melbourne surprised Lady Caroline going
through her desk and wrote Byron a very angry note about it.

> I cannot bear her having got that letter whether she opened
> it, or found it, 'tis all one, it will be long before I forgive it,
> if it was either on my Table or in my Drawer, she has added
> falsehood to her other iniquities, for in that case she could not
> think that it was for her.[16]

How many times Lady Caroline may have gained access to
Byron's letters without being caught is and can only be a guess.
What is clearly established is that she did have access from time
to time and had no scruple about reading someone else's mail.

It is curious and interesting that of the many letters and notes Lady Melbourne must have sent to Byron, this is one of the very few that have been preserved. Byron must have destroyed most of the others, but this one he saved. He may very well have had good reason.

Having given Lady Caroline the slip in favor of the calmer but equally attractive Lady Oxford, Byron found that his first lover was not prepared to relinquish him so readily. From that time in early January 1813, Lady Caroline never ceased to intervene in his affairs except during the brief period of his marriage. Her state of mind by the end of June has to be inferred from some of her actions and from some of Byron's replies to letters that seem not to have survived.

In the autumn of 1812 Lady Caroline's parents had carried her away to Ireland for a prolonged visit in an effort to separate her from opportunities to continue her affair with Byron.[17] For a time she was fairly placid, to all appearance, but she was not long back in London before she forged a note to Murray, as though from Byron, directing the publisher to turn over to her a favorite miniature of the poet at the moment in Murray's possession. Murray, not suspecting the forgery, did as Lady Caroline wished.[18]

Hardly had Byron returned to London from his halcyon days with Lady Oxford before Lady Caroline renewed her pursuit. Letters to Lady Melbourne containing various messages of dismissal for Lady Caroline apparently were of no avail. On 29 April 1813, Byron replied directly to a letter from Lady Caroline:

If you will persist in meeting me in opposition to the wishes of your own friends and mine, it must even be so. I regret it and acquiesce with reluctance. I am not ignorant of the very extraordinary language you have held not only to me but others, and your avowal of your determination to ob-

tain what you are pleased to call "revenge"; nor have I now
to learn that an incensed woman is a dangerous enemy.

Undoubtedly, those against whom we can make no defence, whatever they say or do, must be formidable. Your
words and actions have lately been tolerably portentous, . . .
more especially as I believe you fully capable of performing
all your menaces. . . . You say you will *"ruin* me." I thank
you, but I have done that for myself already; you say you
will "destroy me," perhaps you will only save me the trouble.
It is useless to reason with you. . . .[19]

After the break, Lady Caroline is known to have visited Byron's
apartment on several occasions. Some of these visits unquestionably took place in his absence, and to what extent she may have
acquired entry into his desk and his letters no one knows. Certainly she could easily have appropriated note paper, writing materials, and an imprint of his seal (as if she hadn't plenty of his
letters from which to make a duplicate). In short, in the game
Lady Caroline played, there was no such thing as her commit-
ting a foul.

COMMENTARY I

This was the cast that toward the end of June 1813 converged to play out the near-melodrama. Three of the four principals were in London, where the "season" was nearing its end; no one knows where Colonel George Leigh was. Byron, prevented by Augusta's arrival from a final leave-taking of Lady Oxford, was at amatory loose ends. Augusta, after prolonged and very domestic rustication at Six Mile Bottom, had come up to London in search of funds or credit or for other never expressed reasons. Lady Caroline was ready to commit almost any folly to reassert her dominion over Byron. Within the next two or three weeks the lives of all these people became hopelessly entangled.

The function of this study now becomes to examine as minutely as published material will allow the evidence bearing upon the supposed incest of Augusta and Byron. The first point to establish is if the poet had developed a modus operandi in his relations with women, how he usually applied it, and if his m.o. was suited to this specific situation. Next, since the product of their incest (or of Augusta's adultery with someone else) has been identified as the child Medora, it is essential to determine as exactly as possible the date of her birth, since that date sets limits upon the time and place of conception. Both time and place in turn have a bearing upon possible paternity. Hence, we must try to discover how often and under what circumstances Byron and Augusta were associated during the interval rendered appropriate by the child's birth. Alternatively, so far as recorded events and reasonable inference permit, we must consider other putative paternity. Regrettably, none of the principals kept a daily log; every bit and shred of evidence derived from recorded comments and from discerned behavior will have to be analyzed.

61

❧ 8 ❦

HIS LORDSHIP'S M. O.

Once one establishes a reputation as a rake, his opportunities increase. At the same time, if he is a logical man, he tends to repeat techniques that have hitherto been successful. Byron was a logical man—sometimes. The purpose of this section is to examine Byron's amatory technique and to see if he followed a consistent mode of operation in his dealings with the ladies.

From the available information it seems Byron followed two quite different styles. If he dealt with young women of no standing—barmaids, servants, farm girls, and perhaps some actresses, as the records of such women as Susan Vaughn [1] of Newstead indicate—his approach was evidently direct and simple. So far as he was concerned it was all in good fun. If there was a rebuff it meant nothing except that the girl was not in the mood, or that she wasn't the type.

His relations with various women in Venice apparently followed a similar pattern. Byron never clearly described his technique and probably would have denied he had one. It is well documented, however, that the poet, in his cups or out, among his social inferiors was something of a roisterer, and the probability is rather strong that his first step was to establish a jesting relationship and to follow that with a very earthy series of advances. A pat on the bottom, a glass of wine, a good laugh, and the girl was perched on his knee. It is a technique in general use and has the virtue of calling for no pretense.

With women of his own class Byron's technique was quite different. Hobhouse wrote of him in 1812, "Those, indeed, who are acquainted with his lordship are aware that no one requires more encouragement from any woman, and that no one is more easily abashed than himself." [2] And Byron's own account agrees—"I have neither the patience nor the presumption to advance till met halfway." [3] Again, he wrote to Lady Melbourne, ". . . now as I never swim unless I tumble into the water, I don't make love till almost obliged." [4] And he refers again and again to his shyness, which he regarded as a family trait.

It is possible, of course, that Hobhouse meant his comment as an apologia and that Byron was exaggerating his innocence for Lady Melbourne's benefit. The record, however, seems to bear out rather exactly the truth of their assertions. Among the women of his own class, his technique—if it can be called anything so deliberate—consisted of waiting about until some lady decided she wanted him. Such certainly was the situation with regard to Lady Caroline Lamb. Byron just went around to some parties and sat quietly apart until Lady Caroline decided she had to have him, overpowered him, and dragged him off to her bedroom. Just how the affair with Lady Oxford developed is not documented. That lady had had affairs with Sir Francis Burdett and Lord Archibald Hamilton, [5] and possibly several other gentlemen. Byron, according to the record, attended some house parties at which the lady was present, and she seems to have induced her lord to invite Byron along for a visit at their place at Eywood.

Even the highly respectable Miss Milbanke seized the opportunity afforded by his rather general inquiries to invite him to propose marriage. To put it in a paraphrase of Elwin, she accepted him before he managed to propose.[6] Claire Clairmont clearly threw herself at him, and the Gambas, father and son, did all they could to advance his interest with the Countess Guiccioli, their daughter and sister.

His letters to Tom Moore with respect to Lady Adelaide Forbes[7] and his account of his introduction to Lady Charlotte Leveson Gower[8] demonstrate how readily Byron abandoned a quarry that did not try to get caught.

The inconclusive affair with Lady Frances Webster is a case history in how not to accomplish a seduction. In this instance Byron apparently began the advance, though his letters to Lady Melbourne make it appear he was reasonably sure of her fascination before he made any show of his own interest.[9] The ineffectual conclusion of this small affair may reflect the fact that Byron was unwilling to pursue an advantage if it occurred as a result of his own efforts. Equally it demonstrated how inept he was in the face of less than cordial acquiescence. It is only fair to add that the correspondence with Lady Melbourne bespeaks a totally different attitude from that Byron related in his journal of 1813–14. He was probably much more romantically involved than he was willing to reveal in his cool and humorous letters to his confidante. If he was as serious as the journal indicates, it is as well the affair came to no fruition, for Lady Frances's temperament would have proved in a prolonged association as incompatible as Miss Milbanke's in fact became.

There are two accounts that suggest a departure from his usual method. One of these, that of Harriette Wilson, is surely fictitious.[10] The other, assembled by Lovell in *His Very Self and Voice,* is a relation by Eliza Francis of an encounter with Byron. If Miss Francis's account is accurate, Byron's technique on that occasion lay somewhere between that of his manner with servant girls and that with ladies. Miss Francis was in need of money and literary support, according to her story. He gave her the money but not the support. She in turn employed the faintness routine and wound up sitting on his lap. She protested and he let her go, but subsequently she returned and there was another episode of near miss.[11] The whole account seems pretty overdrawn and it is possible Miss Francis created a pretty piece of fiction out of a trivial encounter.

Susan Boyce's letter, also in Lovell's book, has elements of a similarly overheated imagination. Miss Boyce was an actress at Drury Lane when Byron was one of the board of that playhouse. Her letter implies that she expected a far greater interest on Byron's part than he actually showed and that he had led her to believe he had quite serious interest in her. Miss Boyce also appears to have grossly exaggerated the meaning of a little courtesy.[12] This was one of the perils, to match the opportunities alluded to earlier, of being known for a rake.

If Byron had elaborated, either consciously or otherwise, a successful approach to ladies, it is appropriate to guess what happened with respect to Augusta, if incest really occurred. All biographers seem agreed on the fact that he was relaxed and at ease in her company, and his own statements bear this out. The relationship, certainly in the beginning, was one of easy familiarity. As adult man and woman they had had little association and hardly knew each other, except through their earlier shared memories. Augusta may have been overly demonstrative or she may have behaved in a pattern of their very much earlier association when Byron was a mere boy. A bit too much physical contact at the right moment, and reflexes may have taken over for both of them. This kind of interpretation certainly seems reasonable if Byron's letters to Lady Melbourne may be accepted as accurately reflective of events, and if his reference is to Augusta.

Byron's complexity as a man renders the problem all the more difficult. In many of his amours it seems that love followed sexual activity, and that he was able to view love as both a romantic and an idealized situation and at the same time as an ironic and comic foible. Finally, Byron would pretty surely have been capable of an experimental curiosity: would the product of an incestuous union be necessarily different from other offspring in the Byron family, among whom first-cousin marriages had been so frequent? This would have been an afterthought, a part of his speculative reflection. If incest occurred, it more likely would have been impulsive and unintended, possibly the result of potation and proximity.

❧ 9 ❧

MEDORA'S BIRTH AND BAPTISM

The reason for the attempt to set limits on the birth date of Medora Leigh is obvious: normal human gestation requires 280 days, and the date of birth therefore sets a time and place in which conception could have occurred. Within limits the time and place may also establish possibilities as to paternity in a disputed case.

The Entry in Augusta's Bible

Mayne, who did not specifically document her source, stated that Medora was born 15 April 1814.[1] In a much more recent study Elwin offers detailed discussion of the source. The date derives from Augusta's Bible in which the birth dates of all her children were listed, but Elwin notes that not all the entries are in the same script and speculates that one of Augusta's daughters, probably Emily, may have completed entries Augusta herself failed to make.[2] The assignment of the second script to Emily is largely guesswork, and it is not clear whether Medora's record appears in Augusta's or the other script.

The Bible itself, a part of the Lovelace-Wentworth collection, came into possession of Lord Lovelace through purchase after the death of Emily Leigh.[3] But neither the provenance of the Bible nor the handwriting of the entry is as pertinent as the time when the entry was made. There is no evidence to indicate if Augusta or anyone else made the notation of birth soon after the event. If the entry took place at some later time, even if Augusta made it herself, the date assigned to Medora's birth may not be correct. Either incorrect information, inaccurate memory, or conscious or unconscious distortion could affect its reliability. Obviously some kind of support for the date is highly desirable.

Evidence from Byron's Letters

Byron's letters offer some evidence as to the date on which Medora may have been born. They are useful only for approximation, but they serve to set limits, and one of them has received no attention so far as its possible significance is concerned. This letter, dated 8 April 1814, carries the information from Byron to Lady Melbourne that he has just returned from Six Mile Bottom, and adds that all his relations, "that is, my niece and her mother" are well.[4] Such a statement is curious in that Lady Melbourne had not shown any particular interest in the health and welfare of his relatives, and this gratuitous information seems all the more out of place when he adds that Colonel Leigh was not at home.

What appears to be casual reportage may be something more. Byron rarely mentions Leigh in his letters and specific mention of the Colonel at this time and in conjunction with the rest of the letter seems to imply more than the usual trivial family news. Marchand's interpretation of the visit—an interpretation that other biographers have accepted—was that Byron wanted to be near and perhaps to comfort his sister as the time for her confinement drew near.[5]

Another interpretation is possible upon close reading. In this letter Byron referred in the singular to "my niece and her mother." Though his handwriting might allow for failure to observe the plural of "niece," his use of the singular possessive "her" makes it clear that he specified only one of Augusta's children. In all other correspondence when Byron mentioned the children at Six Mile Bottom he wrote "my nieces." (There is the curious discrepancy already mentioned with respect to Augusta's children. Mayne states that in 1813 Augusta had three daughters, but Elwin, deriving his information from the Bible, reports there were two daughters and one son.[6] If there was a son by this time, nothing in any of Byron's correspondence indicates his existence, a fact that further clouds unquestioning acceptance of the notations of Augusta's Bible.) The use of the singular in this letter, therefore, appears to be specific and intentional rather than casual or the result of oversight.

Hence, the alternative interpretation of the letter of 8 April is that Medora had already been born and that the purpose of the visit was to confirm that Augusta and the baby were in satisfactory condition. In this interpretation the notation of Leigh's absence becomes significant in the sense that the Colonel had not yet come back after Augusta's confinement. "Come back," because at that time and in their level of society, there was a general understanding that men were not to hang around during delivery;[7] it was a time for women only, but fathers were expected to return to view their offspring within a brief time after the confinement was over. Leigh's absence was noteworthy.

Obviously one consideration that might lead the Colonel to absent himself would be either known or suspected illegitimacy of the child. In subsequent years, however, there was nothing in his conduct toward Medora that would indicate that he treated her with any less affection than his other children, and indeed there is a little evidence that she was something of a favorite with him.[8] Since his dislike for Byron is well attested,[9] Leigh's behavior toward the girl would hardly seem compatible with even a suspicion of the poet's paternity and might reinforce the idea that he regarded the illegitimacy as something of an honor, and if not an honor, then something of an advantage.

As to the reason for Byron's visit to Augusta at this date, Mayne's suggestion that he went out of affection, to reassure and comfort his sister as she approached confinement has always seemed forced and remote. It is much more plausible that he would have gone down to Six Mile Bottom to view a delivered infant than to assure Augusta that everything would work out well, an assurance he certainly could not have offered. Furthermore, if the birth of the child was a prospective consideration, it hardly seems likely that Byron on 11 April would have agreed to go with Hobhouse to Paris,[10] even though it is true he reneged on his promise the day following.

If a few days before 7 April should be accepted as the earliest possible date for Medora's birth, Byron's letter of 25 April sets the latest possible date, so far as his correspondence is concerned. In this letter, obviously a reply to Lady Melbourne, he writes that the child is not an *"Ape."* [11] The established interpretation has been that he refers to the birth of Medora, although in no way is that conclusion inevitable. However, if one accepts the Lovelace interpretation, this would set the latest possible date of birth as probably around 23 April, or perhaps a day or so earlier, to allow time for news to arrive in London.

Medora's Baptismal Certificate

The only unassailable piece of evidence with regard to Medora's birth is her baptismal certificate, which bears the date of 15 June

1814. The Rev. Mr. Derek D. Billings, the present vicar of Bottisham, has very kindly prepared a true copy of the certificate from the records of the church at that village. Quite aside from other peculiarities to be mentioned below, the vicar finds this certificate curious. Though the vicar in 1814 was the Reverend William Pugh, known to have been a rather "mean" (i.e. stingy) man and one not likely to pass up a fee for baptism, the officiant in this baptism was the rector of Borough Green, which lies a few miles away, though it is a little closer than Cambridge, where Pugh was a master in one of the colleges. There clings to the substitution of officiants a faint tinge of irregularity.

The certificate is otherwise of more than passing interest in that there is only a check mark to indicate the date of birth. In sum, its information consists of the fact that the child was born, and beyond that lists as her parents "The Honble. Mrs. Augusta Leigh and George Leigh, Esq." So far as the records of the church are concerned, Medora was as legitimate as any other child. As is customary, the list of sponsors follows and, as was also customary, they were relatives: Lord Byron, the Duchess of Rutland, and Mrs. Wilmot.

The sponsors obviously were the choice of Augusta, and it is evident that she must have had fairly recent communication with both the Duchess and Mrs. Wilmot (presumably Mrs. Anne Wilmot, the wife of Robert John, who subsequently played some part in transactions with Lady Byron). The inclusion of Mrs. Wilmot deserves a small notice of itself, for it suggests that Augusta had had occasion to meet the lady somewhere, possibly in London, and to have been on fairly intimate terms with her, since one does not request a relative by marriage to stand as sponsor without some degree of friendly association. Yet, if Wedderburn Webster's account is correct, Byron had not met Mrs. Wilmot until a year later [12]—additional evidence that Augusta in London in 1813 had gone about on her own.

The date of the baptism unfortunately establishes no satisfactory reference point with respect to the birth. Although it was customary to baptize a child within about two weeks of birth, Augusta's record for promptness was not exemplary. As Elwin gives the dates of birth and baptism of the other children who preceded Medora, Augusta usually permitted at least two months to pass before she managed to induct her children into the fold. This may not have been the result of indifference or poor management. It is entirely possible that, with Leigh away from home as much as he was, Augusta might not have had any conveyance suitable for a trip of three or four miles with a new baby.

The widest limits for the date of Medora's birth, therefore, appear to be from the first few days of April to as late as 1 June, if one allows that Augusta, uncharacteristically, rather promptly brought her baby over for baptism. But if the "Ape" letter of 25 April is authentic and if it refers to the birth of Medora, 23 April (to allow time for news to reach London from Six Mile Bottom) seems to be a much more realistic late limit. The date entered in the Bible, 15 April, is thus about midway between the earliest limit and the most realistic late one.

In the record, therefore, there are three contradictory dates. Byron's letter, for reasons already presented, seems to set about 5 April for Medora's birth; the Bible gives 15 April; the letter to Lady Melbourne on 25 April implies a later date for the following reasons. The "Ape" letter not only seems to announce a birth but to express enormous relief that the child is not a monster. If the birth of a normal child was an event of so much significance, it would be hard to explain a delay of several days (from 15 April) in transmission of the information to Byron. If in turn the intelligence was such as to relieve him of a great burden of anxiety it is unlikely he would have further delayed in communicating the news to Lady Melbourne. If it is difficult to reconcile the "Ape" letter with the date inscribed in the Bible, it would be impossible to account for so much delay if Medora was born around 5 April. The possibility has to be entertained that the "Ape" letter may refer to the birth of some other child—who was born at a time closer to 25 April.

If the earlier date of the first week in April appears preferable, it leaves the date in Augusta's Bible insufficiently explained. As Elwin observed, there were entries in more than one hand, and the Bible had been in the possession of the second Lord Lovelace for many decades. Some possibilities of error have already appeared, but one may add yet another. If the actual date of birth happened to be 5 April rather than 15 April, it is obvious that an accidental stroke of the pen or any unintentional error of recording could easily have shifted the birth date by ten days. But also, since the alteration constitutes only a single vertical stroke, a subsequent "correction" or "editing" could be not only very easy but entirely inconspicuous.

≈ 10 ≈

THE TIME AND PLACE
OF CONCEPTION

With probable limits established for the date of Medora's birth, it is possible to work backward to the probable time of conception. Unfortunately human pregnancy lacks the precision of physics and engineering. While normal pregnancy may be expected to last about 280 days, the duration is subject to a certain amount of variation. Rarely does pregnancy exceed this limit, unless it is associated with serious difficulties and complications, none of which seem to have developed in the birth of Medora. A shorter period is much more common, and this is particularly true of a woman who has had several babies in fairly close succession. Prematurity with survival, however, has its own limits, and it is probably safe to suspect that prematurity of more than three or four weeks would have been incompatible with survival of an infant in the early nineteenth century.

The possibilities for the time and place of Medora's conception —and therefore the possible paternity—can best be represented in the form of two tables. The first assumes a full-term delivery, within 2 or 3 days of 280 days; the second assumes a prematurity of 15 days. Statistically, the tables seem to favor Six Mile Bottom or some other place in the country as the site at which conception occurred, for Augusta was in London from about 27 June to about 10 or 12 July. The last absolute date for her London season is 8 July,[1] and it is probable she left soon, perhaps immediately, after this. There is no solid information at all as to where she was and in fact only two clues exist. One of these is Byron's relation of his journey at night through Epping Forest, described in a letter of 25 July to Moore, and the other is a note to Lady Melbourne on 30 July in which he states he has received a letter from his sister.[2]

Table 1. Full-term Delivery

Birth	Conception	Place of Conception
First week of April	5–10 July	London
15 April	15–20 July	SMB; X
Last week of April	25–30 July	SMB

Table 2. Prematurity of 15 Days

Birth	Conception	Place of Conception
First week of April	20–25 July	SMB; X
15 April	30 July – 6 August	SMB
Last week of April	7–12 August	London; SMB

Note: SMB = Six Mile Bottom. X = some other place "in the country."

By 5 August, again according to information from Byron to Lady Melbourne,[3] Augusta had returned to London. It is uncertain how long she stayed on this occasion, but probably not for a very long period, since she had taken lodging in a hotel and was well aware how little she had with which to pay her bills.

To dispose of Colonel Leigh as rapidly as possible, it is enough to say that there is no record of where he was during any of this time. He could easily have appeared at Six Mile Bottom during any of the dates at which Augusta was also at home—if she was at home. Nor is there any compelling reason to suppose he may not also have appeared in London during any of the periods when his wife was there. And if she went to some other place when she left London he could have joined her, or not.

Supporting Evidence

From the foregoing it seems that any of the earlier dates of Medora's birth favor conception sometime in early to mid-July when Augusta was in London or had just left. Obviously these dates derive from a purely arithmetical estimate produced by the date of birth. Other types of information, however, support the earlier dates of conception. The first suggestion of pregnancy should be apparent within two or three weeks after exposure to opportunity. While none of the principals, it is assumed, wrote anything as forthright as the date when Augusta first missed a period, by 22 July Byron had received some kind of notice to which he seems to have responded by going "into the country" (see the discussion in chapter 11).

Yet another bit of information points toward the later weeks of July as the date when Augusta discovered that she was pregnant—if the reference is to Augusta. On 22 August Byron wrote that he was "in a far more serious scrape" than he had ever been, and six days later to the same correspondent he stated that he felt the only possible solution would be for him to marry.[4] He would, he wrote, "incorporate" with any suitable lady, and then he corrected himself by adding that he would have incorporated a month ago. This letter to Moore of 28 August, therefore, seems to set the end of July as the time at which Byron became aware that he had produced a pregnancy. The accepted version is that the unlucky lady was Augusta.

Obviously the mere fact that brother and sister were in London at a crucial time is insufficient to lead to the presumption of incest, nor is it incriminating that both of them found themselves in trouble at about the same time. In order to establish incest as the "trouble" of Byron and Augusta, it is necessary to exclude other possibilities, to show that opportunity presented itself for their amorous activity, and—as in any fair hearing—to establish that no one else was or could have been involved.

☙ 11 ❧

AUGUSTA'S LONDON SEASON

Her Hostess

Augusta, acutely short of funds, apparently had received an invitation to spend her time in London with a relative. In an undated note, sent immediately after Augusta's arrival, Byron wrote, "Between one and two be it—I shall in course prefer seeing you all to myself, without the encumbrance of . . . *your* (for I won't own the relationship) cousin of *eleven page* memory. . . ." The allusion is quite clear. She was a woman, for Byron goes on to remark that she made one of "the finest busts I have seen in the Exhibition, or out of it." [1] The fact that she was a relative whom Byron refuses to acknowledge clearly identifies her as a member of the Carlisle family.

The Earl and Countess of Carlisle had three daughters, Lady Cawdor, the Duchess of Rutland, and Lady Gertrude Sloane.[2] Lady Gertrude, the youngest, had apparently been a particular favorite of Augusta, for Byron much earlier had written his half sister chidingly about the length of her letters to Lady Gertrude and in fact had referred specifically to the eleven pages of one of them.[3] Though this note establishes clearly the identity of Augusta's hostess, and includes a proper recognition of one of her striking attributes, it does not specify the house.

While it may have been Lady Gertrude's own, it is possible that she was occupying the house of relatives during the London season. Her father owned a house in Grosvenor Place, and her sister the Duchess also had a house in town. Since Byron made an appointment to meet his half sister at the place where she was staying, it is likely not to have been the Earl of Carlisle's place, for the poet would have tried at all costs to avoid a meeting with the head of that clan. It seems probable, therefore, that the meeting took place either at the Duke of Rutland's or at Lady Gertrude's town residence. In either location, opportunity for sexual relations would not have been very favorable: it isn't terribly easy for a house guest, even in a large house, to take a man off to her bedroom without attracting some degree of attention.

For several reasons the best probability seems to be that Lady Gertrude may have been staying with the Rutlands. The Duchess was approaching termination of a pregnancy (the infant was born 13 August) and would likely have chosen London rather than the country as the place for her confinement. It might be reasonable that the Duchess would have liked a sister to be on hand for the forthcoming event and that Lady Gertrude would have arranged to come up and remain with her for several weeks. Furthermore, if Augusta's actual hostess was Lady Gertrude, one might have expected some kind of recognition. On the contrary (cf. the naming of Medora) everything Augusta subsequently did implies obligation to the Duchess.

Byron's Affairs

On 27 June, apparently even before the first meeting of the siblings, Byron sent a note to Augusta to inform her that he had obtained for her an invitation to dinner at Lady Davy's.[4] During the first several days, though the poet seems to have been pleased at the reunion with his half sister, he found her arrival inopportune, for he wrote Lady Melbourne on Tuesday, 29 June, that Lady Oxford sailed that day and he had not had an opportunity to see her off, "all the fault of my sister's arrival."[5] The next evening, that of 30 June, Byron attended a dinner at which the Bedfords, Jerseys, Ossulstones, and Greys were present, but there is no record that Augusta was also a guest.[6] However, on Thursday he requested of Lady Melbourne a "she-voucher" that would permit him to take Augusta to a party at Almack's that evening. He adds, "I have got to stand for my picture, and to sit with my sister and to drive to you."[7] Byron implies that his time was fairly well occupied. The following day, after the party at Almack's, he had to attend Chancery Court. Meantime he was working at intervals on revisions and additions to *The Giaour*.

The weekend, Saturday and Sunday, 3 and 4 July, are unaccounted for. On the evening of 5 July, Lady Heathcote gave a party, the noted one at which Lady Caroline Lamb made a gesture at suicide and created a scandal. Almost every account differs and probably none of them is accurate, but Lady Bessborough's, which if slanted at all should be in her daughter's favor, as given to Hobhouse states, "She cut herself with a razor and would have done more had not Lady Bessborough laid hold of it and defied her to draw it through her hand."[8] In brief, at the height of the ball, Lady Caroline injured herself in some fashion, with some kind of an object, to the extent that she managed to do a good bit of bleeding. The milieu was such that the ladies of her circle could only interpret the action as a response to the obvious lack of interest Byron had displayed. It is about as certain as anything connected with her can be that this was no genuine suicidal effort; she was certainly not laid up as a result of the injury, and there is nothing to show that she made other similar attempts. Byron was Lady Rancliffe's escort the entire evening and there is no indication that Augusta was in attendance. During at least a part of 6 July Byron was sending off notes to Lady Melbourne reassuring her that Lady Caroline's act had been no fault of his and that it probably would not have created such a stir if Lady Ossulstone and Lady Y (probably Yarmouth) had acted with any discretion.[9]

On some date very near this time, immediately following the affair at Lady Heathcote's, Byron attended a dinner for men at Frere's.[10] Augusta was certainly in town on 8 July, for Byron wrote Moore on that date indicating that Augusta's presence was a "great comfort." [11] When she left London is not recorded, but it may well have been not long after this, for by 13 July Byron's eye was roving and he wrote Moore, "I am amazingly inclined . . . to be seriously enamoured of Lady Adelaide Forbes." [12] He went on to catalogue her obvious beauty and to inquire concerning her disposition and temperament. According to Mayne he continued to pay special attention to this young lady during the next several weeks following the Heathcote contretemps. After this letter there is a hiatus corresponding to 13–18 July. Letters 312–318 in Prothero bear dates of 18, 22, 25, 27, 28, and 31 July, and all either carry London datelines or clearly indicate that Byron wrote them in London.

The foregoing is the most complete account that can be developed of Byron's activities during the time at which the supposed incest should have occurred. Obviously there are many hiatuses about which there is no information. In addition to his social activities there were several other functions that required his attention. He apparently continued to pose for portraits by Phillips; letters to Murray make it clear that this late he continued to work on various emendations and additions to *The Giaour;* [13] the

Chancery suit was still in progress and required some portion of his time.

Doris Langley Moore's new volume, *Accounts Rendered,* adds another preoccupation of an absorbing character: during at least the latter part of this time, the poet was buying all kinds of clothing, uniforms, equipment, saddlery, and camping requirements (not to exclude embellishments).[14] By 15 July, she reports, he thoroughly gave himself over to this operation. Her records of his purchases also make it certain that he was in town on 16, 17, and 19 July.

Augusta's Activities

It is evident that Byron attended several different gatherings at which Augusta was not present. One supposes conversely that she must have been present at a number of parties to which he was not invited. Her relations with the Carlisle kin had always been most friendly, and as a guest of one of the daughters it is expectable that others of the family invited her. To none of these family gatherings would Byron have been welcome, nor would he willingly have gone if he had been invited. At some of these, it is reasonable to suppose that she met Mrs. Wilmot, as suggested in the section on Medora's baptism.

Furthermore, if Augusta's principal concern in coming up to London was to obtain some type of financial reinforcement, she must have recognized very early that Byron was in no position to assist. With the rapid and conclusive elimination of that possibility a determined woman would not have retired in defeat, but would have turned to other possible sources. In addition to the Carlisle connection, Augusta could well have turned to her half sister, the Countess of Chichester, or her half brother, the Duke of Leeds, both of whom were sufficiently affluent. It is but reasonable to guess that without a Byronic encumbrance Augusta may have sought out and visited with all these prospects during her season in London. To suppose that she was so completely dependent on Byron, or he upon her, as to appear in company only as a pair is to disregard not only the character of the two but the commitments and purposes of each individually.

To be still more specific, there are only three occasions when it is established that Augusta and Byron were together in the evening: the dinner at Lady Davy's, the party at Almack's, and the gathering at Glenbervie's. If he "sat" with his sister, it would have been in the afternoons probably—perhaps for tea. It is not conspicuously a time for flaming immorality.

Finally, one should not overlook the fact that she may have requested an audience with the Prince Regent himself. Though Colonel Leigh was in disgrace, Augusta might possibly have undertaken to restore him to favor or at least to seek compassion for the family. Later letters of Byron indeed suggest that she had on one or more occasions intervened to find some kind of position for Leigh. Whether Augusta made such an approach directly or through some intermediary, or even that she sought help from the Regent or possibly from the Duke of York, as commander in chief, does not appear. Under any of these conditions Augusta would have placed herself in a vulnerable position. Far better men than any of these have known how to take advantage of such a situation and to exact a *quid pro quo*. For reasons to be demonstrated later, there is cause to think that Augusta's mission may have resulted at once or possibly somewhat later in important financial aid. To what extent Byron assisted in her efforts is unknown, but certainly by this time his own attitudes and activities would not have provided him with very much influence in Court, which represented almost the only source of benefits.

Postlude to Augusta's Season

The exact date of Augusta's departure from London is unknown, the last assured date of her presence in the city being 8 July. The preceding review of Byron's and her activities makes it clear that the two were by no means constantly in company, but that each pursued his own goals. If Augusta's purpose in coming up to the city had been to find some kind of succor, one may assume that by mid-July she had been successful or that the mission had ended in hopeless failure.

Nor is it certain that she returned to Six Mile Bottom at once upon her departure. Since it appears almost certain that she had been a guest of Lady Gertrude Sloane or the Rutlands, and since the season was nearing its close, Augusta may have accompanied some of her kin to a country place. In the case of the Duke of Rutland, one country place was at Chevely, very near Newmarket, where apparently he kept his horses and where Augusta may first have encountered the name Medora, that of a two-year-old filly.

≫ 12 ≪

AUGUSTA SENDS SIGNALS

Byron remained in town, and within a week had indulged in a thoroughly documented shopping spree in anticipation of his intended departure to the Mediterranean area.[1] Both the records of his purchases and the letters he wrote make it almost certain that he was in the city till 22 July. Between that time and 25 July, when he wrote Moore that he had been "into the country," he had made a very rapid excursion to some place or places. With respect to this trip the only other significant information is that he traveled by night and passed through Epping Forest.[2] While he did not specifically state whether one or both legs of the journey passed through the forest, the assumption has been that the return was by that route.

The significance of the information is (1) that he was moving rapidly though not necessarily furtively, and (2) that Epping Forest lies along the road to Cambridge, Six Mile Bottom, and Newmarket. If only his return was by this route, the information suggests that he had gone to some other place, come around to Cambridge (presumably to Six Mile Bottom), and then returned to London along the usual road. What seems important is the haste he showed. Even if the journey were solely to Six Mile

86

Bottom and back, he allowed himself a very short time at his destination, for he would have left the city on 22 July and left Six Mile Bottom on 24 July.

The generally accepted view is that Byron, madly in love, could no longer endure separation and dashed into the country to visit Augusta. But while lovers suddenly and impulsively may hasten to their amies, they usually linger if they can. Byron's return, however, seems to have been as precipitous as his departure from London.

On the other hand, if Byron had received some kind of message—perhaps only a very brief note that he may have destroyed —from Augusta, and if her signal indicated trouble, his temperament would have led precisely to this kind of response. Especially if she were at some other place than Six Mile Bottom, a sign of distress and an appeal for help would have appropriately produced the kind of journey he made. It may not be unreasonable to suspect that in fact she had gone to some house party in the country, discovered that she was in trouble, and appealed to her half brother to fetch her home promptly.

Immediately upon his return to London the poet resumed his preparations for the East, as though he had not suffered the interruption. It is important to observe that, as of 25 July, he gave no evidence at all of any change in the plans he had entertained since as early as May—or even much earlier. His purchases were of the same order as they had been before his incursion "into the country." [3] Then there came a second interruption, this time in a verified letter from Augusta, which he reported to Lady Melbourne on 30 July and which may have arrived a day earlier. [4] This message evidently was of a different type from the earlier (and hypothetical) signal. For Augusta specifically instructed him not to reveal its contents to his confidante. Furthermore, the information in Augusta's letter also seemed to be less urgent—

or alternatively to have called for extensive rearrangement of his plans.

At all events Byron's response was much more deliberate, for he did not leave London until 2 or 3 August. When he returned he brought Augusta with him and installed her in a hotel.[5] Hardly were they back in London when the poet on 5 August wrote Lady Melbourne that Augusta was in town and would soon go with him to Italy. Conditions were such that a week later, from some other place "near London," as he described it, he informed James Wedderburn Webster that he and his sister were planning to leave England to go to Sicily—again, so he explained the situation, to relieve Leigh's financial difficulties.[6] Meanwhile Lady Melbourne had written the poet in some alarm and apparently had objected strongly to his emigration with Augusta. Whether it was her intervention, a change in some external relationships, the difficulty of going abroad, or yet other entirely unknown factors, by late in August the whole project was thrown over and Augusta was back at Six Mile Bottom. Such are the facts and the sequence of events.

In the light of the *Astarte* thesis, all this scurrying about and the adoption and abandonment of plans are completely intelligible. Later actions and statements, although they are intimately connected with these events, adjust less readily to the hypothesis of incest, and no one has offered explanations of events of early August. One wonders, for example, where Byron and Augusta were when they were "near London" and why they went to wherever they were. Since Six Mile Bottom is about seventy miles from the city, "near" hardly seems an appropriate description for that place. It would seem more plausible that if Augusta had earlier spent a few days in the country with her hostess of the London season, she and Byron may have gone back to the same house.

This would be reasonable if the place to which they went was Lady Gertrude Sloane's, for her husband's place was nearer to London than that of any other relative. Lady Gertrude and Augusta had been closely associated during their girlhood, and if Augusta was in trouble she presumably would have sought out her old friend and confidante, who may also have been her recent hostess and sponsor in London. The poet might have served well enough when action was essential, but probably would have been of little use when hysteria threatened. If Byron had been her lover, his own consolation should have been sufficient, but it looks as if Augusta's tribulation required the sympathy of a woman. The point may receive further substantiation from the fact that the following year Lady Caroline Lamb complained that Lady Gertrude was exceedingly cool toward her.

It is entirely understandable that Augusta would have called upon Byron in the event of difficulty. Not only had she had little association with her half siblings the Duke of Leeds and the Countess of Chichester, but Byron had specifically reminded her that as Lord Byron he was head of the family and that she was to turn to him with any problems.[7] Quite aside from his assumption of the role of family protector, Augusta, with or without impropriety, had more recent association with him than with any of her kin on her mother's side.

One can only speculate on the nature of the information Augusta transmitted in her communications. Undoubtedly both (if there *were* two, as I think probable) contained news of some gravity, judging from Byron's reactions. The second message, the content of which Augusta directed her brother not to reveal, evidently carried the more distressing news since it led to the more drastic reaction—that of taking Augusta away from her home and her children.

In the section on Medora's birth it was suggested that the first letter may have brought the information that she was pregnant, since the time would have been about right for a conception in the second week of July. Because there is no proof that she returned promptly to Six Mile Bottom when she departed London, there is a possibility that the first of the two communications may have contained an urgent request for Byron to come for her and convey her home. In that case the second letter would have imparted the fact that she suspected she was pregnant.

Was pregnancy, even though contracted extramaritally, an affair of so much concern that Augusta would have warned Byron not to reveal it to Lady Melbourne? Certainly situations of that kind were far from uncommon among the upper classes, and though they might occasionally produce some messy scandals, disgrace resulted from the fuss rather than the fact. The general statement, however, does not sufficiently establish that Augusta may have regarded the situation so lightly when it applied to herself.

By 5 August, she was ready to leave England and accompany Byron to some place in Italy. This represented a radical decision indeed. To the followers of *Astarte,* the obvious explanation of both letters and Byron's plan to emigrate has been that their relations had continued as often as Byron could get away from London, and that they were on the point of eloping with the intent of spending the remainder of their lives in inexpiable sin. This hypothesis has the gratifying lurid quality that would appeal to those who regarded *The Giaour* and the other heroes of the Eastern tales as replicas of the author.

The ostensible reason for Augusta's accompanying him, as Byron informed Lady Melbourne on 5 August and Webster on 12 August, was that her husband's financial affairs were so bad that it was necessary to emigrate to escape the duns. Nevertheless, Leigh would not go with them. (This was not a rare expedient for the English upper classes. Living on the Continent was cheaper than in England and one was much more secure from creditors, who could go so far as to attach household goods or even, for people of lower birth—not so much lower, at that—demand prison sentences. Lord and Lady Oxford had found it convenient, quite aside from Byron, to take refuge in Italy.)

If the purpose of Byron and Augusta was elopement rather than emigration they gave it up rather readily—certainly in part prompted by the vigorous intervention of Lady Melbourne, whose disapproval was instant and emphatic as judged from Byron's replies to her. Perhaps Augusta had entered into the scheme reluctantly and regretfully. Certainly she proposed first "Lady C." [8] and then one of her children as a member of the emigrating menage, undoubtedly to provide the appearance of propriety. That they were by no means impetuously eloping is clear from the fact that instead of taking the first coach to Dover or Southampton or anywhere, both brother and sister spent at least a week in examining a series of plans and exchanging—on Byron's part —several notes with Lady Melbourne. When, after all the debating and changing of plans, Augusta abandoned the whole idea and went home, one would have expected Byron to have been frustrated and infuriated if his basic purpose had been to remove to Italy for a life of sin in the sun.

There is another plausible explanation for the two letters, Byron's reactions, the plan to go to Italy, and the rather ready abandonment of the plan. Without the original information, certainty will never be possible, but the following interpretation of the events seems compatible with established dates, as well as with the attitudes and emotions of the principals. Unfortunately the obstetrical clock is not a very accurate timepiece. Suspicion of pregnancy as the subject of either the first or the second letter from Augusta, about 20 July or about 29 July, would allow of birth as early as 5 April or 15 April. The earlier report of pregnancy would accord most readily with an earlier date of birth, with conception probably in the period 5 July to 12 July, with its occurrence in London, and pretty certainly with the exclusion of Leigh's paternity.

On such a hypothesis, Augusta's first communication may well have carried the information that she was pregnant. What message would the second carry that would lead Byron to go down to Six Mile Bottom and bring back his sister with the announced intention of taking her abroad with him? The most obvious answer seems to be that Leigh had returned home for a visit, learned of Augusta's problem, been certain that he had no part in it, and told her to leave his house. Tidings of this type would certainly call for the injunction of strictest confidence. The situation would also be disastrous enough to lead a hitherto devoted English wife to consider housekeeping for her brother in Italy.

If this was the situation on 5 August, the rather ready abandonment of the plan and Byron's slightly later "exquisite good humour with" himself and "two or three other people" become understandable. He almost surely had effected a rapprochement between the estranged spouses. Since, as Augusta later wrote, Leigh was quite jealous about such matters,[9] it would not have been out of character for him to send her away if she had proven unfaithful.

This explanation seems to meet the requirements of available dates and to be compatible with the behavior of the various principals—with one exception. If Byron had been the agent of Augusta's pregnancy he could not readily have had part in the reconciliation; he could not have been in a very good humor; and it is most unlikely that Leigh would have found him a suitable guest at Christmas or would have been content in the January following for Augusta to spend three weeks at Newstead with him.

⚜ 13 ⚜

THE SEASON OF HIS DISCONTENT

Not long after the Carolinish demonstration at Lady Heath-cote's ball and the exquisite good humor of mid-August, Byron's behavior takes on an entirely different character. Whereas he had before this moved with sufficient aplomb among the great soirées, he began to avoid his previous haunts. The season was just ending and he was thoroughly aware how frivolous and meaningless were his associations in the haut monde, but as this section will demonstrate the poet subjected himself to a striking degree of ostracism for a period of several months. If his behavior in any way clarifies the nature of the problem that faced him in late July, it does so only by inference and deduction.

There is no question that Byron had been hoping to leave England as soon as he could arrange his affairs. Hardly had he returned from the East when he expressed the wish to go back, and his desire had been steadfast. No one, not even he, would deny that he had enjoyed his notoriety and the activities that derived from it. But as of the end of June 1813 there was little to keep him in England. He had broken off with Lady Caroline, and Lady Oxford had already departed. There were only some Chancery proceedings and Augusta's presence in town to delay his departure. His only other obligation would have been the completion of his sittings for his portraits by Phillips, which had certainly begun as early as 2 July.

Perhaps the change in mood dates from Caroline's injury. Byron's notes in the early morning and on the day following made light of the episode. However, he was writing to Lady Melbourne, and his attitudes as he revealed them in his letters to her do not always correspond in every respect with comments he made to others, or perhaps with his genuine but suppressed reactions. How much Caroline's gesture may have frightened him, or if he came to consider it as a far more serious attempt at suicide never becomes clear. At any rate it gave rise to a lot of gossip and, worse, to newspaper reports.[1] Taking the lightest possible view, Byron could only have considered the episode as most annoying.

If it had no other effect, the affair seems promptly to have crystallized his decision to go abroad. On 13 July he wrote Croker requesting passage to the East, and apparently for some days he set about providing himself with what he regarded as necessary for a long absence in remote places.[2] On 8 July Byron had written Moore the letter which contains the curious statement that Augusta's presence in London was "a great comfort," and only five days later he was discussing with Moore the possibility of becoming "seriously enamour'd" of Lady Adelaide Forbes.[3]

These deflections of interest, however, in no way interfered with his basic design to get away, and he continued to provide himself with a lot of useless and expensive equipment for his expedition.[4] To what extent all this activity may have merely occupied him, may have diverted his mind from other problems of a far more immediate and serious complexion does not emerge. Since he had learned already that plague in the Eastern ports had resulted in quarantine and that passage was at best uncertain, it appears as if the poet may only have been busying himself.

At this point occurred the two letters from Augusta and her return to London for a stay of probably seven to ten days.[5] During this time she stayed at the St. James Hotel, whether because she had obtained a source of funds or because no other choice was available. The season was over and it is possible that none of her friends was still in town. If her relations with the ladies of the Carlisle clan had deteriorated, no subsequent events would seem to support such a possibility.

Byron's letters during this and the next ten days contain almost no information as to what he was doing, but on 20 August he wrote from London to Lady Melbourne, who seems to have been at the country place at Brocket, a very cryptic report.[6]

> When I don't write to you or see you for some time you may be very certain I am about no good—and *vice versa*. I have sent you a long scrawl, and here be a second, which may convince you I am not ashamed of myself, or else I should have kept out of the way of one for whom I have so much regard. . . . I happened just then [when he answered two letters from Lady Caroline] to be in exquisite good humour with myself and two or three other people.

And he continues with the significant addition that he was at the time of the note "in very good plight and spirits." By that time Augusta had returned home. His evident high spirits and relief, as well as his clear statement that he had nothing he would be ashamed of, do not support the contention that he had reluctantly abandoned the idea of migration with Augusta only as a result of Lady Melbourne's urgent dissuasion and Augusta's preference to return to her family.

It is pretty certain that all events connected with these decisions took place in London, for Prothero states that Byron was dining almost nightly at the same restaurant from 7 August to 27

August.[7] Thereafter he missed a few meals, but resumed his custom from 2 September to 10 September, when a new problem, which seems to have been gathering force, took him away from London to some place near Cambridge. By this time the "good humour" and "good plight and spirits" had vanished and his letters had acquired a grim, even morose tone.

The "Fancied" Duel

Many years later Byron told one of his friends that as a consequence of the contretemps at Lady Heathcote's, Lady Caroline had promised "young ——" that if he would challenge Byron to a duel "she would ——."[8] There is nothing in the record to substantiate the story except the poet's activities throughout the autumn, his obvious effort to take himself out of regular circulation among his acquaintances, and a series of cryptic letters to Lady Melbourne, if they are in the main authentic. So far as consistency with known characteristics is concerned, Byron's behavior with respect to a possible challenger would be acceptable. Just about everything he ever wrote and some recorded instances of his behavior indicate that if he received a challenge he would feel compelled to answer. It is just about as certain, as his letter about a possible duel between Scrope Davies and a peer demonstrates, that he regarded the activity as foolish.[9] That Byron would have found it more reasonable either to kill a young man or to allow himself to be killed over Lady Caroline than to see Davies and the peer shoot each other over a card game seems implausible. In this context his absences from his usual haunts may have served a very necessary purpose.

The letters to Lady Melbourne of later August and September are consistent with the idea that he expected a duel, and not very consistent with anything else. On 8 September Byron informed her that he was determined to leave London for an unspecified place, regardless of the fact that she disapproved his going and had attempted to dissuade him from it. "I leave tomorrow for a few days, come what may; and as I am sure you would get the better of my resolution, I shall not venture to encounter you. If nothing particular occurs, you will allow me to write as usual. If there does, you will hear *of,* but not *from* me (of course) again." [10] It is possible to infer that Byron was going to Six Mile Bottom and that he and Augusta would leave for the Continent promptly, but such an interpretation is most unlikely, since by early September their idea of going abroad together seems to have been abandoned. Certainly he was about to depart from London to meet someone, and the outcome of the meeting was quite uncertain. If the meeting went off without some kind of major incident he would continue his correspondence as usual. His underscoring the prepositions ("you will hear *of,* but not *from* me") and adding "of course" suggests that the meeting could in fact have been a duel and that he expected not to come out alive. Some months later, in the journal, he speculated on the subject of a duel (by that time he may have had Webster in mind) and stated that he had abstained from pistol practice and that if he were in a duel with an aggrieved challenger he would not return the fire.[11]

His letter of 9 September, the day after the first of this series to Lady Melbourne, seems to reinforce this interpretation. "Something has occurred that prevents my leaving town till Saturday —perhaps till Sunday [12 September]; later than that I cannot well remain. Without as A says being in a state of *despondency,* I am nevertheless very much perplexed; however that must end one way or another." [12] There is no indication of the reason he could not leave town, unless it may have had something to do with continued Newstead litigation. Certainly an inflamed lover on an elective visit to his *amie* would hardly have written in this fashion: it is evident he did not at all relish the prospect of the trip.

"A" almost certainly refers to Augusta. If the identification is correct she had very probably written something about his emotional state. But he seems to have reached a kind of resignation: he was not despondent but "perplexed"; and that state, he informed Lady Melbourne, would soon end "one way or another." If confrontation with an injured and challenging man was in prospect, some conclusion would surely occur—either in the form of retraction, or possibly of compensation, or in the death of one of the principals.

Apparently the trip outside London was brief and to some point not far from Cambridge. The dates are a little confusing, but they seem to indicate that Byron left London on 12 September, while his letter of 15 September to Augusta states that he left Cambridge "last night" and arrived at London at 3 A.M. He also reported that he and Scrope Davies had dined in hall at Cambridge and in the course of the evening had consumed six bottles of wine.[13] Of course the dinner with Davies may have been no more than a reunion of old friends, but that he chose to report in some detail seems to give the meeting added significance.

The relationship between Byron and Davies had begun in university, and at a later time Byron had borrowed a considerable sum from him. By 1813, Davies had become a Fellow, but it appears that he may not have been often in residence, since he was an inveterate gambler and opportunities for his kind of stakes were far better in London. Byron's letters and journals do not refer to Davies as often as to many of his other university friends, but he records two occasions when his friend was to act as his second in a threatened duel and one occasion when the poet acted as Davies's second.[14] (None of these reached the point of gunfire, it may be noted.)

Cambridge, of course, is quite near Six Mile Bottom, but the fact of geographic proximity is not sufficient to establish that Byron's visit had been to that place—or, if a duel was in prospect, that the challenger was Leigh. The terms of Byron's will were such that if a duel between Byron and Leigh should have occurred, the Colonel would promptly have come under suspicion of conspiracy to murder for the sake of Augusta's inheritance.[15] It seems almost certain that Byron did not see Augusta at all during this trip, since on 15 September he wrote in almost commercial style, addressing her as "My dear Augusta" and concluding with "yours very truly." In this letter he inquires if she will visit him in London before his anticipated departure for Europe, a question he surely would have had no occasion to ask if they had recently met.

This point receives confirmation from a letter to Murray on the same day, in which Byron wrote that he wanted passage overseas for himself, a friend, and three servants.[16] As an afterthought he added that he expected to see Augusta before his departure. The identity of the "friend" remains completely obscure. It is evident, however, that by this date Augusta had abandoned any thought of flight to the Continent, and since the flirtation with Lady Frances Webster had not yet begun, if his friend was a lady the only possibilities are Lady Caroline or some hitherto unidentified lady.

Unless Byron was inventing the whole story, therefore, it seems that he in fact faced a real possibility of a duel, that Davies characteristically was his second, that a meeting and some kind of reconciliation occurred about 13 or 14 September, that Byron and Davies celebrated the averting of bloodshed, and that the poet was eager to leave England and his previous associates as quickly as possible.

Whether the aborted confrontation involved "young ———" is a different question. Obviously one turns serious if he is about to let someone shoot him, even if he considers the occasion of the quarrel as trivial. Byron's later reference to young ———— appears to be a rather airy dismissal of the entire affair. Another possibility, therefore, is that the occasion of the meeting arose from a far more serious situation, and that Byron was more than pleased to come out of it without injury to either party. But his mind found no peace, and perhaps for the want of anything else to do, as well as from a desire to take himself away from his usual environment, he joined the Wedderburn Websters in a prolonged house party at Aston.

The House Party

If Byron chose this invitation as a means of avoiding undesirable encounters, he chose well. Most of his associates had their estates either in southern Yorkshire or in the south and west of England. Webster had not moved in the same circles as Byron and their acquaintances were for the most part quite distinct. So far as there is evidence the two men had not seen much of each other for some time, and it thus seems likely that Byron's choice of a host in the country was well designed to avoid the embarrassment of encounters.

After some ten days in the house party, at a time when his hosts and their party were on the point of attending races at Doncaster, Byron broke away and returned to London. He may have deserted the party at this point through concern over the possibility of an unfortunate collision with some man at the races. Since nothing that Byron ever wrote or that was written about him indicates any interest in racing, his departure may only have been to avoid boredom and to attend to some business in London. But his own statement, "The Doncaster races drove me to town. . . . I had reasons of my own, some bad, others good, for not accompanying the party to Doncaster," certainly seems to indicate a number of motives.[17]

The race Byron avoided was the St. Leger Stakes, run on Monday, 27 September.[18] Characteristically, the St. Leger drew enormous crowds—for the time—and people who attended converted the occasion into a very English type of fête champêtre. Members of the royal family often appeared; and country houses, to say nothing of the few inns available, were packed with guests. The race of 1813 was marked by rather heavy betting, and the favorite, Altisidora, owned by a Mr. Watts and ridden by Dick Andrews, paid 5 for 2. Among owners of colts and fillies entered in the race appears the name of the Duke of Leeds with two entries, but none of the other owners is recognizable in any connection with Byron's activities. Lord Archibald (by this time Duke of) Hamilton frequently entered colts in the St. Leger, but seems to have had no entry in 1813, though he may well have been in attendance. Lord Darlington, the familiar associate of Colonel Leigh, likewise had no entry in this race, though he had entered in 1812 and may have attended. One cannot, therefore, pick out from the records the name of a particular person whom Byron wished to avoid, but the absence of a name among the list of owners, of course, does not imply that he may not have attended.

Byron did return to London and on 29 September reported that he had completed the signing of his will.[19] The new will changed the provisions, which previously had divided his estate equally between Captain George Byron and Augusta, and now established Augusta as his sole beneficiary. On the *Astarte* hypothesis, the interpretation of the change is that it constituted a monetary acknowledgment of his paternity of Medora and compensation to Leigh and Augusta. If this were true, his meeting at or near Cambridge should have been with Leigh or his representative, and the provisions of the will in accord with an hypothesized indemnification should have ended any further concern.

After three or four days in London to conclude his business, Byron rejoined the Websters at Aston Hall. It appears that some of his acute problems had been relieved—at all events, his relationship with the lady of July (if she was not Augusta) had reached its conclusion and on 12 October he informed Lady Melbourne, "Anything, you will allow, is better than the *last* . . . but recollect, the circumstances which have broken off the last and don't exactly attribute their conclusion to caprice." [20] In short, that affair had not terminated through any whim of his own or as a result of his interest in Lady Frances but out of necessity. His continuing discussion of this topic, in his letter of 23 October, is even clearer in reference to a duel and to a final conclusion of the affair. "Come what may, I can hardly regret the untoward events; . . . you have preserved me from *two,* one eventually and the other had been immediately fatal." [21]

If the letter of 23 October has any literal meaning, it indicates that Lady Melbourne in some fashion had prevented a duel between Byron and some other man, a duel in which Byron would have received but not returned his opponent's fire. Her intervention could have involved political, financial, or personal sanctions or rewards. Of these the only one to which Leigh would have responded would probably have been financial, since he had no interest in politics and since social preferment in Whig or any other circle meant little to him. It appears equally certain that during the next several years he himself received no sort of preferment, sinecure, or annuity. If he was determined to kill Byron on account of Augusta, probably the only person who could have influenced him would have been among his associates in racing or gambling. It appears unlikely one of these would have bothered himself over the shooting of a poet.

The visit at the Webster's country house continued and Byron apparently persuaded his hostess to invite Augusta to the house party. The letter to Lady Melbourne in which this information occurs goes on, "I have also reasons for returning there on Sunday, with which they [the Websters] have nothing to do; but if C. takes a suspicious twist that way, let her—it will keep her in darkness. . . ." [22] While this letter makes it appear that he wanted to renew his relations with Augusta—superficially a sound interpretation if one accepts unquestioningly the *Astarte* hypothesis—the circumstances of the house party would have rendered any trace of affection blatantly conspicuous. The house was small [23] and there were only a few people; Webster was excessively jealous and had been watching Byron narrowly with respect both to his wife and to her sister, Lady Catherine Annesley. The ladies themselves were very much aware of the poet, as almost the only unattached male around, and were closely observing him for interest in each other. That under such continuous and close scrutiny he would have risked discovery of his infatuation for Augusta strikes one as inconceivable—even for Byron. It appears at least reasonable that he may have had some other motive for requesting her invitation. As it chanced, however, Augusta could not or did not accept the invitation, and there followed the poet's rather aimless—so he represented it to Lady Melbourne—courtship of Lady Frances Webster, his host's wife.

Without much doubt Byron was prone to like whate'er he looked on, and in this small party Lady Frances and her sister constituted the horizon. In some respects he found agreeable the rather hesitant manner and demure, pale good looks of his hostess; he was impatient with Webster's boastful possessiveness; there was very little to do. Though he may have begun his approach to Lady Frances in cynicism and out of ennui, the young woman proved rather more fascinating than he anticipated. If he never loved her—in some one of the many meanings of "that wide word"[24]—she came to preoccupy quite a bit of his attention and thought, as his journal of that winter reflects far more accurately than his letters to Lady Melbourne.

If the poet had been a truly cynical rather than a romantic man the story would have followed quite a different course. As it was, Lady Frances fell in love with him and was ready to elope—if he would propose it. The fact that she was tearful, rather metaphysical, and perhaps becoming a bit hysterical about the possibilities may have had something to do with Byron's self-denial. At any rate he exhibited quite unexpected kindness and consideration, and withdrew before either of them was too far committed. It may be questioned whether he would have behaved so well without the experience of the previous few months. But perhaps, in view of the mode of operation attributed to him, he was not capable of forthright seduction, particularly if the lady exhibited concern and a kind of resigned and sorrowful compliance.

Fortunately for both of them the house party broke up in mid-November and Webster and his lady set out to spend the winter in the Grampian Hills.[25] Byron returned to London and began his journal. In a state of semiseclusion he remained until the arrival of Augusta about mid-December. Now and again he went to Holland House and occasionally he joined some of the Whig aristocracy for an after-theater dinner, but for the most part he avoided society and saw but little of the brilliant set with whom he had associated so much during the earlier part of 1813.[26]

Family Interlude

In mid-December Augusta returned to London; abruptly the journal stopped. Whether she came at the urging of Byron, prompted by her passion (if it existed), or again in search of some palliation of her chronic insolvency does not appear in any published record. It is even possible, as later discussion will suggest, that her affairs were temporarily in somewhat better order and that she just came up to town for Christmas shopping, a not unheard-of activity even among ladies of limited means.

Byron still retained his cramped quarters in Bennet Street, and Augusta at first found lodging with Byron's old friends, the Harrowbys; but after a time she moved to stay with her friend, Mrs. Theresa Villiers, who lived much closer to him. Augusta's presence in London started the gossip, and more than one lady began to snoop about. The poet wrote Lady Melbourne that "Lady Holland had been guessing and asking about Mrs. Chaworth," and Lady Mountnorris, the mother of Lady Frances Webster, "was seized with a sudden penchant for A and called on her at Vlrs and asked her to some party. . . ." [27]

Not unexpectedly Lady Caroline Lamb was suspicious. She first tried the rumor factory; as Byron wrote, "The separation and express are utterly false . . . so you see her spies are ill-paid or badly informed." [28] The meaning of the sentence is not crystal clear, but it seems to be that Lady Caroline had spread the news, obtained from some of her sources in and out of London, that the Leighs were on the point of separation. When this failed to gain support or interest, she then began to spread the word that Augusta was staying at Byron's flat. At this point the poet replied that Augusta not only was not there, but had stayed with his friends, and that even if she visited him in his flat it would have been far more seemly than Lady Caroline's incursions into his previously decent house.

Just when Augusta returned to her own home is not recorded, but almost certainly she would have gone back before Christmas. Shortly before or just after Christmas Byron came down to Six Mile Bottom to join a small party, which contained, among others, Sir John and Lady Frances Shelley.[29] While Byron left no comment, Lady Frances presents a rather sharp etching of the crowded house near Newmarket. The picture is that of a hostess attempting a house party in the face of difficulties—"The house is far too small even for the company it contained. . . ." As for the hostess herself, she evidently had her hands full. "She looks very much older than her brother, and does not make the most of herself. She is dowdy in her dress, and seems to be quite indifferent to personal appearances. She is extremely good, and I like her much." [30]

One should recall, as he reads this description, that Augusta was pregnant and not altogether well, that she had three young children to see to, and that she had recently faced severe financial strain, even as at the moment she was trying to entertain guests in a pretty inadequate situation. Nor is it entirely out of place to mention that Lady Frances recently had been circulating in rarefied society and playing the belle at the most select gatherings of the Regency.

However vain and socially ambitious she may have been, Lady Frances had a rather sharp perception of people, and her comments on Augusta are illuminating. In 1813 she observed of the relation between Byron and Augusta, "Her manner toward him is decidedly maternal; it is as though she were reproving a thoughtless child." And this early appraisal reinforces her commentary of 1870 when she dismissed out of hand the story of incest, "The preposterous accusation which has lately been brought against Mrs. Leigh seems to me, who knew her well, as the height of absurdity. She was what I would call a religious woman; and her feeling for Byron was that of an elder sister towards a wayward child." If Lady Frances was mistaken she was at least consistent in her reading. (As for Lady Byron, upon whom she called in company with Augusta in April 1815, her hostess "received us courteously, but I felt, at once, that she is not the sort of woman with whom I could ever be intimate. Mrs. Leigh seems to be fond of her. . . . I was not sorry when the visit was over.")[31]

The significance of the party at Six Mile Bottom is far from certain. While Sir John and Colonel Leigh were old comrades in arms and apparently enjoyed each other's company, there has been no trace of information that Augusta and Lady Frances previously had known each other. Further, while the Shelleys had been leading a very glittering existence, the Leighs had been desperately insecure. What strikes one as odd is that at Christmas of 1813 Augusta had felt prosperous enough—at least for the moment—to set up a house party. The possible implication of this minor and temporary affluence will appear in later discussion.

On an uncertain date, probably after New Year's Day, Byron returned to London and his solitary ways, but he did not resume his journal. Instead, on Wednesday, 12 January 1814, he wrote Augusta, "On Sunday or Monday next, with leave of your lord and president, you will be *well,* and ready to accompany me to Newstead." [32] Well or otherwise, certainly well into her sixth month of pregnancy, Augusta got herself ready. They arrived at Newstead just before a record snowfall that kept roads almost impassable till 5 February. During the interval, Claughton came by to examine the property before he should bid on it. Byron, while he failed to carry out his original purpose of visiting Mary Chaworth, who was attempting to renew their ancient romance, received mail and finally saw *The Corsair* into print—about which, more will be said later.

Financial Reprieve for the Leighs

In the absence of balance sheets, speculation as to the financial condition of the Leighs has to be very careful. However, the record seems quite clear that in the spring of 1813 Augusta had been desperate with respect to her finances. That her visit to London, beginning in late June, was for the purpose of obtaining relief seems pretty certain. Byron's letters to Lady Melbourne and to Wedderburn Webster during the first two weeks of August imply there had been no improvement in the interval. At none of these times was there any indication that Byron was able to assist in any important manner.

What seems interesting is that after about 15 August, nothing indicates that Byron received any further solicitation. The date corresponds fairly closely with the letter to Lady Melbourne in which Byron informed her that he was in "exquisite good humour," not only with himself, but "with two or three other people," one of whom may have been a man of considerable fortune. It was suggested that as a result of Byron's intervention around the first two weeks in August, the Leighs were not only reconciled but indemnified.

If they were in financial straits as late as October, Byron behaved in a very remarkable fashion, either for a brother who was at last willing and able to assist a sister or for a madly infatuated lover. He began to receive some money, apparently as the result of litigation during July. There is no indication that he sent Augusta so much as a shilling, but it is certain that he loaned £1,000 to Webster and a bit later gave Hodgson £600–800.[33] Even if his position with respect to his half sister was merely that of head of the house this behavior is difficult to construe, except on one premise—that Byron knew she had already obtained enough money to put off her more pressing creditors.

In addition Augusta had found the means to come up to London before Christmas, possibly with no other errand in mind than Christmas shopping, and just around Christmas she had felt sufficiently secure to set out a party for the Shelleys. And while a house party in the country represents no great outlay, it requires more expense than day-to-day domestic operations, especially with guests like the Shelleys, who had been accustomed to a very high style of life. The fragments of evidence seem to accord well with the suggestion earlier in this chapter that one of the results of Augusta's pregnancy and of her trip to London in August had been significant indemnity. How much would have been required to mollify their most urgent creditors can only be guessed at: probably a minimum of £2,000, but more likely a larger sum.

An alternate explanation may be that Augusta had resorted to blackmail. If the biographical assessments of her temperament are at all accurate, however, this would be completely out of character. It is true she could have received information from George Leigh, who had acted as a courier between members of the royal family, but the blackmailer insists upon a prompt settlement, and then returns again and again. There is, indeed, evidence that the following spring (1814) the Leighs approached Byron for money and received £3,000; this could indicate either that the original assistance was not in response to blackmail or that it was Byron himself who was being pushed. However, if Byron was the blackmailee, he could not have secured other benefits for Augusta (see chap. 19, "Augusta's Appointment").

But Byron, whatever his defects, was not the sort of man to have tolerated a resort to blackmail. Nor did Colonel Leigh, though he might well have had information useful for such ends, apparently ever so far debase himself. Even if he may have felt tempted, the fact that he and Augusta never ceased to anticipate some kind of favor from the Regent would have constituted sufficient restraint. As for the possibility that blackmail had been directed toward Byron, his letter describing his excellent humor should be adequate disproof. In short, the known facts suggest that some gentleman, finding that he had made Augusta pregnant and that in consequence the Leigh family was on the point of dissolution, undertook to make what amends he could.

Acknowledgment of "Lines to a Lady Weeping"

In 1812 there had appeared anonymously a two-stanza poem addressed to the Princess Charlotte, daughter of the Regent. The first stanza is pertinent:

> Weep, daughter of a royal line,
>   A sire's disgrace, a realm's decay;
> Ah, happy if each tear of thine
>   Could wash a father's fault away.

The second stanza was nothing more than a complicated compliment to the Princess.

Because publication was anonymous the verse aroused relatively mild interest for a few days, and then everyone forgot it in enthusiasm for some more instant bit of scandal. Certainly Byron did not regard the stanzas as significant poetry, and, though admittedly a poor judge of his own work, if he knew anything at all he recognized them for what they are—trivial and very topical material. And so they should have remained, a very small problem of attribution, hardly worth a doctoral candidate's notice, but for the fact that Byron deliberately called attention to them.

Late in 1813 Byron sent instructions to Murray to publish the lines in the same binding with *The Corsair,* which he had just completed.[34] During the time the poet and Augusta were snowed in at Newstead, the volume appeared and the outcry from the Tories was shrill and instant. Even the Whigs were not happy. When Murray prepared the second printing, he withdrew "Lines"; Byron quickly learned of it and sent him a sharp note with peremptory instructions to put "Lines" back in the next printing.[35] Murray put them back.

Such are the bare facts of the acknowledgment of the poem. Byron himself has left nothing in the record that explains why, after a minor bit of verse had floated about for almost two years, he should have chosen to call attention to its existence and to augment by the weight of his established reputation its republication. Nor do any of his correspondents offer any explanation.

Obviously, the first question is whether the acknowledgment merely represented one of his "caprices," as he termed them. His original instructions to Murray were quite definite, and there was time enough between the first direction and the binding to have allowed full reconsideration. Moreover, when Murray became frightened by the uproar that resulted and attempted to withdraw the verses from the second printing, Byron very angrily and curtly ordered him to replace them. The answer to the first question, therefore, is in the negative. Manifestly, Byron had chosen deliberately to acknowledge "Lines" and persisted in his purpose.

His letter to Moore, dated 12 March 1814, reinforces the opinion that the attack on the Regent was calculated. "I have nothing of the sort you mention, but the *lines* (The Weepers). . . . I wish to give them all possible circulation." He continues that he has in mind still other material to be delivered *at* him, or *to* him (the Regent). "I shall perhaps read him a lecture he has not lately heard in the Cabinet. From particular circumstances, which came to my knowledge almost by accident, 'I could tell him what he is—I know him well.' " [36]

There can remain no question that Byron meant battle, and that the attack had received full consideration before he undertook it. Of course, personal attacks were by no means rare in the politics of the time: nearly all political ephemera were vituperative and frequently were scurrilous. Only the authorship attached any real interest to such material. The second question, then, is whether the publication signaled that the poet was about to reenter politics or corresponded in any fashion with a governmental crisis in which he manifested more than passing interest.

The answer to both parts of the question again is in the negative. Nothing he wrote during the period suggests any intent to return to political life, even such as existed in the House of Lords. There seems to have been no governmental or ministerial crisis of unusual character, nor was there any significant election at all related to the time of publication. So far as the verse might extend beyond the Regent to his ministers, again there appears not to have been anyone in the Cabinet toward whom Byron felt any fresh or specific animus; he merely entertained for most of them a general disdain. So far as political damage to a party might accrue from the acknowledgment of "Lines," it appears their republication would probably damage the Whigs about as much as the Tories. In short, the vendetta appears to have been personal.

There was no specific occasion which might have aroused Byron to a violent antipathy toward the Regent. They had met only under the banal circumstances of a levee, and their personal relationship had been bland, if not cordial.[37] Nor, indeed, had Byron, so far as anyone knows, seen Princess Caroline, the estranged wife of the Regent, in well over six months. If any particular new difficulty had arisen with respect to Princess Charlotte, that also is not evident. Hence there appears to be no explanation in the direct relationships of the poet to the royal family to account for the attack.

Other explanations may exist, but are too remote and unlikely to merit attention; and one is therefore compelled to conclude that republication of the "Lines" was a calculated retaliation for something the Regent had done or failed to do. There is no indication that Byron was replying to anything directed at himself, nor does the Regent seem to have injured any public figure closely associated with the poet. Not only the circumstances of the attack but the absence of any apparent provocation of a public nature suggests that Byron may have acted on behalf of the Leighs. His letter to Augusta on 24 June 1814 seems to support such an interpretation. At that time Byron had just transferred £3,000 to Augusta's account and informed her that Colonel Leigh did not have to concern himself about repayment unless "this Prince should *come* forward at last, or the General *go,*— he can then repay it or not as he likes." [38] In short the remittance, which some biographers have regarded as a purchase price for Leigh's acceptance of Medora, was a loan and Leigh had signed a note. Byron reassured Augusta, however, that it was not subject to call unless the Prince (presumably the Regent) should provide for her or them, or unless the General (presumably Leigh's father) should die and Leigh should inherit enough to pay off the loan.

Return to London

As soon as the roads began to clear a little after the January snowstorm, Byron set out for London; and from Newark-on-Trent on 6 February he informed Lady Melbourne that he had succeeding in crossing the flooding river.[39] Whether Augusta was with him in this part of the journey he did not say; possibly he passed by Six Mile Bottom to deposit her in safety before proceeding on to the city. Having arrived there he found the excitement over "Lines to a Lady Weeping" at its highest pitch. Characteristically he refused to enter the battle with his critics and only resumed his solitary life and his journal, with frequent exchange of letters with Lady Melbourne, to whom he remarked in a letter of 11 February that all the disturbance created by "Lines" was as nothing "to that within, on a subject to which I have not alluded." [40]

Later in February Hobhouse returned from a lengthy tour of the Continent and remarked that he found Byron very withdrawn and solitary. Nevertheless the poet was very glad to welcome him home and kept him up half the night to hear his confessions.[41] Thereafter Hobhouse made a number of efforts to distract Byron from his morbid preoccupations, but with little success. The most he could persuade Byron to do was to attend a few dinners with men—literary or political figures, among whom Hobhouse at times included Sir Francis Burdett, with whom he had a rather warm association. On 3 March, still in self-imposed solitude, Byron wrote to Moore that he could tell him a "tale of present & past times"—but he would have to wait till "we are veterans." There is nothing on the spot, he writes, to love or hate, but sufficient for both at no great distance; he goes out very little and sees no one.[42]

Entries in his journal throughout this time are only slightly, if at all, less morose than those of the autumn. However, the reflections on suicide and the nightmares that afflicted him during the autumn were either less persistent than they had been, or Byron ignored them so far as possible. With respect to his poetry, he wrote Moore, "I have done with [it] forever."

On 8 April he noted in his journal that he had just returned from Six Mile Bottom, where he had been for the preceding six days.[43] This period has already received attention as the time during which he may have been on hand for the birth of Medora. On the same day as the journal entry he also wrote Murray a short note to convey Augusta's thanks for a copy of *The Corsair* the publisher had sent her, and he promised that she would write her own "letteret" of thanks within a day or two.[44] Murray's present, as well as Byron's confident prediction of Augusta's own acknowledgment within a short interval, fits conveniently into a confinement and delivery.

Up to this time Byron's mood had undergone no significant change. On 8, 9, and 10 April he made brief entries in his journal, most of which allude to his dismay that Napoleon failed to die in battle, if he had to lose his war. Then he concluded his diary on 19 April with some of the bitterest sentences he ever wrote.

> There is ice at both poles—north and south—all extremes are the same—misery belongs to the highest and lowest only, to the emperor and the beggar, when unsixpenced and unthroned. There is, to be sure, a damned insipid medium—an equinoctial line—no one knows where, except upon maps and measurement.
>   . . . To be sure I have long despised myself and man, but I never spat in the face of my species before— "O fool! I shall go mad." [45]

But he didn't. Instead, within another week or ten days he had begun to resume his attendance at levees and assemblies. Tom Moore came to town and together they resumed circulation among the Irish lords, and were frequently at the Rancliffes.

The change in mood is specifically exemplified in his letter of

25 April to Lady Melbourne. There is a brief paragraph about
the possibility that he may encounter Lady Caroline. Then he
turns to an entirely different subject, in a mood that seems exu-
berant.

> Oh! but it is "worth while", I can't tell you why, and it
> is *not* an *"Ape"*, and if it is, that must be my fault; how-
> ever, I will positively reform. You must however allow that
> it is utterly impossible I can ever be half so well liked else-
> where, and I have been all my life trying to make someone
> love me and never got the sort I preferred before. But posi-
> tively she and I will grow good and all that, and so we are
> *now* and shall be these three weeks and more, too.

Byron then continues with a flippant account of a musical
evening at the Princess of Wales, and describes a visit of his
physician. Finally, after setting down his list of engagements for
the week, he concludes—

> I don't often bore you with rhyme,—but as a wrapper to
> this note I send you some upon a *brunette,* which I have
> shown to no one else. If you think them not much beneath
> the common places you may give them to any of your "al-
> bum" acquaintances.[46]

Clearly his letter is a reply to a quite serious one from Lady
Melbourne. Since Byron was careful about the use of quotation
marks, one can reconstruct from the quoted words and the
sense of his letter that Lady Melbourne had written that he was
lucky the baby was not an ape, that the risks he had taken were
certainly not worth his while and that she most sincerely hoped
the affair was finished. To all of which he replied that he and
his love were good at the moment and would remain so for
three weeks, or perhaps longer.

The consensus of biographers holds that "Ape" refers to a newborn infant. It is evident that Lady Melbourne introduced into the correspondence the superstition which held that a child of incest would be a monster of some type. Byron's reply is not a model of lucidity. "It is 'worth while'" and "it" also is *"not an Ape."* The pronoun must be supposed to have different (unexpressed) antecedents. Then having asserted, with emphasis added, that it was not an "Ape," he continues, "and if it is, . . ." Since Byron used "and" as the conjunction and since he had emphasized the non-apeness of "it," then he may have had in mind some other "if" for which he would take responsibility ("that must be my fault").[47]

The rest of the paragraph seems to connect the "Ape" with a love affair that is in abeyance, perhaps as a result of recent accouchement ("these three weeks"). The final paragraph of the letter seems to refer back to the second. If it does, the wording may imply that the recent mother is a brunette, a point Byron chose to emphasize. The poem used for the wrapper was not preserved with the letter, according to Quennell's footnote, and the only identification of the lady remains the fact that she was emphatically dark.

Both his use of the present tense with respect to his (their) good behavior and his use of the future tense for "these three weeks" imply the lady was accessible. If that is correct, she should have been in London; certainly it suggests that he had seen her quite recently, since he underscored "now." But Augusta, of course, was at Six Mile Bottom and it had already been three weeks since he had seen her. Further, if the argument that Medora may have been born as early as 5–6 April is correct, the elapsed time between Byron's announcement of the birth, Lady Melbourne's reply with its references to an "Ape," and Byron's reply on 25 April is rather hard to explain. Even if one accepts the date of Medora's birth as 15 April, the interval is quite long, since Lady Melbourne was in London residence, as evidenced by the fact that Byron expressed the hope they would encounter each other at some of the parties.[48]

Whatever the letter means, it establishes the return of Byron's normally high spirits: there is not a hint of remorse and but little of repentance. The adventure had been eminently "worth while." In this mood of exuberance he entered the glorious summer, and the mood endured till autumn when he found himself passively and unexpectedly engaged to Miss Anna Isabella Milbanke.

⊰ 14 ⊱

"____'s", "*****'s", AND "X's"

There can be little question that Byron fully expected almost everything he wrote to be published eventually. In 1814 he turned over to Moore, whom he had designated as his biographer, the Journal he had kept from November 1813 to April 1814,[1] and later sent to him another journal that seems to have dealt mostly with his own version of the events that led to his separation from his wife. Finally, in 1822 Byron directed Moore to see if he could obtain letters the poet had written to Lady Melbourne.[2] If the assumption is correct that Byron expected all this material at some time to appear in print, there obviously would be names he would prefer to conceal, and there were many.

The purpose of this chapter is to examine Byron's techniques of obfuscation of names and events, and to compare the concealments employed in the surviving journal with methods he used in various correspondence. The result may perhaps identify some of those whose names or actions he wished to conceal. Cross comparisons between his correspondence with Lady Melbourne and that with Moore and his Journal of 1813 establish at once that Byron was extremely inconsistent both in the kind of symbols he used and in the degree of concealment he employed in the three accounts of himself and his affairs. (Correspondence with other people is of no import: with none of them did he reveal his private life to the extent that it appears in the cited material.)

The letters to Moore contain only the vaguest references to his exploits, and names seldom appear except as they refer to friends in common or to other literary people. There is here and there a reference to his "serious scrape" and to other involvements, and once, on 6 January 1814, Byron refers to two affairs, one of which he says may bring him to Moore's county with "hackbut bent". He writes of his autumn and "a strange summer adventure . . . (I don't mean **'s, however, which is laughable only)." [3]

If he is more circumspect in his letters to Moore than in those to Lady Melbourne, a study of his journal of 1813–14 also will give some idea of Byron's attitude toward the mention of other people, particularly ladies. In that journal Augusta's name in full appears five times, if there is no error in the arithmetic, and nearly always in relation to a frank expression of affection. As for her identification in any other context, it is most difficult. The original manuscripts from which Moore worked have been lost for a long time. Moore (or his printer) chose to represent in asterisks whatever squiggles Byron may have used to conceal identities. The asterisks appear in sets and suggest a pattern of replacement. Thus, "**" clearly denotes Lady Frances Webster ("Ph." in the Melbourne letters)—most of the time. Once the set seems to identify a place and once, perhaps, Lady Oxford. On the other hand "****" and "*****" regularly seem to refer to some lady far more significant with respect to events of the summer. That Byron did obscure names is evident in his letters to Lady Melbourne, the originals of which survive. Thus, though the symbols may be Moore's, the concealment presumably was Byron's and the problem of identification is the same.

In comparison with this frequent but inconsistent use of concealing symbol, the journal clearly identifies Lady Holland,
Lady Melbourne, Lady Jersey, Lady Charlemont, Lady Heathcote, in addition to the clear reference to Augusta and to a
number of ladies of no suspected significance. Lady Catherine
Annesley, toward whom Byron seems to have felt some attrac-
tion, is inadequately covered as "Lady C. A—."

In contrast with these, there is one clear instance of careful
concealment. In the journal under the date of 17 November
1813, Byron made a curious entry.

> Called on C** to explain**. She is very beautiful, to my
> taste at least; for on coming home from abroad, I recollect
> being unable to look at any woman but her—they were so
> fair, and unmeaning, and blonde. The darkness and regu-
> larity of her features reminded me of my "Jannat al Aden".
> . . . She was very good-tempered, and everything was ex-
> plained.[4]

Then on 10 December he recorded that he had attended a
dinner at Lord Holland's two days earlier (8 December) and
that among the guests were the Cowpers, Ossulstones, Melbournes, and Staffords. Under the same entry he added that he
went to the playhouse the following evening (9 December) and
was invited to the after-theatre dinner. "I was much tempted;
C** looked so Turkish with her red turban, and her regular, dark
and clear features. Not that *she* and *I* ever were, or could be, anything. . . ."[5]

The two references unquestionably apply to the same lady, and
her identification may be of some importance, whatever the
validity of the disclaimer that concludes the second passage. In
the first place she appears to have been most attractive and to
have suited well the "Orientalities" Byron said filled his mind. In
the second place, he mentioned her in the journal not as "Lady

C**" or by some other title, but referred to her by her Christian name. This point is very exceptional in all that Byron left: the only other individuals to whom he applied first names were Augusta, Annabella, and Lady Caroline Lamb, though he must have known a good many other ladies fairly well. Within the circle of regnantes in which he moved, many were near his own age and had pedigrees no better than his; but in his journals and correspondence he regularly applied to all these ladies their titles. The appellation by first name therefore signalizes exceptional intimacy.

It is evident that "C**" was not Lady Caroline, for her features and coloring in no way correspond, and yet the lady had moved for some time in the same society as Byron, since he mentioned noticing her so particularly after his return from the East. Second, she appears to have had some kind of special relationship, since in addition to his use of what is apparently a Christian name he felt that it was necessary to explain something to her. "**" does not identify the subject explained. If the second symbol indicates Lady Frances Webster, then it seems he was reporting to one intimate on his romantic attachment to another.

If the premises and exclusions are correct, "C**" should identify Lady Ossulstone (later, Tankerville). Elsewhere in writing to Lady Melbourne, Byron described her "pretty, black face." [6] "C**" and Lady Ossultone, therefore, had the same brunette coloring. Certainly the Ossulstones were among the early connections Byron formed when he began to attend parties at Holland House, Melbourne House, and at the Jerseys'. Finally, her Christian name was Corisande, the first of some five baptismal names. (She was the daughter of the Duc de Gramont and as a child had been brought to England to escape the Terror.) [7]

But the final evidence for this identification occurs in a note to

Lady Melbourne on 22 November, five days after the journal entry of 17 November.

> Yesterday the Lady Ossulstone sent for me to complain of you *all*. We had met at Lord Holland's the night before. . . . We had a kind of squabble at the Argyle, which I could not help tormenting her a little by reminding her, not of *that*, but of that evening when we were all wrong-paired. *She* wanted to sit by Mildmay at supper, and I wanted to have been next anybody . . . but a person who had serious concerns to think of.[8]

There is evidently a discrepancy in dates, with respect to which Byron usually was rather accurate. A possible explanation is that while his first journal reference to "C**" occurs under the entry of 17 November, it is rather late in the various comments of that date, and the next date of entry is 22 November. It seems possible that he may have added short notes from time to time without setting out the precise date on which each was entered. Otherwise one may presume there were two separate meetings with Lady Ossulstone.

There is further the discrepancy between the nature of the interview as Byron entered it in the diary, and that which he reported to Lady Melbourne. In his journal he wrote that he called upon the lady to explain something. To Lady Melbourne he asserted that the lady sent for him to complain. He then elaborates the complaint: that the people of Melbourne House had been antagonistic ever since the affair of Lady Caroline's injury at Lady Heathcote's ball, that the Melbournes indeed blamed her for the spread of gossip and scandal.

This interview with Lady Ossulstone is, to say the least, murky. In the first place, within a few hours after Lady Caroline's scene at the Heathcote ball, Lady Melbourne had sent a note or message to Byron with Lady Ossulstone as the messenger.[9] This fact in itself is a bit strange, since Lord Melbourne had written of the lady that she was a "frivolous little woman who doesn't know what she is about. . . ." [10] If this was her reputation it strikes one as somewhat odd that Lady Melbourne would have chosen her as a messenger on quite a sensitive subject, unless she had some reason to think Lady Ossulstone enjoyed a special relationship to Byron. Assuredly, Lady Ossulstone was not a confidante or an intimate of the Melbournes. If subsequently she became indiscreet, she might well have incurred the annoyance of the Melbournes and the Lambs.

Perhaps Byron's call was for the purpose of mollification or reassurance. Whatever he had to explain, he expected some kind of outburst but found that the lady accepted what he had to say in good humor, and "all was explained." If the subject of Lady Ossulstone's behavior with respect to Lady Caroline's injury was not the matter of the interview, it may have had something to do with Byron's teasing her or, in spite of his denial, with the squabble at the Argyle. In the context in which the entire entry occurs, however, it seems a more probable reading that Byron was undertaking to explain a present infatuation to a lady who might have had a particular interest in such a problem.

In summary, that Lady Ossulstone held or had held some special position with respect to Byron seems indicated by three pieces of evidence. The first as already mentioned, is his very exceptional use of the Christian name. The second is Lady Melbourne's selection of a person regarded as unreliable to carry specific instructions or sentiments to Byron with respect to a scandal that affected her son very closely. The third is a curious reference in a letter to Lady Melbourne on 22 November 1813, a date that falls closely upon the other dates at which the poet appears to have been preoccupied with "C**." He wrote of Webster's jealousy and Lady Frances's desire in no way to upset his assurance that she was absolutely faithful, and then continued, "Next to Lord Ossulstone's voucher for her discretion [presumably C**'s], it has enlivened my ethical studies on the human mind. . . ." [11] The implication certainly appears to be that Byron knew, quite as accurately as he was informed about Lady Frances, that Lady Ossulstone was not above an occasional peccadillo and had been equally skillful in deceiving her husband.

The correspondence with Lady Melbourne presents quite a different set of symbols and imposes some other difficulties. One can, very much as Lord Lovelace did, identify all obscure references as concealing the name of Augusta, or one can deny that any refer to Byron's half sister, or concede that there are inconsistencies and variable identifications. The problem is compounded by the fact that "Augusta" appears openly at various times, and at others is clearly identifiable as "A," "A^a," or "My A." One cannot even be entirely certain that these refer to Augusta in every instance, though the probability is that they do. Certainly, various other designations do not invariably serve to identify Augusta beyond a reasonable doubt.

"My A" enters the correspondence after Byron began to refer to Miss Milbanke, whom he had designated as "your A," [12] but even under these conditions the usage was inconsistent, and not rarely Augusta's name appears without any attempt of concealment. To add to the confusion, in a letter of 25 November 1813, at a time when his affair with Lady Frances was preoccupying much of his emotion, the poet introduced "——," and this symbol occurs repeatedly in the Melbourne correspondence up to 2 July 1814. But "——" overlaps in the correspondence with "X," to whom he first referred in a letter of 1 May 1814. (In that letter, "A^a," "——," and "X" all appear, the latter two only in postscript.) [13] It is necessary to sort out these various usages and attempt identification.

During Byron's pursuit of Lady Frances Webster, which began

in early October 1813, he usually referred to her by the appellation "Ph." As already indicated in the section on his journal, in that manuscript she usually appears as "**" though the two-asterisk sign is not reserved exclusively for her. By 25 November, how-ever, when Byron wrote to Lady Melbourne about the possibility of his death, he noted that while Lady Caroline would be upset because it wasn't on her account, and Lady Oxford would be philosophical, "poor ——" would be "really uncomfortable," and then he added "that perverse passion" was probably "the deepest of all." In February of the following year, "——" appears again, this time allowing him a free rein to see whom he pleases and to do what he pleases. Then on 1 May 1814, in postcript, he writes Lady Melbourne that he finds it difficult to account for "——," who had insisted on marrying a fool, but "they get on very well" together.[14]

On 16 May he notes that he will write to "——" the following day; on 26 June he states that if Caroline continues to plague him he will leave and take "——" with him, whatever the out-come. (The editor's note indicates that Byron had written the name and then carefully expunged it.) On 2 July the poet ap-parently had just received a letter from "——" and he indicates that she "is very much astonished and in very good humour" with regard to some information he had conveyed.[15]

The clues in this correspondence permit a few fairly clear in-ferences. The first is that Byron regarded his attachment to the lady of the concealed name as a "perverse passion." Approxi-mately synonymous are "wrongheaded," "obstinate," and "will-ful." As poet and man of letters, he had a keen sense of meaning, as his comments to Lady Melbourne on "essential" and "lovable" indicate (see below, p. 204); he did not mean or imply "per-verted." The other clue is that "——" had married a fool, but that they got on well enough. Without much doubt Byron re-garded a good many of the men in Whig society as fools, but there were not very many of whom it could be said that they maintained a reasonably harmonious marriage. The lady in question would be really uncomfortable if something fatal happened to Byron; that is, she loved him. The final determinant of her identification is that he continued to correspond with her through sometime in July 1814, and that she would have been willing to elope with him.

Earlier identification of this lady has been with Augusta. The whole tenor of the journal, however, indicates that for several months after the visit with the Websters, Byron's imagination was pretty well preoccupied with Lady Frances. There can be little doubt from his journal and from his letters to Lady Melbourne that Lady Frances was very much in what she regarded as love with him. Other evidence makes it unmistakable that Byron continued a surreptitious correspondence with Lady Frances,[16] and there is no question at all that he regarded Webster as a remarkably foolish man. Finally, as he had remarked in other letters to Lady Melbourne, Byron did regard this affair as particularly "wrongheaded."

The problem of elopement deserves a bit more comment. In August 1813, it had been Augusta who was openly considering going to the Continent with Byron, but that arrangement had completely collapsed. Her affairs were considerably relieved by July 1814, and indeed she was already making efforts to arrange a marriage for Byron. On the other hand, the poet had referred repeatedly to the possibility that he and Lady Frances might at some point flee to some other land. In summary, if "——" refers to any lady whose name is clearly associated with that of Byron in the time span under consideration, the most probable identification is with Lady Frances Webster. If the symbol does not identify her, it may refer to some other, hitherto unsuspected lady.

"X" makes her first appearance in the letter of 1 May 1814, in a postscript that bears what is in Byron's entire correspondence the unique designation of "PS. *ad.*" Occasionally he employed "PS. *nd.*" or "Ps. 2d," by which one would suppose he wished to signify that it was a second afterthought (and it might be easy for a forger to mistake Byron's "n" for an "a"). Furthermore this postscript of 1 May is such as to make the identification of "X" impossible to mistake.[17] He had asked his mother when he was a child why he might not marry "X," and the author of the postscript made it clear that the bar to the marriage lay in its incestuous nature (see text of the postscript in note 17, below). Since about the only little girls Byron may have known at the time other than Augusta were cousins, with whom the Byrons intermarried very regularly, and neighbors, it is evident that no other identification is possible.

"X" does not appear again in the correspondence until October, when in a period of one month this symbol occurs in each of eight letters to Lady Melbourne.[18] The timing of "X's" appearance coincides with the general knowledge of Byron's engagement to Miss Milbanke and lasts until his visit at Seaham with her family. A reference to "X" occurs only one other time, in a letter to Lady Melbourne, 2 February 1815.[19] Scattered among these letters, Augusta's name appears in full several times and once she is designated as "Ax."

Not only is the time during which this symbol appears a very restricted one, but in all but one of the references "X" appears in connection with the failure of efforts to form a match with Lady Charlotte Leveson Gower. Byron, in effect, appears to be writing Lady Melbourne that he was completely indifferent with regard to whom he married, that perhaps he had favored either of the Ladies Leveson Gower, but that as luck would have it Miss Milbanke accepted him almost before he knew what had happened. All of this is more or less true, perhaps, but none of it agrees well with letters of the same period from Byron to Moore, Hobhouse, the Countess of ——, or Miss Milbanke. Nor does the attitude coincide with Byron's sentiments as expressed to Lady Melbourne before and after this series.[20]

The penultimate letter in which "X" appears, that of 31 October, states that the poet has stopped with her on the way to Seaham and adds that he has "made X my heiress." These two statements establish unquestionably the identification of "X" with Augusta, though the repeated references to her intervention in the effort to find a wife for Byron could have left little doubt.

The final appearance of "X" is just after Byron's "treacle-moon," when in reply to a rather elaborate reference of Lady Melbourne, he wrote that if "by 'C——noir' you mean X," he still must take omens from her flight, whether she be raven or griffin. This part of the correspondence is thoroughly opaque, allusions and metaphors become inextricably confused, and one is far from certain that either writer was responsive to the other.[21]

The only other known instance of the use of "X" applies to a lock of hair, purportedly Augusta's, which she supposedly sent to Byron in 1813. The symbol, however, is not truly "X," but appears much more as a plus sign or a cross, and it accompanies the packet's label, "La Chevelure of the one whom I most *loved*." [22] The script only partially resembles Byron's but he could have written it at a much earlier age; it resembles as much in form his later script as some of his earlier schoolboy poems resemble *Don Juan*. That it belongs either to a schoolboy or to some copier far less well acquainted with the French language than Byron is further suggested by the fact that the writer seems to have been unaware of the distinction between "chevelure" and "cheveu"; there is also the suggestion of an accent on "La."

As an interesting footnote to these comments, and possibly as further evidence that letters with "X's may not be authentic, a letter Byron sent to Augusta in 1816 should be mentioned. In it he describes a visit to see the mementos of Lucrezia Borgia, and he remarks especially on a page of her writing which concluded with a symbol for a signature. Byron describes the symbol particularly as a cross and adds, "Is not this amusing?"[23] It is amusing. For it suggests that Byron was aware someone had seen letters from Augusta to him signed with what was intended to be a cross—and had mistaken it for an "X."

It is appropriate to summarize the entire correspondence in which the symbol "X" appears. What characterizes this set of letters?

1. With two exceptions, "X" is limited to a single month.
2. One exception occurs three months earlier in a uniquely designated postscript.
3. The other exception occurs three months later in a very opaque exchange of correspondence, in which Byron appears uncertain of Lady Melbourne's meaning.
4. Although the use of a new symbol to refer to someone previously named should be only for the purpose of completely obscuring identification, three or four quite gratuitous bits of information establish identification with Augusta beyond a doubt.
5. The month of October, immediately following announcement of the Byron-Milbanke engagement but well before the final plans for marriage, represented an opportune time for a schemed disruption.
6. The general topic of the entire letters is of a failed effort to procure a more desirable marriage.

No one can question that Byron frequently behaved pretty foolishly in his various love affairs, but outside of these there is no indication that he was completely stupid. If he was going to lengths to conceal from everybody except Lady Melbourne the information that he had had an incestuous liaison with Augusta, it is hardly conceivable that he would include unmistakable means of her identification with "X." Yet it was clearly the intention of the author of these letters that there might be no possible other identification. To be fair to Byron, this simply makes no sense.

The letters of October bristle with "X's" in a style not very characteristic. All too often Byron introduces some person either by name or symbol and then turns entirely to pronouns—not altogether to the greater clarity or comprehensibility of his message. The author of these letters left no uncertainty at all as to what "X" did.

I have remarked on the nature of the correspondence and have pointed out that the sentiments expressed to Lady Melbourne with respect to her niece, Miss Milbanke, were anything but agreeable. Was Byron, then, clumsily attempting to break up his own marriage during the month of October, when in September and November, not only to Lady Melbourne but to all his correspondents, he indicated that he regarded himself as lucky and his fiancée as a talented and highly intelligent young woman? [24] And in order to accomplish this purpose was he deliberately laying grounds for a charge of incest against Augusta?

It is possible, but it is equally possible that the letters are spurious. Not only is there the instance of Lady Caroline's forged note to Murray, but there hang framed in Newstead Abbey several letters known to be forgeries, and they are very good forgeries indeed. If the letters of October are forged, their intent is plain: for a person such as Miss Milbanke they could hardly have been more insulting, and to one of her religious inclination hardly more devastating. Only with difficulty could one design a correspondence better devised to wreck a marriage or to ravage the spirit of a young wife. What would make the vengeance doubly sweet would be the fact that a person with Annabella's pride of logic would construct an edifice of deception for herself. It would not even require a lie.

There is one additional point to be brought forward. When Lady Byron came to London in February 1816 to complete arrangements for the separation, she had a long and surreptitious interview with Lady Caroline, who had promised to show her letters and other evidence that would wholly support her determination.[25] It is not known that Lady Caroline did present the material, but after the interview Lady Byron decidedly changed her manner toward Augusta.[26] If the "X" letters of October were the ones Lady Caroline displayed, it is easy to see how their origin as forgeries would have made them readily available to her, whereas if they were indeed a part of Byron's correspondence with Lady Melbourne it would have been much more difficult to gain possession of them.

≫ 15 ≪

THE PORTRAIT OF A NOBLEMAN
"FOR MRS. LEIGH"

Byron's letter of 1 July 1813 to Lady Melbourne seems to have been written in rather high spirits. He informed his friend that he had to sit with his sister, stand for his picture, and drive to see her.[1] There is no hint of trouble, anxiety, or despair.

Since the only painting of that period that represents Byron in a standing position is Thomas Phillips's *Portrait of a Nobleman in Albanian [or Arnaut or Suliot] Dress* one has to interpret the letter as a reference to that portrait. This picture represents Byron in full panoply of a Suliot chieftain and has the further feature of a rather long mustache. With respect to this adornment there is little doubt that the artist supplied it, since there is no indication that the poet tried the effect of a mustache earlier than about 1820, since other contemporary portraits represent him as clean shaven, and since the length of the Albanian mustache would have called for several months of careful nurture.

Shortly after the letter of 1 July, Byron's mood began to change. Within a few weeks he had become very restless, had left London at least once, and had begun to eat very heavily, a pretty sure sign that he was quite upset.

Then, it seems, a curious change in Phillips's activities took place. Both the poet's letter to Lady Melbourne and a much later letter from him to Miss Elphinstone establish the approximate beginning of the portrait in Suliot costume.[2] The painter's sittings book indicates that this painting was not finished and signed until April 1814.[3] In the meantime, indeed by 23 September 1813, the sittings book indicates that he had begun and completed *Portrait of a Nobleman* and specifically records that it was "for Mrs. Leigh."

This portrait, apparently the one now in the possession of Lt. Col. R. Geoffrey Byron, resembles the portrait at Newstead Abbey in position, dress, and technique. What makes it interesting is the fact that Phillips, after having begun "Albanian Dress," seems to have laid it aside and completed the one "for Mrs. Leigh" in a relatively short time. Of one point we may be sure: Phillips would not have interrupted the first painting to begin and complete another without the poet's consent. Unquestionably, the priority given the portrait for Augusta would have resulted from Byron's insistence.

This line of reasoning leads us to ask why the poet changed his mind and hastened the portrait specifically intended for Augusta. So far as we know, she already possessed a miniature, probably that by Sanders of about 1812, a rendition that her half brother did not like. But unless there had been some reason for urgency Byron's normal behavior as the subject of a painting would have been to allow his appointments to drag along and his sittings to occur at his "caprice."

The relationship of dates may furnish a possible explanation. In the section in chapter 13 on the "fancied duel" (the term was applied by Miss Mayne) the argument was that far from being "fancied" the encounter was a very real and potentially deadly one. It developed further that the expected time of the encounter was very near 12 September. It seems reasonable, therefore, to argue that Augusta, knowing of the approaching duel and of her situation as heiress to half of Byron's estate (so the will stood at that time), had wished for a better and larger formal portrait of her brother. It is important to emphasize that Byron had evidently received the challenge and just as evidently—since he regarded himself as having wronged his challenger—had resolved to receive but not to return the fire.

There does not appear to be any other acceptable explanation for the supersedure of "Albanian Dress." At the same time, if the argument is sound, it reinforces the evidence that a potentially fatal duel was imminent. The fact that the duel did not occur and that the original of the painting was still present in the flesh may well explain the fact that this portrait seems to have remained with Phillips at least until after exhibition at the Royal Academy in April 1814,[4] and possibly until Augusta took over her apartment in St. James.

Reasons against Colonel Leigh's identification as the wronged husband have already appeared. One need only add the exquisite irony involved in the haste to provide his wife with a fine portrait of her half brother whom the Colonel was just about to exterminate. This would be a bit too much even for a family far more eccentric than the Byrons.

≫ 16 ≪

THE PORTRAIT OF THE JOURNAL

Byron wrote to Lady Melbourne on 22 November 1813: ". . . she ["C"—presumably Lady Caroline] sent me Holmes' picture for a *friend leaving England,* to which friend it is now making the best of its way. . . ." [1] In a journal entry dated "November 27, I believe," he wrote: "***** has received the portrait safe; and in answer the only remark she makes upon it is, 'indeed it is like'. . . . this portrait was not a flatterer, but dark and stern—even black as the mood in which my mind was scorching last July, when I sat for it." [2]

On one reading, the entry in the journal seems to provide a good clue to the identity of the lady of midsummer, since it appears to imply that she was familiar with his sternness and knew the cause of his black mood of July. One biographer has indeed conceived this argument and contended that the portrait in question was either one of the Phillips paintings or a Westall portrait. Augusta has been named as a possible recipient. [3]

In the entry, however, are several points that aid in identification of the painting. It had been sent in some fashion and had arrived safely; it was what Byron considered to be a very good likeness; the painting had been started in July. Though it may be open to question and perhaps to doubt that the references in the letter to Lady Melbourne are to the same painting as those in the journal, the agreement in time and in references to be presented shortly make it fairly convincing that the subject is the same picture. If they are identical, the additional information from the letter to Lady Melbourne is that the "friend" was leaving England and that the painter was James Holmes.

Several points argue that the painting on its way was a product of the miniaturist Holmes. The first is that the shipment of an easel portrait of the sizes Phillips and Westall painted in 1813— about 36 × 28 inches, without the frame [4]—would not have been a very easy thing to arrange, even if it were taken off the stretchers and rolled. The size of the parcel would have attracted attention and made much less certain its "safe" arrival—undetected, presumably with respect to the anticipated disapproval of an irascible husband. Furthermore, once having reached the inamorata safely, a large easel painting would hardly be the sort of thing she could keep at hand for fond reveries, while a miniature could easily be dropped out of sight at any hint of interruption.

More than this, though Byron sat for a number of portraits and to several painters during the spring, summer, and autumn of 1813, he seemed never to have been too well pleased with the renditions of any of them except that (or those) of Holmes. Of that painter he wrote that he alone could produce "inveterate likenesses." [5]

Finally, even though there is no evidence that either Westall or Phillips ever painted miniatures, it is perhaps inappropriate to dismiss so readily the possibility that the painting on its way may have been one of their easel portraits. The subject of the various portraits of Byron during 1813 is a difficult and intricate study in itself. If ***** and the friend leaving England were not the same lady, it is possible that ***** received not the Holmes miniature but an easel painting. And several recent ones were available, at least in theory. The question is if any one of those we know of disappeared from view about this time.

In the early part of the year Byron had been sitting to Westall.[6] The result was a full profile, half-length painting—maybe two, one facing left, the other right. But it or these seemed to have remained in Westall's studio as late as December 1813, when Byron wrote T. Asham of Cornhill, London, regarding it or them.[7]

The Phillips portraits, as discussed in chapter 15 and note 3, seem to have remained in the artist's studio until the following April. Indeed the only one that may have been finished by November was the one "for Mrs. Leigh," if Phillips followed the usual practice of entering a painting in his book only after he had completed, varnished, and signed it. (At least such is the custom among present-day artists; the succession of dates with respect to *Portrait of a Nobleman in Albanian [or Suliot or Arnaut] Dress* fairly certainly establishes that Phillips followed the same custom. The portrait was begun in July 1813, but it was not entered in the sittings book until April 1814.) Finally Byron's letters to Murray in December 1813 and even as late as February 1816 leave no doubt that some of Phillips's portraits were still in the painter's possession.[8]

Since most if not all of the easel portraits are accounted for, it seems reasonable to conclude that the secretly posted and delivered portrait was most likely a miniature. If there were any completed easel paintings, they were still in the studio of the artist. Byron's comments suggest the most likely painter of the miniature to have been Holmes.

If Byron's two references are to the same painting, that painting was on its way to a lady about to leave England. If there remains a shadow of suspicion that he may have sent it to a man,

his use of the pronoun "she" should dispel doubt. Moreover, surreptitious posting to a man would hardly have been necessary.
The point is reinforced by a letter to Lady Melbourne about the
same time in which the poet states that four of his ladies now
have pictures of him.[9]

To an Englishman, "leaving England" may signify no more
than going to Ireland, Scotland, or Wales, though the term might
also refer to a trip to the Continent. Fortunately for purposes of
identification, it was far from comfortable for the English to
travel outside of Britain in the autumn of 1813. Throughout the
earlier part of the season many ports were quarantined; Napoleon's activities added to the hazards of travel, except in the
north of Europe, which would have been pretty cold and unpleasant for a winter holiday.

If the lady was then on the point of departure, it seems fairly
reasonable to conclude that her travel might take her somewhere
within the British Isles. Of the ladies about whose plans any information is available, only Lady Frances Wedderburn Webster
appears to meet the requirements, for as Byron informed Lady
Melbourne she was on the point of departing to The Grampians.[10]
Augusta—if there had ever been a love affair—had long since
abandoned any idea of emigration; and if she had contemplated
it at all her departure would surely have been in company with
Byron. But if the painting was on its way to her, there would
have been no occasion for secrecy since a present of a portrait to
a sister—even to a half sister—would not appear in any way remarkable. And while Lady Caroline Lamb could have been on
the point of departure for Ireland, where her family had large
holdings, she seems not to be in question, since Byron had just
recovered the Holmes miniature from her. Unless some hitherto
entirely unsuspected lady was involved, this pretty well leaves
Lady Frances as the person who received the painting safe.

The final piece of evidence that supports the position is contained in a letter of Byron to Murray on 25 November. In this letter the poet confides that he is continuing a correspondence with Lady Frances. By a kind of relay in which a third person received and rewrapped the original letter before posting it on to Lady Frances, it had been possible to continue correspondence without arousing the suspicion of Webster. Then he added in his note to his publisher, "She had this picture sent the same way." [11]

The identification of the recipient of the painting thus only reveals Lady Frances, in whom there is no great interest. Only in the event that "C," who sent him Holmes's picture, may refer to some hitherto unknown lady rather than to Lady Caroline, could this clue lead to the discovery of Byron's activities during July. If the "C" of the letter to Lady Melbourne, and of Holmes's picture, should perchance be the same as "C**" of the journal (Lady Ossulstone) the entire problem will require reevaluation.

≫ 17 ≪

SEALS

"Mem. I must get a toy tomorrow for Eliza, and send the device for the seals of myself and *****" (Journal, 14 November 1813).

"Got my seals *****" (Journal, 16 November 1813).[1]

These cryptic entries, like so many others Byron left about, promise to provide important clues to the identity of some lady with whom he was in love but whose name he would never enter in his journal *en clair*. No other references to seals appear elsewhere in his journal and mention of them occurs only in two or three letters. Adjacent entries in the journal, for example, furnish memos to himself to buy some toys for his little cousin Eliza, the daughter of Harry Byron, who was visiting in London at the time. He remembered the seals and, as the entry indicates, had them in hand two days later.

Records of two establishments from which Byron might have ordered the seals—he maintained accounts in both houses and made frequent purchases from them—were destroyed during the bombing of London. It would have been exciting to find sketches Byron himself may have furnished, but it might have been of immense significance to learn the name of the lady for whom he had the seals made.

One has to depend on the surviving, sometimes fragmentary impressions in wax on letters from Byron to his various correspondents for any information as to the seals he used. Unfortunately none of this correspondence deserves to be called clandestine, and on all the available samples the impression has been consistent. The seal produced an impression of a script *B*, marked by a certain amount of flourish, surmounted by a baron's coronet.[2] In one impression a shield bearing the *B* appears beneath the coronet, but it is impossible to decipher the quarterings, if they were in fact represented.[3] A third and later impression bears the coronet, the shield, and supporters on either side of the shield. This appears on a semiofficial piece of correspondence that deals with the problem of a British sailor in Italy, and Byron signs himself "Peer of the Realm." [4] At Newstead a single seal, one with *N.B.* in simple capitals, is of interest only in connection with later correspondence after he had adopted the name "Noel."

Lt. Col. R. Geoffrey Byron has in his collection a number of seals of the family. Some of these seem to have belonged to the sixth lord, although it is not possible to be quite certain which is which (the reading of the interior of a small seal is not highly accurate). The designs of most of this collection reveal what appear to be dolphins as supporters on either side of the shield and therefore probably derive from the seafaring side of the family—"Foul Weather Jack" and the seventh lord, possibly. Certainly there are no very unusual or unrecognizable types such as one might use to conceal the identity of the sender.

The poet's only other reference to seals occurs in connection with Mrs. Mary Chaworth Musters (or Mrs. Chaworth, as she was usually known, by virtue of the large inheritance she provided). Dates, however, make it rather certain that the seals of the journal do not correspond with the seals mentioned in the Byron–Chaworth exchanges. Unless, of course, Byron had undertaken to deceive Lady Melbourne.

The statement is clear that he had received the first set of seals, those for himself and "*****" about the middle of November. Late in the following month Mrs. Chaworth addressed him anonymously suggesting that a lady whom he had once known might be interested in renewing a friendship. In spite of the pretense of anonymity, she evidently expected Byron to recognize either her style (atrocious) or her script—and he did. Very soon he received a second letter from her in which she confirmed his original identification of the sender.[5]

One or the other of her letters, more probably the second, suggested that he should provide her with a set of seals in order that they might carry on their correspondence without danger of interception or discovery. Evidently soon after, he replied that the seals were ready. As soon as she received this news Mrs. Chaworth, perhaps a little deviously, suggested that if he would be at Newstead any time soon, he might bring the seals to her rather than trust them to post.[6] (Since he did not go across to her estate during the time he stayed at Newstead with Augusta and since there is no record that he sent the seals, one wonders if she ever received the devices.)

The sequence of dates, therefore, creates a rather turbid situation. If the seals of the journal are the same as those referred to in the Chaworth letters, Byron and his old inamorata had been communicating for at least a month before he made any record of it. While he certainly was under no compulsion to record his various affairs immediately or even to relate all of them, his letters to Lady Melbourne about Mrs. Chaworth seem to be straightforward.

Obviously the only reason for the creation of a set of new seals is to conceal the identity of the correspondent in the event there should be any surveillance. It is pertinent to determine what other correspondence at this time may have required surreptitious transmittal. Certainly his exchanges with Augusta required no cover, for they had written to each other openly for many months, and recently had not sent letters more often than about once a month. The distinctive seal that Lord Lovelace stated Augusta had used —on only one letter, so far as available information goes—appears only a year after this time.

The only other correspondence about which Byron might have experienced any concern was that with Lady Frances Webster. This exchange of letters began almost as soon as he had left Aston and continued for almost a year. Their communication was indeed clandestine, since a third person acted as intermediary, since Webster had manifested extreme jealousy, and since he had received enough letters from Byron to be thoroughly familiar with the poet's regular seal. Thus it seems highly probable that the "seals for myself and *****," unless they involved some hitherto unsuspected correspondent, eventually found their way to Lady Frances Webster.

To dispose of the Chaworth problem, it lasted very briefly. If the poet correctly informed Lady Melbourne, Mary's efforts to resume their friendship were quite unwelcome,[7] not only because there was the problem of her rather violent and unpredictable husband in the background, but because Miss Radford, acting as go-between and friend, was a person he did not trust. He found it particularly objectionable, he continued, that Mrs. Chaworth had chosen to employ an intermediary, since the correspondence contained nothing that called for concealment. As he pointed out a bit testily, the only questionable thing about their letters was the surreptitious transmittal.

The purported seal of Augusta mentioned above is of special interest. On the title page of the second edition of *Astarte*, that prepared by Lady Lovelace, it appears as a strange-looking cartouche or colophon. A note appended by either Lord or Lady Lovelace asserts it is the design of a seal Byron had prepared

and procured for Augusta. Whichever of the editors is responsible for the information is of no importance. The statement, however, is that the seal appeared in wax on a letter Augusta sent Byron in December 1814.[8] Since its presence on earlier letters is not mentioned, this may well have been the first occasion of its use. If that assumption is correct, it could have no connection with the seals Byron referred to in his journal.

The reproduction is somewhat deficient in definition and clarity, but the main features are unmistakable. Within a fairly large oval appears a representation of an Eros riding in a chariot and lashing at two running horses, certainly an unconventional equipage for Eros. The horses are shown in full career and have, in the positive imprint, the same orientation, positions, and gait as the running horses on all the coats of arms of the Hanoverian line. The resemblance may be accidental; maybe all running horses, as they appear on seals, look alike.

The chariot is most remarkable in that the body of it incorporates the body of a bird, with head and beak forming a part of the front guard. The head and eye are readily identifiable and markings along the side of the chariot unquestionably are conventionalized feathers. The only major uncertainty pertains to the length of the bird's beak, which projects forward from the upper part of the dash. It is not entirely certain if the beak is long or short. If it is relatively long, the body of the chariot was clearly meant to represent a goose—and therefore Augusta.

If that attribution is correct, the only possible interpretation is that the design was meant to signify something understood by Byron and Augusta, but perhaps not readily apprehended by others. If this is an ideogram, as it seems, one could read it as "Love drives two racing horses to convey Augusta or Augusta's chariot." At this level, the implication can only be that someone connected with horse racing is under the lash of love in some connection with Augusta Leigh. If identification is limited only to associations with the turf, the reference could extend all the way from the royal dukes and the Duke of Rutland through a long series of wealthy nobles and commoners to such hangers-on as Leigh. However, if the delineation of the horses was not an accident—and in so elaborate a jest it may seem unlikely to have been—the ideogram must refer to two of the sons of George III. If the author of the legend in *Astarte* correctly attributed the seal to Byron and if it was made up sometime in late 1813, or early 1814, one suspects strongly that the poet was celebrating in a rather poor joke Augusta's activities in London during early July.

It is appropriate to ask, in the face of this interpretation, if two royal dukes had been in love with Augusta. No direct evidence exists, and the probability of double Hanoverian devotion seems slight. But the figure of Eros could symbolize not only the spirit of erotic love, but also the man whom it possessed. In that case the man would have to be someone who enjoyed powerful influence with members of the House of Hanover. Very high on a list of such men would be the Duke of Rutland, who corresponded often and most cordially with the Regent[9] and with whose wife the Duke of York was said to have been in love.[10]

≫ 18 ≪

THE NAMING OF MEDORA

The statistical probability that on a given date, or any date, an upper class English female child would be baptized Medora is so remote that some inquiry into the choice of such a name is entirely justified. First, it is noteworthy that the name was in fact the second name, the first, as it appears on the baptismal certificate, being Elizabeth—which is not particularly exciting and is associated with a reasonable probability. The other recorded Leigh names show Augusta and the Colonel to have been not terribly original: both the older girls had received Augusta as the second of their two names. By the time of Medora's arrival the Leighs may have decided that was quite enough Augustas.

As related in the chapter on Augusta's London season, it is possible she may first have heard the name in London in July 1813 or maybe—if she had spent some days in the country at Cheveley with the Rutlands—a little later. As of that time the only other known Medora was a two-year-old filly that the Duke of Rutland regarded as being potentially a very good racer.

Later in the year, when Byron began to cast about for a name for one of the forlorn females of *The Bride of Abydos,* he chose "Medora." On second consideration he decided to abandon that

name for Genevra. After some reflection upon the fact that recently he had written two sonnets addressed to a lady with that
designation (in fact a pseudonym for Lady Frances Webster), in
January he notified Murray that the name was again Medora.[1]
Meantime, of course, he had attended the Christmas party at Six
Mile Bottom. Since both Leigh and Sir John Shelley had a considerable interest in the turf, it is possible one or both could have
referred to the promising young filly of the Duke. Or at some
point Augusta may have mentioned the animal, but it seems unlikely that Byron would have had any direct knowledge of it.
There is no evidence that his naming one of his heroines Medora
was more than a curious coincidence. The naming of the Leigh
baby was surely not a coincidence, but we can only speculate
whether it was the lady in the poem or the horse that the Leighs
had in mind. Perhaps Augusta was thinking of one, the Colonel
of the other.

Before the baptism of the baby, the filly had achieved some distinction. At a mile and a half, The Oaks was a long race for a
young animal, but Medora won it in 1814.[2] If Leigh happened to
have had a well-placed bet, he may have had more than poetic
reasons for making the selection of the name himself. Children,
unfortunately, have received unusual names for far less cogent
reasons.

The child's other name, Elizabeth, is probably of far more significance. That name was uncommon in the Byron family, nor
does it appear among the contemporary Godolphins, the family
name of Augusta's half siblings on her mother's side. It was, however, the baptismal name of Lady Elizabeth Howard, who had
become the Duchess of Rutland. Both the selection of Elizabeth
for a name and the nomination of the Duchess as one of Medora's
sponsors deserve examination. If during her short London season
Augusta had been primarily the guest of Lady Gertrude Sloane,

and if the selection of name and sponsor signified recognition of
friendship and hospitality, it would have been appropriate to have
selected Gertrude for the name and her namesake for the sponsor.[3] The choice of Lady Gertrude's sister, concerning whom no
reference appears in any correspondence, implies some exceptional
affection, gratitude, or acknowledgment of obligation. It seems
inescapable that the Rutland relationship was prominent in the
mind of Augusta when she named her infant daughter, and to
postulate that the combination of names—one associated with the
Duchess, the other with the Duke—was fortuitous or purely
whimsical is to stretch plausibility.

     As it turned out, the child was never known among her own
family as Medora, but rather by the diminutive Libby. Nor is it
clear at all when the use of her second name became so accepted
a convention that the girl has come down in biography as
Medora. At some point she became Medora, perhaps because the
name has an exotic ring more appropriate to the career of the girl
and woman than so commonplace a name as Libby. Of course
her uncle's widely read poems established dark and disastrous
connotations, and it would have suited Lady Byron, for example,
to consider "Medora" far more appropriate than her familiar
name. The popularization of the name Medora, however, may
owe as much to Lady Caroline Lamb as to anyone else. In 1816,
at the height of the troubles, that lady quite abruptly recalled that
sometime in 1814 Byron had told her a woman was pregnant by
him and the child would be called Medora if it was a girl.[4] If she
happened instead to be called Libby, but had the other name, it
became essential to Lady Caroline's purposes that she should
wear Medora as a mark of her origin.

≽ 19 ≼

AUGUSTA'S APPOINTMENT

Among the many unexplained features of the Byron–Augusta affair is Augusta's appointment to the household of Queen Charlotte. While the position was not a highly honorific one, it carried with it enough advantages to be quite desirable—a "grace and favour" apartment at St. James's Palace, an allowance of about £300 per year, and probably a reasonable amount of free food and drink, as well as some—possibly boring—social life. The duties were insignificant and consisted mainly of being available for companionship if the Queen wanted a quiet evening, of filling a place at dinner or at a card table, and of constituting a part of the Queen's entourage at major social or Court functions. Furthermore, there was a general arrangement among the several attendants in the same grade that there should be a rotation of duties, so that it was something of a month-on, month-off type of obligation.[1]

In short, the appointment was well worth seeking and a good many ladies were in competition for positions of this type. What gives rise to interest is that Augusta received such an appointment at all, especially in view of the Queen's established propriety. Of course, for a good many months Augusta had been seeking almost any sort of favor that might allow her a small revenue and reasonably reliable protection from creditors. Since there have been rather loose accounts of Augusta's position and rank in the household, it is as well to record that the date of her appointment was 20 February 1815 and the title was Woman of the Bedchamber.[2] So far as the evidence appears, however, Augusta did not take possession of her apartment until April or May 1816, shortly after Byron departed, hard upon the cuts she had sustained at Lady Jersey's ball and at the nadir of her own reputation (see chapter 20).

Appointments such as this were at the behest of the ruler, usually under the urging of the highest ministers or chief courtiers. In consequence, a whim on the part of the Regent, a Cabinet change, or the death of the royal personage led to changes in the personnel of the Household. In 1817, upon learning of Queen Charlotte's illness, Byron wrote to inquire of his half sister whether the Queen's death would terminate her position as what he designated—incorrectly and pretty certainly ironically—as "Maid of Honour."[3] The Queen survived that illness, but succumbed the following year. With her death Augusta's position as Woman of the Bedchamber came to an end. Strangely enough, however, she retained the use of her apartment well into the reign of Queen Victoria, indeed until her own death in 1851. Still more surprisingly, in 1820 the Prince Regent, having just acceded to the throne as George IV, provided her with a stipend of £300 per year,[4] which continued in effect until Lord Melbourne, in the reign of Queen Victoria, abrogated it.

If one reflects that the original appointment followed by only a few years the Regent's dismissal of Colonel Leigh in something close to disgrace and that as soon as it lay within his power as King he provided for the Leighs a lifetime domicile and support, this highly beneficent favor becomes yet more surprising. Moreover, not long before Augusta's appointment Byron had publicly acknowledged authorship of "Lines to a Lady Weeping," an acknowledgment that led to a furious attack by the Tories. The events are difficult to account for also in view of the fact that from January 1816 forward the Tory press seemingly operated under directions to annihilate Byron. Though Augusta had never taken any part in politics, she was near kin to Byron and moved in Whig circles when she appeared at all. Nor did her half-sister relationship to the Duke of Leeds afford any support: his mother, the Dowager Duchess, was removed about this time from her position as a kind of governess of the Princess Charlotte.[5] Augusta's appointment, in terms of politics, was impossible.

Manifestly, very great influence would have been essential to her cause. None of Byron's associates, male or female, was in favor with the Regent or his ministers. The power of the Earl of Carlisle had declined to a negligible level. Lord and Lady Chichester were on casually courteous terms with the Regent but held no real power. The Duke of Leeds, as remarked, could not keep his mother in her position.

Alone among her near kin, Augusta's cousin, the Duchess of Rutland, might have had the necessary power and influence. The Duke of York, Leigh's former commander in chief, was in love with the Duchess, and the Duchess's husband was on very friendly terms with the Regent. Only these among the kinship would appear to have possessed enough pluses to offset the Byronic minuses. So far as the record shows, however, there had been no close association between Augusta and the Duchess since they were girls until Augusta came to London in 1813. That the Duchess, rather than her sister and Augusta's hostess, Lady Gertrude Sloane, agreed to serve as Medora's sponsor may suggest that some recent closer relationship developed. Augusta evidently had never met the Duke at all until her visit to London, if she met him at that time. Unless unknown and very special circumstances were involved, this relationship might have been expected to result in no more than a routine appointment, for the duration of the Queen's life, say, or at the most for that of the man who was to become George IV.

One other anomalous fact may have a bearing upon the paternity of Medora. It has been noted that Leigh, who had never liked Byron, regarded Medora as something of a favorite. If he was of a jealous nature, as Augusta informed Hobhouse, the near certainty that Medora was the product of adultery would not have led him to prefer her to his natural children—unless (1) her conception in adultery may have resulted in significant advantage to him or (2) the nature of the adultery was such as to reflect some honor upon the family. It is doubtful that he was quite venal enough for the first alternative.

Possibly one final point deserves notice. The Carlisle clan, with whom Byron had feuded throughout the years, alone among his political opponents sent carriages to the poet's funeral, and the Duke of Rutland who was all set up for a hunt, upon learning of Byron's death, adjourned the sport. It is true the Carlisles were kin, though not close; the Duke of Rutland was not. Possibly the demonstrations were for Augusta's sake. If they were, these marks of respect are hardly what one would expect from a family she had disgraced. In addition to expressions of familial and social solidarity these outward shows may reflect knowledge of the actual events of Augusta's midsummer nights.

And perhaps it is not unfair to quote a lady who observed the Rutlands at Tunbridge Wells in 1803, ten years earlier: "The Duke and Duchess of Rutland are here with two Little Girls. They are not happy together, tho' hoping to have a Son. I have heard the Duke Blamed; but Latterly the fault seems to rest with the Duchess. She is said to be Childish and provoking, and He is not very sensible, and Passionate. . . ." [6]

≥ 20 ≤

THE BONDS OF MATRIMONY

As of June 1814 Byron's situation was apparently improving. He had recovered his spirits and, with Moore and other friends, was experiencing an Indian summer of fame and prestige. Since he had no visible mistress, people began to suspect first one lady and then another. Lady Caroline was consumed with curiosity about what he was doing and whom he was seeing, and resumed her investigations into his private affairs. ". . . she has often belied and sometimes betrayed me; she has crossed me everywhere; she has watched and worried and *guessed* and been a curse to me and mine." [1]

And ten days later he complained again, "She perplexed me very much with questions and guesses . . . there is no conjecturing what she may assert or do." She continues to get into his flat and is making his life miserable and he doesn't know "whatever absurdity, or enormity, her madness may plunge me into. . . ." [2]

Even Lady Melbourne was inclined to wonder a bit what Byron was about, to the extent that Byron replied to one of her notes that he was by no means about to get into a scrape with "R's moiety" (see below). [3] There is, of course, no way to guess how

many other ladies whispered and gossiped but failed to write
reminiscences. Without question in the aimless upper class in
which he moved it was quite inconceivable that a normal young
man, even though a poet, would not have some kind of an affair
in process, since by definition the ladies of the set were attractive.
Byron, of course, had had no visible attachment since Lady Oxford left in June of 1813, the affair with Lady Frances Webster
having been in so remote a place and conducted with such discretion that people in London knew nothing of it.

This inconceivable situation could only mean that he was engaged in some kind of highly secretive romance, and it became
the duty of the ladies to find out what was going on. As early
as January 1814, according to Maurois, Lady Caroline had
started stories of incest.[4] About the same time Lady Holland had
employed one of her sons as a special investigator around Nottingham.[5] And when Lady Melbourne became curious, Byron
replied that he accepted only what was offered and that that lady
had offered him nothing. "R's moiety," not better identified, in
the opinion of Prothero was Lady Milbanke. That identification
is inconceivable, since Byron had resumed an intermittent correspondence with Annabella, and since every piece of evidence
that exists indicates that he and Lady Milbanke thoroughly dis-
liked each other. It seems far more probable that as a result of
Moore's return to town and Byron's reëntry into circulation
among the Moore clique, the lady in question was Lady Rancliffe.
Byron apparently liked her—or had liked her—before she abruptly
rebuffed his interest in her sister Lady Adelaide Forbes.[6] The
Rancliffes were particular friends of Moore and some of Byron's
reports indicate that together they had been to Rancliffe parties.

During all this time he apparently continued a rather desultory
and very well concealed correspondence with Lady Frances,
another indication that his attachment to her by no means was

as superficial and amused as he had represented it to Lady Melbourne.[7] Though he had written Moore in March that he was
permanently finished with versifying, the return of Moore and
the pressure of Douglas Kinnaird was on the point of leading
him into the composition of *Hebrew Melodies,* a series of short
pieces designed to be set to music and used as songs by Isaac
Nathan.[8]

Leigh seems to have been off about his usual pursuits during
much of 1814, but Augusta came up to town, bringing with her
some of her children.[9] During this relatively short visit she had
space at the London Hotel in Albemarle Street, fairly good indication that she had a little money left after paying off some of
her more pressing creditors. Soon after her arrival, Byron having
leased a house at Hastings, he, Augusta and her children, and one
of their cousins (regularly stated to have been Captain George
Anson Byron, the heir presumptive to the title) went to the sea-
shore for a summer holiday and remained for three weeks.[10]

The family holiday seems not to have differed very much from
any other seaside visit *en famille.* They swam, sailed, and idled.
Hodgson, Byron's old friend from college, looked in from time
to time and Byron wrote a little. About the only things that broke
the monotony occurred, as Byron wrote Moore, when the poet
got in a rage with an ink bottle, hurled it out the window and
smashed it on a white statue of one of the Muses. And there was
a little difficulty, entirely by correspondence, with Murray, who
was on the point of bringing out a new edition of Byron's collected works. To illustrate the new volume Murray wanted to
use an engraving of a portrait (which was never specified). Augusta and the cousin thoroughly disapproved of the engraving;
Byron's response was indifference, but he insisted on deletion of
the engraving to please the others.[11] (That Captain Byron would

have been at all concerned seems very improbable; another cousin may have been on hand part of the time.)

There must have been a lot of idle chatter and perhaps a few serious talks between Augusta and Byron, for soon after the holidays had ended and Augusta had returned to Six Mile Bottom, she undertook to act as marriage broker and to arrange a wedding between Byron and her friend Lady Charlotte Leveson Gower.[12] This effort failed, for the Lady Charlotte or her friends had found a far more promising husband than Byron. Shortly after this, brother, sister, and children again spent several days together, this time at Newstead.

At the same time as Augusta's inquiry went to Lady Charlotte, Byron very tentatively raised the question of marriage to Miss Milbanke, with whom he had maintained sporadic correspondence and far from ardent acquaintance almost from the time of his return to England. In early 1813 he had gone so far as to request Lady Melbourne to inquire of the young lady if she might be interested in a more direct proposal. The young lady replied that she would not, and Byron had regarded himself thereafter as a rejected suitor.

Of his selection of Miss Milbanke—if Byron selected her rather than she him, for she certainly was not passive in the strategy that led to their marriage—one of the more attractive features that Byron could find in the situation was that he would become Lady Melbourne's nephew.[13] However, viewed in the light of marriage as interpreted and understood by his class, this should have been quite a successful arrangement. The lady was an heiress, came of good family and better connections, and was generally regarded as highly intelligent.

There is no record of Lady Caroline's opinion of or reaction to the news that her late lover was now engaged to her husband's country cousin, Anna Isabella Milbanke. Certainly in comparison with Lady Caroline, the country cousin was dull and pedantic; and furthermore, if one can judge from the available likenesses, Annabella was rather less attractive physically. There was not a lot Lady Caroline could do openly, particularly since Annabella was a niece of Lady Melbourne. That fact in itself may have played a decisive part in Byron's choice of Annabella: he may well have regarded her, by virtue of her connections with the Lambs, as the best possible protection against further torment by Lady Caroline.

Miss Milbanke's acceptance was prompt, and by 15 September the engagement was official.[14] Byron made all the necessary announcements, and from that time till December a lot of his time and effort went into the numerous legal arrangements that were essential to marriage among the upper classes. The entire process was annoying, and probably, like many another young man, he was a bit frightened by what he had undertaken. It is only just to add that Hanson, his solicitor, pursued the necessary legalistic procedures to marriage with very flagging zeal.

When all the details finally were completed, Byron set out for Sir Ralph Milbanke's place at Seaham, where the marriage was to occur. It became apparent at once that Byron was not pursuing the trip in burning haste.[15] Hobhouse remarked that he hardly expected to encounter again a less eager bridegroom.

Toward Christmas of 1814, as Byron loitered along his way to Seaham, he stopped at Six Mile Bottom and found the household, as usual, chaotic. As Marchand writes, "It was not a very happy Christmas there, either, for Colonel Leigh was at home and Byron felt restrained. He could play with the children, but his sister had to divide her time with a sick and complaining husband."[16] It was of this visit that Byron wrote Miss Milbanke, "Colonel L. is opposite me making so many complaints of illness and calls for medicine that . . . the rest of my letter will be like a prescription if I don't leave off." [17]

Domestication, More or Less

The ceremony took place with no more than the usual errors, and Hobhouse, who was best man, handed the bride and groom into their carriage, not without a considerable reservation with respect to their future happiness.[18] For the duration of the "treaclemoon," as Byron called it, adjustments were no more unstable than they usually are. Beyond a doubt Byron was pretty demanding sexually, and later remarks of Lady Byron indicate that fairly soon he may have initiated her into some of the more exotic activities.

Upon their establishment in London troubles began. Annabella's company was not sufficient to offset Byron's inclinations to resume bachelor dinners. In taking over 13 Piccadilly, the two had assumed a cost of living far beyond any visible income. A married couple of quite limited income, no matter how grand the address (rented), were simply not as attractive socially as an unmarried literary lion. Furthermore, within a short time Annabella found herself pregnant and, since she was something of a hypochondriac anyhow, the normal discomforts of pregnancy became marked impediments to their social and domestic life. To add to the complications, Kinnaird induced Byron to become a member of the board of Drury Lane, and the poet began to spend more and more time in the green room, where one of the actresses in particular became the object of a brief attachment.[19]

During this interval and indeed until separation occurred, Lady Caroline remained, so far as the world could observe, placid. There is no record of her interference during any part of the period while Lord and Lady Byron lived together.

With the progression of her pregnancy Lady Byron became increasingly unhappy with Byron's mode of life. He in turn made no effort to conceal his indifference to his wife's charms and exasperation with the creditors who collected about their house. Matters had reached such a point by October 1815 that Lady Byron wrote to Augusta some of the details and asked her to come up to see if she could ameliorate her brother's conduct and language.[20] Augusta came, and she remained in the house in Piccadilly through the final months of the pregnancy, the delivery of Ada, the separation of Byron and his wife, and the social obloquy that followed. Augusta herself was pregnant during this interval of residence in London, and Leigh made several visits to Byron's house during the months Augusta remained there. Indeed he urged Augusta to remain in London—because he feared if she returned to Six Mile Bottom Byron would follow.[21]

It is unnecessary to repeat the accounts of Byron's behavior toward Augusta and Annabella during the final month or so of the marriage. From the beginning the two partners had been incompatible in almost every respect, but one aspect of their incompatibility has not received the degree of attention it deserves. Byron, as the section on his earlier life demonstrated, was basically a very vigorous and healthy man, and men of that type are prone to manifest very little sympathy toward an individual who complains constantly of malaise. Yet persistent malaise was one of the outstanding characteristics of Annabella, despite an external appearance of glowing health and quite pink cheeks.[22] (That her malaise may have had psychological sources is quite evident; what those sources were is entirely speculative.) Certainly with this type of psychological and physical organization she must have found pregnancy profoundly uncomfortable.

Byron, in contrast, aside from his obvious annoyance, seems to

have felt as well as ever, if Gronow's description of his appearance and behavior in mid-1815 is accurate. "Byron was then a
very handsome man, with remarkably fine eyes and hair; but
was, as usual, all show-off and affection [sic]. . . . Byron, on this
occasion, was in great humour, and full of boyish and even bois-
terous mirth." [23] This description portrays Byron at a dinner for
men, among whom were Sir Walter Scott, Lord Caledon, John
Wilson Croker, and Sir James Bland Burgess. The contrast between his vitality and Annabella's lassitude could hardly be more
vivid, and she may have responded as ladies of her type not in-
frequently do, by resenting this overflowing health in contrast
with her own state of utter misery—as she perceived it. Nor could
she have taken any comfort from the fact that her lord so obviously preferred evenings of conviviality of this type to sitting
at home to hear a catalogue of woe.

The situation steadily worsened. To add to other difficulties,
the Byron household achieved a state of bankruptcy and bailiffs
began to move in and even to take up residence.[24] At this point
Lady Byron was confined and on 15 December gave birth to a
daughter, Ada. Byron accepted the arrival of the infant with
what must have seemed to his wife exceptional sangfroid. The
serious and unremitting harassment of his creditors may have
played a part in his relative indifference; at any rate Annabella
perceived a striking lack of enthusiasm compared with the kind
of demonstration she evidently expected.

Affairs were, indeed, critical, and as soon as Annabella was
able to travel, Byron suggested that she should rejoin her parents
until he could make essential changes in their domestic arrangements. Accordingly she left London and Byron on 15 January
1816. During the next several days Augusta sent Annabella almost
daily letters, with descriptions of the state of Byron's health (bad,
she said), his troubles (overwhelming), and reports from his

physicians (not insane).[25] The last information convinced Annabella that her husband's conduct during the preceding two or
three months had not arisen from mental aberration but from
innate wickedness.[26] Her mother and father, totally dismayed by
the miserable experiences of their only child, refused to consider her return to Byron, and by late January the Milbanke
family had determined on a legal separation.

Rumour Peynted ful of Tonges

With the news of their separation, rumors began. Augusta
wrote Lady Byron in late January that, thanks to Lady Caroline
Lamb, gossip was flowing from Melbourne House, "a fine affair
in their imagination your absence—and my stay!" Lady Byron in
turn wrote her mother, ". . . I very much fear that she [Augusta]
may be supposed the cause of the separation by many, and it
would be a cruel injustice." [27]

Just after Lady Byron's withdrawal, Lady Caroline wrote to
Byron offering her good offices and assuring him of her support.[28]
His reply was brief and polite, but firm. Immediately she prof-
fered her support to Annabella, with the information that she
knew things about Byron that would prevent his ever taking
Ada away.[29] She accused him of incest and homosexuality, and
when Lady Byron came up to London to confer with Dr. Lushington, her counsellor, Lady Caroline went into detail. According
to Elwin she passed on such evidence for incest as she had
gathered, but cautioned Lady Byron on no account to inform
Mrs. Leigh of the character of the accusation, since Augusta
would only try to disprove it.[30]

There is nothing to prove or disprove that Lady Byron suspected incest before this time, except some of her own belated
notes; but after her conference with Lady Caroline it became, in

Lady Byron's opinion, a proven fact, and if rumor and talk would make a thing true, these followed promptly, together with a few other charges of sexual depravity to reinforce the lesser ones. About the same time Mrs. Villiers, Augusta's good friend and former hostess, wrote to Lady Byron that rumors of incest were about and that her silence seemed to lend credence to the gossip and was unfair and unjust to Augusta.[31]

As news of the separation spread and especially after it became apparent that Lushington regarded the secret charges against Byron as beyond any negotiation, London gossips seized upon anything Byron had ever hinted, either in speech or in poetry, as evidence of uncontrollable and perverted lust. Augusta wrote to Lady Byron in mid-February, "There are reports abroad of a nature *too horrible to repeat*. Every other sinks into nothing before the MOST horrid one." [32] The people around Byron, and Byron himself, were perfectly aware of the nature of the slander. Augusta wrote Hodgson, 4 March, "Now I have borne patiently and indeed laughed at all of the reports I have heard against myself—and it has been a good deal for some days past." [33] Six days later she wrote again reporting that Lady Byron had produced "a *written contradiction* of the two principal and most horrible reports." [34] (In fact, Lady Byron had done no such thing. Apparently under the guidance of her solicitor she had framed a statement that was designed to lead Augusta to draw this inference, but that in fact set forth no more than that incest was not one of the charges against Byron.) Hobhouse and, no doubt, both Captain George Byron and Mr. Robert Wilmot were completely familiar with the charges. Hobhouse wrote that Augusta had "staid long enough to *give the lie* to all rumours respecting herself," and that Colonel Leigh had behaved very handsomely in rejecting all the gossip as malicious lies.[35]

Biographers are in accord that Lady Caroline originated and

propagated most of the stories, as Byron himself maintained. She alone, in addition to having first-hand experience of his sexual prowess, would have been thoroughly conversant with everything he had published and would have enjoyed at least partial access to his otherwise private correspondence with Lady Melbourne. But Lady Noel, as Annabella's mother had become, contributed her own nasty bit. For transmission to the attorney Lushington, she passed to Mrs. Clermont, her companion, confidante, and former housekeeper, a report clearly designed to add sodomy to Byron's misdeeds: "Ld. B. has told his Wife that in 1813 he had *absolute criminal* connection with an *old Lady,* at the same time as with her Daughter in Law—that *She* absolutely *proposed it* to *him*— . . ." She added, "this *explains much,* which before was *inexplicable,*" whatever she may have meant by that.[36] About the same time Annabella wrote Mrs. Clermont, "Besides *you* might have a return of *Love*" for Byron.[37] This is one more remarkable and *"inexplicable"* ingredient in the correspondence among very unusual people: Byron and the aging Mrs. Clermont, so far as information reveals, had always viewed each other with suspicion and hostility.

During early February, Lady Melbourne, whom biographers presume to know more about the putative incest than anyone else, was ill. On 5 February, she promised Byron she would pay a call on Augusta,[38] a note that indicates the poet may have requested the visit as a partial offset to rumor. Her continued illness prevented the call, but on 14 February she reassured Byron ". . . at all events I shall call upon Mrs. Leigh tomorrow or the next day,"[39] and apparently she did what she promised.

It took a pretty strong person to side with Byron in those days. After Annabella started her campaign even Mrs. Villiers defected, as Marchand reports,[40] and shortly was scheming with Lady Byron to extort a confession from Augusta. It was Lady

Byron's contention that only an open confession could atone for the guilt and that it was her Christian duty to obtain that confession, preferably signed and in front of witnesses. Robert John Wilmot, Byron's cousin, joined sides with Lady Byron as soon as the trouble began, though there appears no good reason why he needed to take any position at all. Captain George Byron, another first cousin and heir to the title, sided with Lady Byron from the beginning. He at least had the advantage or disadvantage of first-hand observation of Byron's language and behavior toward her.

Hobhouse made a number of entries in his diary during the time in question. Though anything he committed to paper may be prejudiced, unimaginative, dull, or humorless, the strongest partisans of Lady Byron have never claimed he lied. One of the entries is particularly significant since it bears the date 22 December 1815, before any of the allegations, even before there was any indication Lord and Lady Byron might separate. He dined at Holland House and in the course of the evening Lady Caroline came in. She "defined the truth to be what one thinks at the moment. . . ." She also "cooed a good deal, very good-humouredly." [41] The other pertinent entry occurs on 27 April 1816, after all was finished and Byron was on his way to exile. Hobhouse called on Lady Melbourne and learned from her that a Miss Doyle, an intimate of Annabella and sister to the Colonel Doyle who had been active in Lady Byron's behalf, had said "she should burst, and that if she might speak she could tell such a story. Whilst we were talking, in came Lady Caroline Lamb. She was ready to sink. I said in her hearing that I trusted that Lord Byron's enemies would condescend at last to perch upon a fact." [42] Unfortunately, Miss Doyle did not burst, at least not into any memoir anyone has reported, and it is completely unknown why she might not speak or what story she could have told. Since just about everything that could be said had already been told, one suspects her story would merely have added some additional lurid detail, suspected or rumored. As for Lady Caroline's loss of aplomb, if Hobhouse was correct in his observation, one can only guess that she knew when she had been caught in a lie.

During all this period, while erstwhile friends were destroying reputations and imposing true ostracism, lawyers were busily at work on both sides. Although Byron at first demanded a trial in order to force the Milbankes to produce the grounds for their action, he eventually capitulated (see chapter 22). The final papers were drawn and all necessary arrangements were achieved to provide for a variety of contingencies with respect to death, inheritance, and other acts of God or man.

All the principals were emotionally and physically exhausted, with the possible exception of Byron himself, who retained enough vigor for anger and bitterness. By March 1816, Hobhouse found Augusta near collapse and distraught by her need to return to Six Mile Bottom to see to her children.[43] Feeling she had stayed long enough in London to discredit the rumors, she was ready to go home. Leigh had already gone back to the country, as Augusta wrote Hobhouse, and "He has never pressed my return since he quitted London and on the subjects of reports has only been indignant and vexed. . . . and you know he is suspicious on these sort of things." [44]

The extent to which lawyers may have influenced the actions of the principals cannot be fully known. In addition to such usual details as inheritance and fiscal affairs, one of the essential problems in separation is custody of the child. Apparently this problem lay at the bottom of much of what Annabella did and tried to do, since she was resolved that Ada should not pass into Augusta's care.[45] The law in England probably gave a slight edge to the husband in usual cases (particularly if the child was male), and only flagrant and established misconduct might offset his claim. But even if he did not receive custody, the law recognized that, as head even of a broken house, he had certain powers over the management and rearing of the infant. Though Byron specifically had stated that he would not separate Ada from his wife, except for most serious cause,[46] Lady Byron perhaps never quite trusted the assurance. It was almost certainly to forestall any demand for control of Ada that Annabella in the next several years undertook to act as her own investigator and barrister. The result, as so often when an amateur undertakes the function of a professional, was a compulsive accumulation: no proof was ever good enough; the QED demanded by her mathematical training could never be satisfied.

By April, social ostracism of Byron was complete. What seems remarkable is that it extended only partially to Augusta. Lady Melbourne seems to have called on her, as she had promised, and Mrs. Villiers accepted her in her house. On the other hand, at Lady Jersey's ball, which she attended in company with Byron, she had to accept the cuts of all the ladies with the exception of Lady Jersey and Miss Elphinstone.[47] Thereafter, and following Byron's departure for Italy on 25 April, Augusta's position seems to have promptly returned to normal except for the harassment Lady Byron offered, which she regarded as very much for Augusta's own good.

During the entire interval the press had done its duty effectively. Chew, particularly, has underscored the degree to which the ostracism of Byron had both a political and a religious-moral basis.[48] That Augusta neither lost her place in the Household nor suffered persistent social obloquy seems strongly to reinforce Chew's point.

COMMENTARY II

The events just narrated call for closer scrutiny on a number of points. If, as Byron thought, Lady Caroline Lamb was the only begetter of the story of incest, where did she pick up the idea for it and how much did she herself believe it?

Augusta's appointment took place during this interval, but the chain of events that produced it may begin with her London season and may involve, somewhat later, Byron's acknowledgment of "the Weepers," as he described "Lines to a Lady Weeping" in his letters to Moore. If Byron and Augusta were outcast, how did it come about that she was able to continue so valuable an appointment, which proved to be impervious to attack?

Just after Byron's departure into exile, Lady Byron entered upon a campaign to secure—probably for forensic reasons—a confession from Augusta that would protect Ada and herself from any action Byron might bring. How good was the confession and to what exactly did Augusta confess?

Byron at first insisted that he would bring the Milbanke side to court to force them to state charges, and then consented to a separation decree without proceedings. Why?

Finally, some authorities have considered, as did some of his contemporaries, that parts of his poetry constitute an acknowledgment of incest. To what extent is this view correct, and to what extent may the contents of the suspect poetry receive other interpretation or have other purpose?

These are the subjects that now come under examination.

≫ 21 ≪

LADY CAROLINE'S REVENGE

The odium that attached itself to Byron after the separation arose from a variety of sources—political, religious, and social. The special circumstances, together with Lady Byron's refusal to specify the grounds on which she demanded legal separation, left plenty of room for horrid imaginings. This chapter will attempt to investigate the possibility that Lady Caroline Lamb took advantage of the situation for her own purposes. In order to accomplish this aim it will be necessary to show that she had never acquiesced in Byron's dissolution of their liaison, that she resented it fiercely, and that she had determined to punish him for it.

Unfortunately—or maybe not—her letters seem not to have survived and it is possible to know how she thought only by reference to the poet's letters to her. The following one is pertinent because it was written on 29 April 1813, before any involvement with Augusta could have occurred, and almost two years before his marriage. The letter was sent under an address to Lady Melbourne with the request that she deliver it to Lady Caroline.

If you still persist in your intention of meeting me, in opposition to the wishes of your own friends and mine, it must even be so. I regret it and acquiesce with reluctance. I am not ignorant of the very extraordinary language you have held not only to me but others, and your avowal of your determination to obtain what you are pleased to call "revenge"; nor have I now to learn that an incensed woman is a dangerous enemy.

Undoubtedly those against whom we can make no defence, whatever they say or do, must be formidable. Your words and actions lately have been tolerably portentous, and might justify me in avoiding the demanded interview, more especially as I believe you to be fully capable of performing all your menaces. . . . Perhaps I deserve punishment, if so, you are quite as proper a person to inflict it as any other. You say you will "*ruin* me." I thank you, but I have done that for myself already; you say you will "destroy me," perhaps you will only save me the trouble. It is useless to reason with you . . . I tell you, that it is in great measure owing to this persecution; to the accursed things you have said; to the extravagances you have committed, that I again adopt the resolution of quitting this country. . . . I once wished, for your own sake, Lady M. to be present [at their meeting]—but if you are to fulfil any of your threats in word or deed we had better be alone.[1]

This was by no means the only letter in this general vein that Byron sent to his former amie. One can only guess at the terms of the epistle he was answering, but the nature of it was evident enough. She was threatening him with just about everything she could think of. Nor was the character of the exchange significantly altered for the better in the next year and a half. Until Byron announced his marriage, Lady Caroline never ceased to attempt to gain his attention—perhaps, more properly, to regain her hold over him. She burned him in effigy, she made an apparent suicidal gesture, she invaded his rooms.

The marriage with Annabella resulted in an armistice, so far as Lady Caroline was concerned. It would have been exceedingly difficult for her to have taken any visible part in destroying a marriage between Lady Melbourne's favorite and her niece. Temporarily, he was out of reach. The separation, a process of destruction which he had confidently predicted for himself, provided the opportunity for which Lady Caroline had waited. Her reaction was prompt.

Since Byron by the act of separation was free again, there was a possibility of recapturing him. Almost as soon as she knew of the separation, Lady Caroline offered her assistance to her former love. What she meant, evidently, was that if he would return to her dominion, her unique talents would be available in any confrontation with the Milbankes. What she, and other ladies, had to learn was that Byron wanted no part of human bondage—for longer than a few months.

The poet, of course, refused her proffer of help, and soon the whispers of all manner of sexual aberration began to circulate, including homosexuality, which under English law at the time was a felony. Once more Byron had rejected her, an affront Lady Caroline could now deal with as she chose. Since she had no reliable information of Byron's activities during the period from the departure of Lady Oxford until the date of his marriage, her imagination had no restraint. He had publicly been with Augusta and therefore he was guilty of incest. Lady Melbourne often invited him, and therefore he had enjoyed perverted relations with her. So far as the poet was concerned, Lady Caroline was the "fountainhead" of all the scandalmongering.

Aside from the fact that charges of this type were not particularly unusual in England of the Regency, Lady Caroline had plenty of material to hand. At various parties Byron had openly speculated on the subject of incest,[2] and some of his poetry— as will appear later—clearly involved incestuous love. For that matter, her own kinsman, Lord Bolingbroke, had fled to Spain with his half sister in 1809,[3] and there were rumors at least that other members of the nobility may have enjoyed very near female relatives. That Byron, in the company of ladies and under his curious compulsion to appear evil, played Satanic and hinted at all manner of dark misdeeds added the element of credibility a persistent rumor requires.

At this distance no one can say how much of what Lady Caroline accomplished represented malice prepense and how much was a quick response to opportunity. Perhaps if the rumors had stopped at the usual Whig and Tory circles they would eventually have died of inanition, but either through a stroke of malicious genius or as sudden inspiration, when she requested an interview with Lady Byron, Lady Caroline found the one type of mind capable of perpetuating the story and of forming an ineradicable conviction. As Annabella reported, their interview converted her opinion into an *"absolute* conviction." [4] In this fashion Lady Caroline not only "destroyed" Byron as she had promised she would, but she also insured that no amount of reformation in the future would be sufficient to lead to reconciliation with Annabella. And she must have recognized that she had finished off Annabella as well.

For Caroline tolerated rivals poorly. Lady Oxford had been a bit too formidable and experienced for direct attack, and Lady Caroline had been rather young at the time. But when she had opportunity to even scores with Lady Frances Webster, she had learned how to employ contempt very effectively: "She [Lady Frances] was most affected. . . . Indeed Lady F. Webster is too ridiculous. Mr. Bradshaw, an amiable Dandy close by me, says it makes him ill for two hours after he has seen her." [5]

This account of Lady Caroline departs considerably from the usual version of her character. But it does so without any denial of the fact that she had great charm, that she was a bright and exciting woman, or that a good many men found her very attractive—for a time. That those who knew her best and were closely associated with her also found flaws in her make-up is well attested. Though one may dismiss William Lamb's intermittent rages as well justified, and though Lady Melbourne's detestation may have reflected primarily her maternal concern, the Honourable Frederick Lamb, the third Melbourne son, a most tolerant and gentle individual, wrote his mother to congratulate her that Lady Caroline was no longer at Melbourne House,

> . . . and [that] you do not see her so continually, but two such curses [as Lady Caroline and Caro-George, the wife of his younger brother] were never inflicted upon a family. . . . I wish I had a receipt to give you against the torment of the little beast, but I know of none, even my patience wd. be of no avail there, for she makes me furious. A settled firm resolution to have nothing to do with her, and not to care a six-pence about what she does, is the best resource. [6]

During the year after his departure Lady Caroline's malignancy toward Byron led her to produce her novel, *Glenarvon* in which in thin disguise Byron appears as the eponymous hero. The book achieved a *succès de scandale,* since it was taken to reveal the truth about the poet's character and exploits. What particularly strikes one is that although the hero proves guilty of a variety of crimes of violence, including infanticide and the murder of a lady or two, and of a considerable amount of general promiscuity and adultery, incest does not appear in the catalogue of his vices.

The meeting with Hobhouse at Lady Melbourne's during which Lady Caroline exhibited a remarkable degree of discomposure when Byron's friend commented on the lies in circulation has been described and it will be remembered that she herself had defined the truth as what she happened to say at the moment. Evidence of her spite for an insignificant rival has been cited just above. But if she really believed that Augusta had been the woman who caused Byron to desert her, it seems incredible that in all the subsequent years she made no further mention of Byron's sister.

At the time Bulwer-Lytton became her lover, about 1824, she informed him that the stories that had circulated about Byron and Augusta were totally false.[7] If she originated them, as all the evidence indicates, there is probably no better authority that they were false. In short, it seems that she had accomplished her revenge, as she had promised. Her "truth," having served its purpose in terminating Byron's marriage, though not in reestablishing her dominion over him, had become "inoperative." That her purpose was originally to have reclaimed the poet for her own seems undeniable in the face of her original offer to takes sides with him against Lady Byron.[8]

≫ 22 ≪

THE CHARGES AND BYRON'S
NOLO CONTENDERE

More than one biographer has made a considerable point of
the fact that neither Byron nor Augusta nor anyone acting for
them made a public denial of the charges of sexual irregularity
brought against them.[1] They make the point further that though
Byron repeatedly challenged the Milbanke interests to take the
case to court, he backed off when court action appeared likely.
The retreat, the argument proceeds, indicates that he could not
have defended himself successfully The purpose of this section
is to examine the merits of this position.

In fact, there were two kinds of charges—the first, the allegations the Milbanke lawyers would take into court; the second,
the rumors and gossip. Since the case never became public
through a judicial process, one can only speculate what the
Milbanke attorneys would have brought against Byron. One
may be sure they would have chosen easily supportable allegations, those for which they could supply witnesses and times
and places, for such is the method of the law. In terms of
similar contemporary actions very likely they would have al-
leged extreme mental cruelty and threats of bodily harm. If

the judge happened to be of a suitable persuasion they could also have brought charges of heresy and even treason, and they knew they had a good case for adultery.[2]

Furthermore, the counsel for Lady Byron followed a very proper and also very effective tactic: they refused to specify the allegations they would bring in court. In adopting this plan they not only left the defense in some state of confusion but tacitly seemed to endorse the rumors, which were certainly a vast deal worse than anything they could prove.

Rumored charges, of course, may be quite specific for the individual, as that such a one has misappropriated public funds or has taken a bribe at a specified time and for a described purpose, or they may be generalized in the sense that numbers of public people may face similar allegations at a certain time. An example of this type of allegation is that of communism or "fellow-traveling" so common during the McCarthy era in the United States. The emotional climate of the time and the public attitudes in the region determine the credibility of rumored charges of this type. England in 1816 was undergoing a conservative reaction: the Napoleonic threat had largely nullified the libertarian ideas of the French and the American revolutions, and English impulse was to settle down and make a bit of money. Evil, therefore, came to signify rebellion, loose living, and religious nonconformity. As a political attack, rumors of atheism and sexual perversion were as potent as McCarthy's allegations of communism, as hard to put down, and as devastating.

The question, therefore, is whether such charges were directed uniquely at Byron or were frequently made against his contemporaries. Only a couple of years earlier, identical charges of sexual aberration had circulated with respect to one of the royal dukes.[3] Shelley, Hunt, and Godwin received their portion of charges with respect to sexual aberrations,[4] and shared no less in accusations of atheism. In short there was nothing original or specific in the accusation against Byron: it was part of the political weaponry of the time, and might be brought against any public figure.

And Byron was unquestionably a public figure. His position in English society and letters in 1814 was more spectacular and more influential than that of Ernest Hemingway in the United States in the middle of this century. Though he was not specifically a member of any political party, his attitudes corresponded fairly closely with those of the more radical Whigs and his writings had identified him as an enemy of the Crown. Several years later the editor of one of the London papers told Byron the paper was under very strong pressure to maintain an attack and to make it strong.[5] So far as the Tory party and the Regent were concerned, Byron was a dangerous enemy, and his separation offered a convenient and effective opportunity utterly to discredit him. But even the Whigs, finding the poet something of a liability, turned on him. This also is no unique political phenomenon.

Thus Byron at the age of twenty-six, essentially a political amateur, until a few months before a lion in Whig society, faced legal action with allegations not specified, a newspaper campaign, and a widespread whispered assault. It would have been a rather tough problem for a seasoned politician; for a poet and man of letters it was catastrophe. Almost certainly Byron regarded the entire situation as a purely private affair, but society would not accept that estimate. He could only counterattack, ignore the entire situation, or attempt to deny everything.

With respect to the categorical denial, it is futile to speculate as to how Byron thought. The only indication we have is what he himself wrote with respect to calumny not only on this but on other occasions.[6] If the originator of the lies was a man, the obvious thing to do was to challenge him and to try to kill him. If it was a woman this kind of correction was impossible. Did it do any good to deny the charge? Obviously if one were guilty he would deny; but if he were innocent and denied an allegation he would not be the more credible. But if the allegation never reached beyond the stage of rumor it was impossible to confront it, since the very nature of rumor is both its anonymity and amorphousness. Hence, Byron concluded, the only position one can take is to ignore it.

Pertinent to this position is the behavior of Byron and Augusta from 1813 up to the time of his departure. On the one hand it is possible to interpret their actions as incredible effrontery, on the other as attempted refutation of possible rumors. Augusta, of course, was in London during the earlier part of July 1813. Byron may have visited her twice in the next three weeks, and on the second occasion brought her back to London with the announced intention of taking her abroad with him. She was again in London in December. In January 1814 the two were together at Newstead Abbey for two weeks or longer. In the summer of 1814 they went together to Hastings, where they remained for nearly a month. Finally, Augusta moved in with the Byron ménage in Piccadilly and remained there until Byron's departure. All of these associations are documented in letters Byron wrote to several correspondents—Moore, Lady Melbourne, and Murray, among others. In no one's interpretation does there appear any suggestion that their visits were furtive or clandestine.

While Byron may have been careless of his own reputation, there is no suggestion that he was indifferent to Augusta's. Their open association may have been a deliberate policy to disarm gossips, if they were involved in a passionate affair. This interpretation calls for a subtlety on the part of Byron and Augusta that does not appear characteristic. Byron may have viewed such open and frank visits as the only possible refutation of calumny. It is apparent that if one chooses to regard them as lovers, any act can be construed as proof of their guilt.

After the separation had occurred, both Hobhouse and Augusta privately denied the charge of incest. Augusta, as one of the victims of the charges, might be expected to give them the lie. In the case of Hobhouse it is another matter. He was a man devoted to Byron but throughout his career a man of scrupulous honor. If Byron requested him not to interfere, John Cam Hobhouse would issue no public denial, whatever his personal view of the decision might be (and it very probably would have coincided, in this instance, with his friend's).

If Byron had been guilty of incest, would Hobhouse have been in a position to know or to have some inkling of it? One can only guess. It is evident that Byron had felt the need of a confidant ever since July of 1813. In his various letters to Moore, he just manages to withhold whatever he has on his mind. Probably because of the pressures of his feelings he undertook to relieve his tension by commencing his journal in the latter part of 1813. None of these expedients was sufficient, apparently. When Hobhouse returned to London in February 1814 he noted in his diary that he sat up half the night hearing Byron's "confessions." But he never revealed what they were. At least, unless Hobhouse lied, incest was not one of the poet's sins.

It is equally striking that Colonel Leigh utterly refused to believe the rumors. His position is the more significant in that he, as much as anyone else, should have had definite knowledge of the events of the summer of 1813. Moreover, he had a considerable dislike for Byron and probably was not greatly attached to Augusta, so that he would not have refused credence out of loyalty to them. If he was a wholly mercenary creature the fact that he owed Byron money and knew that Byron had made out his will in Augusta's favor might have prevented him from antagonizing the poet. On the other hand he could well have expected to reap some reward from the Tories if he denounced his wife. Certainly even a position of nonintervention would have protected his financial interests. In contrast, according to Hobhouse, the Colonel "behaved admirably."

Of other people on more or less intimate terms with Byron, apparently none gave credence to the rumors. These include Hodgson, a minister, who was in correspondence with Augusta during the spring of 1816 and for many years following. It must immediately be acknowledged that Byron had done him a great favor and that perhaps Hodgson's training would have inclined him to discredit rumor. Tom Moore, who knew of the difficulties only from a distance and who had received from Byron letters of the most uncertain meaning, nevertheless did not believe the gossip.

Two other individuals who may well have known quite a lot about the poet and his troubles went to some pains to demonstrate their confidence. Lady Melbourne, who had been ill during a part of the winter of 1815-16, paid a call upon Augusta as soon as she was able to get about. Lady Jersey invited Byron and Augusta to a ball in April. While these two ladies may have had quite mixed motives, in the world of Whig society the two acts were clearly signals from on high. In the particular instance of Lady Melbourne, Hobhouse had visited her on more than one occasion and his diary makes it clear that the rumor of incest had been a subject of discussion. If Lady Jersey had any special knowledge of the situation there is nothing to indicate it. She was not a confidante of either

Byron or Augusta. Very obviously neither she nor Lady Melbourne could expect social, political, or economic advantages from adhering to the Byron side.

The only other person who failed to cut Byron and Augusta at Lady Jersey's ball was Miss Mercer Elphinstone. This young lady was extremely independent, but also apparently of the utmost discretion. Byron's letter to her as he sent her his Suliot costume informed her quite clearly that the clothing had a very unhappy association in his memory and that the period in question was in July 1813. He was not more specific, but it is possible she understood the reference. Though she was in political opposition to the Regent and his party, the Prince apparently trusted Miss Elphinstone very fully and employed her in the recovery of letters and presents his daughter, Princess Charlotte, had sent to Captain Hesse. Moreover, even though she was not considered a politically desirable associate, Miss Elphinstone was the confidante and constant companion of the Princess. As a consequence she would become privy to a considerable amount of information about the royal family. Her refusal to cut Augusta and her brother therefore may either signal an unrequired demonstration of her own independence or reflect some special information contradictory to the rumor of incest.

There remains the question of why Byron, after demanding a court hearing, changed his position and finally acquiesced in private separation. Lawyers were involved on both sides, and it is difficult to know which actions resulted from individual decision and which from legal advice. In the interpretation of some biographers, Byron was attempting a bluff in a maneuver to learn what the other side proposed to bring against him.[7] The Milbanke side called the bluff and agreed to take the proceedings to court, whereupon Byron settled for a private agreement out of fear of what would emerge.

In the meantime Hobhouse had been negotiating with the

Milbanke lawyers and with Lady Byron. After some difficulty and some delay he obtained from Lady Byron a statement that incest and sexual perversion would not be part of the charges brought in court, but he was not successful in acquiring from her a statement that she was satisfied that Byron was not guilty of these practices. While the statement was no major concession, since proof of incest or perversion would have been almost if not entirely impossible, at all events it cleared Augusta so far as any testimony in court might be expected. If this was Byron's principal concern, then once the issue was out of the way his lawyers may have advised him that other charges he might have to face would be indefensible. These could well have been adultery (admitted), failure to acknowledge Christian beliefs (demonstrable from his various written works as well as his private statements), and mental and physical cruelty (probably provable). It wouldn't be the kind of case to arouse a barrister's enthusiasm, and Byron's acquiescence probably stemmed from legal advice.

≥ 23 ⅓

AUGUSTA'S CONFESSION

Very soon after Byron's departure in disgrace in April 1816, Augusta took up her position and occupied her apartment at St. James's Palace. Inevitably her own reputation had undergone some degree of impairment, though apparently never to the same degree as Byron's. Among the friends who supported her was Mrs. Theresa Villiers, with whom she had maintained rather warm relations for a number of years, whose husband's fortunes paralleled those of Colonel Leigh, in that he had been dismissed in disgrace from a post with the Prince Regent, and with whom Augusta had stayed during a portion of her visit to London in December 1813.

When the scandal was at its height, Mrs. Villiers at first flatly refused to believe it.[1] Perhaps her disbelief should carry more than casual consideration. About as well as anyone in London, she had known Augusta, and of course during Augusta's stay in her house, Mrs. Villiers had had unusual opportunity to observe Augusta and Byron in each other's company.

It was to this unlikely associate that Lady Byron turned for assistance. Beginning late in April she initiated correspondence and continued it at frequent intervals throughout the summer.

Her avowed purpose was to obtain from Augusta a full and free confession of incest in order to purify and cleanse her conscience of the heavy burden of guilt under which Lady Byron felt sure it labored. To this end she enlisted the aid of Mrs. Villiers, impressing upon her that it was designed to insure Augusta's peace of mind.[2] (That the confession, if obtained, might constitute a legal protection against any effort Byron might make to acquire custody of Ada was not under discussion.)

Mrs. Villiers, apparently after some hesitation, agreed to assist in Augusta's redemption. On the face of it her acquiescence looks like the betrayal of a friendship. Whether her adherence to Lady Byron's cause was complete or qualified never becomes apparent. Though one biographer has described Mrs. Villiers as a cool worldling,[3] there is no supporting evidence. Her letters throughout the next year make it appear that she sympathized completely with Lady Byron's opinion that something really needed to be done about Augusta's salvation. All the while Augusta continued to visit the Villiers house on a rather familiar basis—behavior unlikely if a busybody is hammering out one's redemption. It is hard to guess what Theresa Villiers really thought, and one cannot quite avoid the impression she may have been playing a role of double agent. Anyhow Mrs. Villiers consented to assist Lady Byron's good works and letters passed between them with great regularity and no undue brevity. At the same time, in letters to Augusta, Lady Byron continued her frontal attack upon the powers of darkness.

Much of the correspondence appears in *Astarte*.[4] One cannot read these letters without wondering, in the face of their elaborate circumlocutions and their pseudo-redemption jargon, if either lady knew what the other referred to. For example, Lady Byron wrote to Mrs. Villiers on 11 July:

She [Augusta] says—"I have *not* wronged you—I have not abused your generosity"—When delusion has once been carried so far, it is difficult to say to what it may extend—[5]

On the same day Lady Byron wrote directly to Augusta, "When I speak of the necessity of confidence, do not suppose I wish to exact any confession—Let the past be *understood* now," and she continues to state that she vaguely knew about it all the time but would not bring it up because it would distress Augusta and might so anger Byron as to make her fear for her life.[6]

Six days later Lady Byron was again at her writing desk, in the meantime having received answers to these two letters. To Theresa, she wrote:

I have an answer—*all* that it ought to be or that I could desire—It thoroughly convinces me of her innocence during all the period with which I was concerned.[7]

To Augusta on the same date, she wrote in a less satisfied state of mind:

It seems to me that you dwell too much on the pain you involuntarily occasioned me, and not enough on the irreparable injury you did *him* by the voluntary sacrifices . . . which you once made to his immediate indulgences.[8]

In return, Augusta on 23 July undertook to assuage the pain she thought Lady Byron suffered:

Don't reproach yourself—or imagine I could ever reproach you for past *doubts*—it was but too natural you should have had them.

And after a deviation unfortunately characteristic of her manner of thought and letter-writing, Augusta continued:

I have said little of *him* my dearest A—— fearing you might mistake ye *nature* of my feelings—I am certain they are & ever have been such as you could not disapprove. . . .[9]

Whatever all these letters refer to—and it seems likely that each correspondent misinterpreted what the other tried to avoid stating—by late July Theresa wrote Lady Byron that she thought Augusta had made a complete confession, although the context and statements are such that they leave considerable doubt as to just what Augusta had confessed to. (It is not at all evident if this style was Theresa's customary mode of expression or if she may have framed a quite nonspecific assurance—without lying—in the hope Lady Byron would at last leave them alone.) Theresa's letter was not sufficiently convincing to Lady Byron and in September she came up to London for the evident purpose of obtaining a complete confession of a type sufficiently abject to relieve Augusta's soul of its unbearable guilt.[10]

The interview must have been a painful one. Augusta's early training under her grandmother and her subsequent adherence at least to the forms of devotion should have made her susceptible to threats of unforgivable sin and other dire consequences. Lady Byron subsequently made notes, apparently extending to as late as the following March, as she recalled various fragments of the interview. Lord Lovelace wrote that her account "is very fragmentary; some interpolations being on very small bits of paper,"[11] which he admits he pieced together to constitute the full confession. It is apparent that Augusta confessed to something, for Lady Byron seems to have been mollified and for a time to have left her in peace.

What Augusta may have confessed or what she may have thought she was confessing is another matter. Two women, with both of whom she had had an affectionate and rather close relationship, had spent several months nagging at her about her sins—unless Mrs. Villiers indeed had gone on about her usual affairs and only written to Lady Byron what she suspected that lady wished to hear. Augusta at her best never possessed an analytical or penetrating intellect: her letters are models of non sequiturs. In light of Lady Byron's careful circumlocution and ponderous imprecision and of Augusta's emotional stress and less than syllogistic processes, it may well be in question if any of her answers were responsive.

Lady Byron's subsequent conduct reinforces the suspicion that the interview in fact was inconclusive. Her summary of the interview as she attempted to set it down almost a year later suggests that she was undertaking to reassure herself that she had in fact obtained a confession of incest, and at the same time assisted in Augusta's redemption.[12] Obviously such a summary could not have been of much value in any kind of a legal proceeding that might involve custody.

If Lady Byron was temporarily satisfied, as the years passed she began to have doubts as to just what had been said. In 1851, more than three decades since any of the events, and after a long period of silence, she learned that Augusta, now in her sixties, was in failing health. Thereupon, though she was in much better health than Augusta, Lady Byron proposed conditions for a meeting. They would each travel halfway to meet at a railroad station. Lady Byron would select and bring with her a minister in whose presence Augusta might make a full and complete confession. Both religious consolation and a credible witness would be at hand.[13]

The meeting took place as Lady Byron commanded. Augusta was broken and ill (indeed she survived only a few months longer), and the entire affair had somewhat the aspect of a deathbed confession. When Augusta concluded whatever it was she had to confess, Lady Byron merely asked, "Is that all?" Nothing in the notes of the meeting suggests that Augusta had anything more than venial errors to confess.[14]

Lady Byron was disappointed and not a little displeased. Within a few days she wrote that she had left her own sick bed, given herself a great deal of trouble, even to bringing along a minister, and that Augusta had repaid all these efforts with only trivial matter.[15] It had not, Lady Byron insisted, been a "good confession" and Augusta had no right to consider herself well shriven. To this letter Augusta replied that she had had nothing to confess except what both had known of for many years. Their own words reveal much about their personalities.[16]

[*Annabella*] As I have received the communication which you have so long and anxiously desired to make—and upon which I made no comment except "Is that All,"—I have done all in my power to contribute to your peace of mind. But I remain under the afflicting persuasion that it is not obtained by such means as you have taken,

[*Augusta*] My great desire for an interview with you arose partly from a desire to see you once more in this world, and still more to have the means of convincing you that the accusations which I had reason to believe had been brought against me to you were unfounded. . . . I had not, and never implied that I had, anything to reveal to you with which you were not previously acquainted on any other subject.

One wonders, in Annabella's words, when delusion has once been carried so far to what it may extend.

≋ 24 ≋

THE LETTERS TO LADY MELBOURNE

Whatever may be true of other evidence and its interpretation, the charge of incest derives its best support from Byron's letters to Lady Melbourne. As Leslie Marchand commented, they seem to confirm Byron's illicit relations with Augusta, if they mean anything at all.[1] Yet, he admits, they are somewhat less than absolute in that Byron never makes the flat statement in any surviving letter that he did in fact have carnal knowledge of his half sister. And perhaps Marchand overstated the situation a little. The letters *may* permit a different interpretation if one allows for the possibility that Augusta was in trouble with one person and Byron with another.

The authenticity of the letters has not been challenged. Stylistically they bear all the marks of Byron. Those of 1813 contain bits of information and expressions that also appear in letters to other correspondents as well as in his journal. But whereas the letters to other friends remain quite vague—to Moore, for example, he mentions "a far more serious scrape," without further characterization except that the scrape involves a lady—those to Lady Melbourne are sufficiently explicit in their references to indicate Byron was thinking of Augusta, at least part of the time.

Six or seven entries in the entire series make masked allusions to a woman who could hardly be anyone else.

What is of greatest importance, however, is less the number and kinds of allusions than the question whether these letters appear in the form in which they were originally written. Those that seem to have bearing on the question of incest cluster around three specific dates. The first suggestions that one may interpret as references to an affair with Augusta occur in letters in August and September 1813, shortly after Augusta's visit to London and during the time when Byron was considering escaping to the Continent in company with his half sister. This was also the period during which there seem to be repeated allusions to a duel. Then for a period he dropped the subject altogether and devoted his correspondence almost exclusively to the affair with Lady Frances. In December and January the topic of Augusta recurs, this time in connection with her visit to London and his short stay at Six Mile Bottom around Christmas. Once more he dropped the subject of his sister, and there is little further reference until a group of letters in April and May 1814, a date that marks the birth of Medora.

Though there were many other letters and notes to Lady Melbourne throughout the period, they contain no references or comments which seem to have pertinence to the problem of his relations with Augusta. Moreover, in those letters that pertain most particularly to the problem, some of the most clearly identifying sentences occur either very early in the letter or in postscripts.

Several other points suggest that alterations could have occurred. The first is that Lady Melbourne apparently retained all or the greater part of the poet's correspondence. Unquestionably she knew the contents rather thoroughly, at least in substance. Yet she made no effort to return his letters before he left England, nor did she ever manifest any particular concern over the disposition or protection of the papers. Though Lady Melbourne was unwell throughout the last two years of her life, she was certainly not entirely incapacitated during much of that time. She was, moreover, entirely familiar with the matter of the scandal of 1816 and was woman of the world enough to know that Byron's letters would ultimately be published. That she took no action to protect pieces of potentially incriminating information seems completely out of character.

Equally difficult to understand in the face of the letters as preserved and published is the indifference of Byron and Augusta. If one postulates that Byron would have shown no concern for his own reputation, holding that it was already destroyed, one can hardly agree that the poet would have been indifferent to their effect on Augusta's position. Yet, so far as any record appears, Byron made no effort at recovery of any of this material until a letter to Moore in 1822.[2] At that time he urged his friend to try to obtain possession of the correspondence in order that he might later publish it. He had delayed so long, he wrote, because he did not wish to trouble the family so soon after Lady Melbourne's death (which was all of four years earlier). There is in the letter to Moore no suggestion that parts might require suppression.

In the same vein, Augusta, if she was "X," knew Byron had been passing on to Lady Melbourne various items of information. However Byron may have responded to gossip and accusations, in Hobhouse's account Augusta found "most horrid" the charges of 1816, and could barely countenance them.[3] They filled her with shock and dismay, wrote Hobhouse. That she should then remain perfectly poised and relaxed about the disposition of the letters after Lady Melbourne's death, and should make no effort to recover them or destroy them stretches credibility. Their publication, or even very limited circulation, could certainly have resulted in the loss of her stipend and position at Saint James's.

One must then choose between two possibilities. The first is that the letters as published are in their original text and that Byron himself, Lady Melbourne, who seems to have been genuinely fond of him, and Augusta, who stood to lose safety and position, were unconcerned about their content of identifiable references. It is true, of course, that both Byron and Augusta were rather unpredictable people. It may be true that Augusta had only limited ability to foresee the results of any action; but the poet had pretty sound sense, when he chose to use it, and all his actions seem to indicate that he had sufficient regard for Augusta to try to protect her reputation.

The alternative possibility is that the letters had undergone some degree of tampering. If any alterations occurred or if any additions or substitutions took place, it is necessary to demonstrate that opportunity could have occurred and to show that someone with opportunity had motive, materials, and skill to make the changes.

With the exception of Ehrsam, other biographers have largely ignored the possibility that some of the primary material may have been forged or altered with forgery. In his very interesting study of the career of a Major Byron, who clearly was a charlatan and impostor, Ehrsam demonstrates repeatedly the skill with which this man imitated both style and handwriting of the poet.[4] What is even more remarkable is the fact that he was familiar with intimate details of Byron's life. That Grub Street contained a sizable collection of clever men with insufficient funds is a familiar fact; that they produced a variety of imitations of Byron from about 1814 onward is well established.[5] For a time some confusion prevailed with respect to *Don Leon,* a very skillful imitation of *Don Juan* by some anonymous and clever scribbler.[6]

That opportunity allowed for alterations of the letters seems
certain. Lady Melbourne died in 1818. The whereabouts of Byron's letters from that time until 1827, when Lady Cowper
showed them to Hobhouse, are unknown.[7] Probably they were in
one of the Melbourne residences, either the house in town or
Brocket Hall. There is no available information with respect to
the protection the papers received in the interval, and it seems
probable that any person who frequented either of the houses
might have obtained access to them without attracting any particular notice.

Obviously the individuals who lived in the two houses had the
best opportunity. These were Lord Melbourne, and William and
Caroline Lamb. One can safely ignore the peer as an individual
who had no interest, and had never shown any, in Byron and his
affairs. Nothing known or reported of the character of William
Lamb would lead one to suppose that he was involved. George
Lamb and his wife were not so often in residence, and they also
seem to have taken little notice of Byron. As for Lord and Lady
Cowper, most of their time was passed at Panshanger, though
undoubtedly they visited in Melbourne House from time to time.
However, it would be difficult to demonstrate that they had more
than a social acquaintance with Byron.

Lady Caroline Lamb, therefore, emerges as the most likely in-
tervener if any alteration in the Byron letters occurred. In the
section on that lady it has been shown that she had sufficient motive, at least in her opinion. She had shown herself capable of
opening mail from the poet addressed to Lady Melbourne. On
numerous occasions she had invaded Byron's lodgings in his
absence. Beyond question she had gained access to his desk and
writing materials, since she left notes when she departed. With
the wealth, power, and charm at her disposal she could easily
have secured a replica of his seal, if she needed it.

In yet another respect the lady demonstrated her capacity to create mischief; she forged a directive to John Murray in which Byron ostensibly directed the publisher to turn over to her a miniature of himself. Murray, who had seen hundreds of pages of Byron's script, seems not to have doubted for a moment that the letter was genuine. Byron, in his account to Lady Melbourne, adds his bit of confirmation, "the hand she imitates to perfection." [8] The poet was shaken up, as well as quite angry with Lady Caroline for obtaining his favorite miniature. When Lady Melbourne replied, perhaps in a somewhat offhand manner, Byron returned this comment: "I confess I look upon the thing in a more serious light than you do. I have seen the forged billet, and the hand very like; now what is to prevent her from the same imitation for any less worthy purpose she may choose to adopt?" [9] It is an entirely valid question, and it may have been prescient.

Stylistic evidence, of course, demonstrates that Byron wrote most of the letters. But there were imitators of his style in abundance. Moreover, it is not necessary to suppose that an entire letter may have been replaced. It would have been sufficient to introduce an idea or two at the beginning or end, without alteration of adjacent sentences. Or, if the sense demanded a more extensive revision it would be simple enough to select phrases from the original and insert them here and there in the "revised" version.

The argument is not that such forgeries did occur, but rather that until most careful study demonstrates that they did not, some of the Melbourne correspondence will have to carry less weight than is usually accorded it. Lady Caroline had opportunity, she had motive, she—or someone she employed—had the requisite skill, and certainly she had no scruple. And, to repeat, Byron warned of such a possibility as early as 1813, before his reacquaintance with Augusta began.

Although biographers have given very little consideration to the problem of forgery, and particularly have not questioned the letters to Lady Melbourne, the principals themselves exhibited a degree of wariness. Notable among the residual comments is one of Lady Byron to Colonel Doyle in a letter of 29 January 1820. (There seems to be little doubt that Lady Byron wrote the letter, since it appears in *Astarte*.) ". . . on the same principle as he contrived to cast on Lady C L—— the suspicion of a forgery in order to destroy the effect of her evidence against him." [10]

Aside from revealing an interesting facet of Lady Byron's character, the letter makes it quite evident that Byron's private correspondence with Lady Melbourne would not remain private very long if Lady Caroline was around (see chapter 24). The poet's accusation appeared in a letter to his confidante well before he renewed his acquaintance with Augusta. Neither he nor Lady Melbourne would have had any particular occasion to discuss the incident and the related correspondence with Annabella. It seems inescapable that she learned of it from Lady Caroline herself. As *Glenarvon* demonstrates, Lady Caroline was capable of constructing highly convoluted plots. It seems most plausible that her "revelation" to Annabella, who was nothing if not literal, served to embellish Byron's villainy and to anticipate any challenge of her own veracity.

Another important point, reinforcing Lady Byron's own statement that her interview with Lady Caroline turned her impression into *absolute* conviction, is the fact this letter points very clearly toward Lady Caroline as the source of the accusation of incest ("her evidence against him"). What the entire sequence implies is that without Lady Caroline's evidence, Lady Byron had very little upon which to base her conclusions—and therefore she was resolved to defend her sources to the uttermost. If one is attempting to pass a forged instrument, the best way to allay sus-

picion of its authenticity, of course, is to state that someone, acting from an ulterior motive, will call it spurious. Lady Caroline
had forewarned her victim.

So far as any other information goes, the only additional time
Byron referred to the possibility of forgery by Lady Caroline appears in the record of a conversation Henry Edward Fox held
with the poet in April 1823: Byron told Fox that Lady Caroline
had "the power of imitating his hand to perfection and still pos-
sesses many of his letters which she may alter very easily." [11] At
the time, the poet seemed to have been thinking only in terms of
the letters he had sent to Lady Caroline, but he could have also
been concerned about the entire correspondence with Lady Melbourne. (It is not known if by this time Byron had learned of
Moore's failure to secure that correspondence from the family, as
Byron had requested.)

⇘ 25 ⇙

BYRON'S POETRY AS EVIDENCE

The use of any writer's literary output to establish proof of a specific event in his life is open to suspicion. Even if the work under consideration is avowedly autobiographical, unless the writer is striving for legal precision, one may question how accurate it is. If beyond this the autobiographer attempts interpretation, precision leaves him altogether and one begins to deal with a species of "truth" that is truth only as that one individual sees it.

But if the work is "literary," in the sense that imagination comes into play and that constraints of form and style appear, uncertainty can only increase. That which is genuinely literary is evocative, and the higher the literary quality of the work the greater become the circles of associative ideas. To that same degree the less exact becomes the particular "fact"—exact in the sense that X and X alone happened and that X cannot be confused with anything else. Human affairs are not so specific—or perhaps they are, but no one is able to describe them so specifically.

The difficulty is even greater in poetry: constraints of meter, rhyme, diction, and assonance produce obstacles of their own, since selection and arrangement may result in the use of the less specific and more general word. Symbolism, imagery, and figures of speech increase the impact, add emotional verity, but do not inevitably result in the precision required of evidence. "The wine dark sea" describes neither color nor turbidity, at least not in terms of contemporary vintages. In addition the emotional envelopment that surrounds poetry produces a quite different species of truth from that of a chemical formula or a prose statement. The manifest content may be only commonplace, but good poetry invests that content with implications that convert it to something much larger. None of these characteristics contributes to the quality of poetry as evidence.

There is also the question of what proportion of a writer's output is autobiographical. In an extended sense, no one can write intelligibly about something he has never experienced, and in consequence everything he produces contains a fragment of his life. But the operative word is "experienced." Even if a fact is completely attested, its passage through the writer's mind, his experience of it, produces connotations and colorings (on the assumption that a poet's mind differs from that of a court reporter). But a creative mind performs in an even more remarkable manner: it is not essential that the specific event have happened to him, but only that he think or feel as though it had. When the intellect operates in such a fashion it is completely unnecessary to ask for whom the bell tolls—"essentially," as Byron used the word, it tolls for thee.

Further, in literary creation one finds, as Freud discovered in dreams, not only a manifest but a latent content. But Freud, Jung, Adler, and some others each discovered a different latent content and each rationalized almost endlessly the accuracy of his own interpretation of the latent material. In interpretation, as in day-to-day observation, one sees that which he is prepared to see: an archaeologist walking across a field discovers a camp site, perhaps can even date it, while a rancher sees only a prairie dog hole. By the same cultivation of vision—and its reverse, restriction—the archaeologist may fail to observe a rattlesnake.

But if in literature one deals only with the question of the manifest content, he may be not much better off. Goethe faced the problem in *Dichtung und Wahrheit*—what is poetry and what is truth, or are they one and the same when the poetry is genuine? But it poses a problem for lawyers. Perhaps in terms of poetic thought the impulse to love is quite as real or as true as the actual consummation. When Byron writes of his feelings toward ——, in his perception of the world and himself is there any "essential" difference between the feeling and the "fact"?

At last to leave guessing and hypothesizing, if one reads Byron's poetry with the assumption that incest occurred, he may find manifest content to support the thesis. Likewise, he can find plenty of material to prove that many ladies died of love for him. Conclusions of this type demand identification of the hero with Byron. Manfred or Conrad or any other hero must = Byron, if Astarte or Zuleika or any other lady is to = Augusta. These identifications were frequent from the beginning of his rise to fame, but neither their frequency nor priority establishes their validity.

There is a good case that Byron imagined himself in these forms, a concept that appeared earlier in the discussion of his ambition. The heroes of the Eastern tales from *The Giaour* through *The Corsair* are men of action at the head of a band of guerrillas. *Lara* tells much the same story, but with a different setting. As Byron wrote of them they are "much from existence," [1] not necessarily his life but some aspect of life he may have seen —perhaps, to judge from some of the entries in his journal, an existence he very much envied. All of these "orientalities" occupied his mind from the departure of Lady Oxford till about a

year later. They appear to be the other side of his profound dissatisfaction with the frivolous life of London, or what he regarded as the inadequate function of a scribbler or a politician,[2]
in contrast with the active life of a hero.

Of these tales the one that signifies most with respect to incest
is *The Bride of Abydos*. Except for the half-sister relationship
that at first appears to exist between Conrad and Zuleika, the
rest of the poem is along the basic lines of the other tales. In one
view it may be argued that Byron was not able to kiss and not
tell, that he had a compulsion for revelation, and that in spite
of himself or because of himself he consciously or unconsciously
publicized his liaison with Augusta. Certainly the writing and
publication of *The Bride* corresponds temporally with the hypothesized incest.

How much is the theme of incest really involved? Although the
affection begins between what appear to be half brother and
half sister, it develops that in reality there is no kinship at all.
The affection, if it was fraternal in the first place, changes toward
connubial as the identity of Conrad becomes evident, and at this
point, before the affair passes beyond the conceptual, both of
them die, according to the theme and pattern of the other tales of
the same period. In short, the blood relationship which was supposed to have existed served only to introduce the principals to
each other, and from that point forward is irrelevant to the main
theme, a variant of the *Liebestod* mixed with some turbans,
ataghans, and extensive mayhem.

If incest, then, is not implicit or germane, why does it appear
at all? Byron's letter to Professor Clarke presents his explanation.
If Conrad and Zuleika were to meet at all or to have any opportunity to fall in love, Conrad had to have access to the harem,
and that would have been possible only in the event that they
were, fictionally, siblings. Under Moslem rules, at the level of

rulers and their families, the only other non-females who might visit the harem were, of course, the eunuchs. Nor would the rules of court or religion have permitted a young man to meet a young woman of noble class except as a result of negotiations for marriage, and then only under the most guarded circumstances.

The story, if it was to take place at all within the theme of love in the East, demanded some mechanism, and Byron's explanation does not appear either lame or disingenuous, though the contrivance itself is pretty strained, a flaw the poet was willing to risk in order to get to his story. Would he then have taken so much trouble to create the necessary encounter between the two? Time and again he indicates in his notes and in letters that while he holds a rather poor regard for his "poeshie," he prides himself on his accuracy with respect to names, places, nouns, cultures, and geography.[3] Finally, there is nothing in the accounts of his contemporaries to suggest that anyone—unless it was Lady Caroline—found anything remarkable in the relationship between the principals.

There are a number of poems addressed to Augusta at various times, and some of these elaborate on his love for her. The difficulty lies in determining the kind of love Byron felt and what he meant by the word. At various times in his letters he defined love as well as he could, but found that the word expresses so many levels of sentiment that without some kind of modifier it is impossible to deal with its meaning at all. He wrote, for example, of the many meanings of "that wide word."[4] Love, as Byron thought of it, was a complicated mixture of different kinds of passion, so that with respect to one lady (possibly Augusta) he stated, "to her my feelings are a mixture of the good and the diabolical."[5] On another occasion he specifies, apparently once again with respect to Augusta, that he uses the word in its "senseless" meaning—i.e., a love independent of the senses or of sensuality.[6] In yet another effort he attempted to define what he meant by "to love essentially." [7] Does this mean a love between essences, or something else? In his usual mood he had an earthy disdain for Platonism and its transcendental shivers.

If all these citations are Byron's own words and not the result of tampering, one can only conclude that he regarded love as a phenomenon worthy of study and not unpleasant in practice. Since he was a man of letters, as a professional the poet was attempting to define as accurately as possible the nature of love. But a logical and analytical approach does not lend itself to poetry. A love poem to Augusta, therefore, expresses his affection but leaves very unclear just what kind of affection it was. In consequence a critic may draw almost any conclusion he wishes from the poems addressed to Augusta.

Finally, it is not inappropriate to observe that in the letters to Lady Melbourne Byron refers to "feeling" fully as often as to "love." On some occasions he seems to equate feeling with an overt expression of it; at others his feeling seems to be entirely subjective and unexpressed. His intricate intellect sometimes appears to hold that impulse does not differ "essentially" from an act, even though the impulse never attains expression except in words. "I wanted to love someone" becomes "I did love someone."

The subject of *Manfred,* however, is quite a different one. The drama—if that is what it is—was written in 1816, after Byron's journey through the Alps. Its sources seem to be an account of the Italian king of that name, who appears in canto 3 of the Purgatorio of Dante. Manfred, the illegitimate son of Frederic II, usurped the kingdom of Sicily from his infant nephew, bore arms against the Guelphs in northern Italy, and was betrayed and died in battle on the plains of Grandella. According to some of the ancient Italian historians, he was a man of superb physical endowment and a phenomenon of learning, including the arcane. Whether Byron may have encountered Manfred in the course of his reading during his traverse of northern Italy in unknown, but it is evident from his notes that he had been reading extensively the history of the region.

The poem is distinctly different from most of Byron's other production. Some time before its composition Monk Lewis had read to Byron, who did not know German, all or a major part of *Faust,* Part I.[8] To anyone familiar with the German drama and with the resemblances in meter, diction, form, supernatural machinery, and the conception of Manfred as a kind of *Übermensch,* it must be evident that Byron owed a considerable debt to Goethe, who himself recognized the kinship and praised the apotheosis.[9] Another literary source appears in Byron's letter of 20 September saying that he had "read a French translation of Schiller." [10] Manfred, he commented later, was very "metaphysical." [11] To Murray in March of the following year, he wrote of it as "a sort of mad Drama." [12]

The first version started on its way to Murray in November 1816. Some of Byron's readers in England objected to the third act, and in consequence during the winter he produced a new third act that went forward to Murray in April 1817. By July the piece appeared in print and Byron wrote to ask Moore, "What think you of *Manfred?*" [13] The question seems to apply not only to the nature of the work as a literary production but to its possible significance in relation to his own life and to the rumors. Moore's answer has not appeared, but to Mrs. Villiers *Manfred* was very explicit and she could not see how poor Augusta could ever hold her head up again.[14]

The story as Byron presents it is that of a rebellious noble who has arrived at point of death. His knowledge has been enormous and he has achieved the power to call up spirits. Remorse for some kind of inexpiable sin preys upon him, but arrogance and pride—or his basic integrity and self-reliance—deny him any of the mechanisms available for solace to people of a lesser order. After one series of spirits upon another fails to provide him with any acceptable solution of his difficulties, he prevails upon Nemesis to invoke the spirit of Astarte. When he inquires of her spirit what he should do, she can only answer by repeatedly calling his name.

In one sense the story is an elaboration of the earlier Oriental tales: Manfred differs in no major respect from Conrad and the others. The theme of death of a woman (Astarte) as a result of the hero's love appears once more. But the relationship is very different. In act 2, scene 1, Manfred rejects a glass of wine the chamois hunter offers him:

> I say 'tis blood—my blood! The pure warm stream
> Which ran in the veins of my fathers, and in ours
> When we were in our youth, and had but one heart,
> And loved each other as we should not love,
> And this was shed: but still it rises up,
> Colouring the clouds, that shut me out from heaven,
> Where thou are not—and I shall never be.
>
> My injuries came down on those who loved me—
> On those whom I best loved: I never quelled
> An enemy, save in my just defence—
> But my embrace was fatal.

In act 2, scene 2, he calls up the Witch of the Alps and presents his problem. He has sought all forms of knowledge and has regarded other humans as insignificant, but there was one:

> She was like me in lineaments; her eyes,
> Her hair, her features, all to the very tone

Even of her voice, they said were like to mine;
But softened all, and temper'd all to beauty:
She had the same lone thoughts and wanderings,
The quest of hidden knowledge, and a mind
To comprehend the universe. . . .

.   .   .   .

Her faults were mine—her virtues were her own—
I loved her, and destroy'd her!
Witch: With thy hand?
Man.: Not with my hand, but heart, which broke her heart;
It gazed on mine, and wither'd. I have shed
Blood, but not hers—and yet her blood was shed;
I saw—and could not stanch it.

.   .   .   .

We are the fools of time and terror: Days
Steal on us, and steal from us; yet we live,
Loathing our life, and dreading still to die.

.   .   .   .

If I had never lived, that which I love
Had still been living; had I never loved,
That which I loved would still be beautiful,
Happy and giving happiness.

In act 2, scene 4, at last he reaches the spirit of Astarte and
addresses her:

. . . the grave hath not changed thee more
Than I am changed for thee. Thou lovdst me
Too much, as I loved thee: we were not made
To torture thus each other, though it were
The deadliest sin to love as we have loved.
Say that thou loath'st me not—that I do bear
This punishment for both— . . .

In summary, he has killed Astarte, who shares the same blood, by a type of love that was forbidden, inferentially incestuous. In the third act, Byron seems on the point of stating the relationship exactly when Manuel recounts some of Manfred's earlier life:

> . . . the only thing he seem'd to love
> As he, indeed, by blood was bound to do,
> The lady Astarte, his ——

One word would have completed the sentence and eliminated any possible doubt. Neither action nor dialogue demanded an interruption.

If the poet's need for confession had driven him to this point, one may well wonder why he stopped at the last word. Instead, as the quotations have demonstrated, throughout the work he chose innuendo. In all of this, does Byron really admit anything or only *appear* to confess? "The pure warm stream" ran in the veins of "my," not "our" fathers; also in ours (as pure and warm) when we were young. Then, "when we were in our youth," we loved as we should not have loved. Does this mean an illicit (i.e. incestuous) or a precocious love?

She (Astarte, presumably) resembled him in all respects, including "the quest of hidden knowledge." A woman who acquired the nickname "Goose" does not correspond very closely with one who had "a mind to comprehend the universe." And then he destroyed her, not physically, but by allowing her to contemplate his heart.

The next selection introduces still more uncertainty. "Thou lovdst me / Too much, as I loved thee: we were not made / To torture thus each other, though it *were* / The deadliest sin" (emphasis added). Byron had studied Latin grammar and understood the conditional. Evidently their love was not the deadliest sin. In short, on a close reading, rather than an impressionistic one, Byron had admitted nothing, but has made it seem so.

Certainly the use of "sister" would not have been any more damaging to Augusta than this amount of revelation. If his letters to her during the entire period from his departure until the completion of *Manfred* reveal anything of the poet's thought, he in no sense wished to damage her or add further to her tribulations. Nor can one think that the omission of the word "sister" was other than deliberate, since he had reworked the entire third act and had considered the material that would appear in it from about November till the following April. Among all the mixed feelings and acts and fragments of sources that went into *Manfred*, Byron must have had some purpose that might compensate for the harm it might bring to Augusta.

In constructing an alternate hypothesis to account for the publication of this specific work, the writer is well aware that he undertakes to read Byron's mind and to understand his motives. Such an undertaking is both formidable and dangerous, and any conclusion at best is subject to doubt. The only justification for the undertaking is that others have attempted alternate interpretations. The test of the hypothesis depends upon the rigor of logic and the compatibility with established facts and statements.

The hypothesis presented assumes that Byron knew what he was doing and that he prepared this allusive reference to incest for a purpose, much as he chose to acknowledge "Lines to a Lady Weeping." In the argument with respect to that poem, it appeared that Byron knew how to use versification for ulterior ends. The argument that follows rests in part on that earlier evidence. It is proposed that *Manfred* appeared with the deliberate intention of leading someone to state publicly, "You see, he has admitted incest." In short, the proposition is that he was attempting to lay a trap for the Milbanke side. That they carefully avoided any public comment may signify that they recognized the attempt for what it was.

The situation, as Byron may have seen it, was somewhat as

follows. He had just sustained a smashing defeat in his dealing with the Milbankes. It is not a condition palatable to a vigorous man, whose normal response is to recover and attack again. Throughout the entire separation, Lady Byron's side, undoubtedly on the advice of counsel, had consistently refused to state the grounds upon which they demanded a separation. In the absence of any clear statement, Lady Caroline had supplied plenty of conjecture, but Byron's dilemma, as outlined in the section on his nolo contendere, was that there was no means by which he could fight back, either literally or figuratively.

When, in an effort at least to clear Augusta's name, the Byron side requested a statement that incest was not involved, Annabella furnished a reply that appeared to satisfy their request, but in fact stated nothing. Throughout the entire time the poet had perforce associated with his own men of law. And one asks, therefore, how a counsel might think, faced with the dilemma of unspecified charges and with a decision not to force divulgence of the charges in an open proceeding. It would require no great astuteness to suggest that if the other side could be drawn into a statement by some means of provocation it would then become possible to take some kind of action. The nature of that action, if the opposing side made the error of public statement, would be a proceeding for libel, the only means of redress available to the Byron faction.

Or, since the idea has occurred to one who is not a lawyer, it could have occurred to Byron himself as a possible expedient. Would such an idea, if it occurred to the poet, have been compatible with his mood in the late summer and early autumn—when he began work on *Manfred?* Although in the conclusion to his journal of the Alpine passage, Byron wrote, "I am past the point of vengeance and I know of none like for what I have suffered; but the hour will come, when what I have felt must be felt, and the— but enough." [15] This mood lasted for a relatively short time, and by 1 October he wrote to Augusta that he had learned Lady Byron projected a trip to the Continent and that she would bring with her Ada. To this plan he objected strenuously, asserting that as a father he had some rights and that he would take the problem to court if necessary.[16] Between this and his next letter in a somewhat similar vein, the poet had also learned from Augusta that if he should return to England, she had instructions not to see him. In it he refers to "Miss Milbanke" and informs his sister he will see anyone he pleases. ". . . I have thus far—as you know—regarded her without personal feelings of bitterness towards her. . . . You know she is the cause of all —whether intentionally or not is little to the purpose. . . ." [17] And on 6 November Byron's mood is about the same, "After what has been said already, I have a right to suspect everything and every body. . . ." [18]

To Augusta again on 18 December her brother comments upon "The tortures of the past two years and that virtuous monster Miss Milbanke, who had nearly driven me out of my senses." [19] Even to Moore, as late as 28 January, Byron expressed his turbulent feelings, "I was half mad during the time of its [*Childe Harold,* canto 3] composition, between metaphysics, mountains, lakes, love inextinguishable, thoughts unutterable, and the nightmare of my own delinquencies. I should, many a good day, have blown my brains out. . . ." [20]

All of these comments allow for many different interpretations, but one mood is common to all of them—frustration that he can find no means of fighting back: one doesn't attack virtue for being virtuous, nor, Byron seems to be saying, attack one's wife for unintentionally—or otherwise—inflicting destruction. Under these constraints, if one can lay a trap or flush the opposition into the open, he can take some measure of reprisal. Since Byron's instinct was not to attack his wife, one must presume he would have chosen as his prime target Lady Milbanke or her companion, Mrs. Clermont, or perhaps best of all, Lady Caroline. What he must have recognized and what would only aggravate his frustration was that his real enemy was a rumor. If *Manfred* contained a snare, it didn't trip, and Byron did not return—as he had planned—to England in the following spring.[21]

⍤ 26 ⍥

SUMMATION

The evidence offered does not represent the final word; there may be highly pertinent material that has not yet come to light. In someone's attic—possibly someone no biographer has thought of—there may be a chest of old papers that will furnish unchallengeable information of some kind. But as of the present writing, this is about as much as exists and it is time to put the argument together for a present verdict.

In the first place it has been demonstrated that the charges of sodomy, incest, and other sexual aberrations were not unique or special with respect to Byron but were in fact standard vituperatives of politics in his day. The Duke of Cumberland had withstood similar charges, and in one fashion or another similar accusations had been flung at political figures of various persuasions.

It is true that Byron and his friends did not publicly and specifically deny any of these allegations. However, one should bear in mind that none of them appeared in any action at law, and that all of them existed only at the level of rumor. Wisely or unwisely Byron chose to ignore them and imposed his attitude on his supporters. His decision was probably the correct one,

since successful refutation of rumors is an impossible undertaking.

All the evidence, both contemporary and that which had appeared subsequently, pretty clearly established Lady Caroline
Lamb as the principal source of rumors and charges. She had
tried without success early in 1814, when she bruited the news—
incorrect in all respects—that Augusta had stayed in Byron's
rooms in Bennet Street in December. The refusal of Lady Byron
and her supporters to specify the nature of Byron's misconduct
added a measure of credibility to the second installment of Lady
Caroline's scurrility.

If Lady Caroline's stories lacked motivation and if her character were such as to make such behavior inconceivable, the evidence would be weak indeed. But to the contrary, it is clear that
she regarded herself as jilted, and she did not bear that condition
lightly. Though there is no record that she felt any great an-
tagonism toward Lady Byron, the spectacle of Byron's marriage
to the prim and unprepossessing Lamb cousin would not have
lowered the titer of her resentment toward Byron. It seems fair
to conclude on the following grounds that Lady Caroline deliberately sought Byron's destruction by spreading rumors of
incest.

1. She was completely unscrupulous in any matter related to
Byron.

2. To others than the Byron faction she was well known to
have no respect for veracity—at least in respect to amatory affairs.

3. On the record, she had threatened him with ruin and destruction.

4. Upon Byron's rejection of her support in January 1816, she
promptly undertook to provide Lady Byron with material, some
of which may have been forged, in support of some of the charges
that she herself originated.

5. In a clandestine meeting that followed her offer, Lady Caroline showed Lady Byron letters, purportedly of the poet, that effectually cut off any further consideration of compromise.

6. In the faintly disguised personalizations of *Glenarvon* Lady Caroline accused Byron of infanticide and the murder of women, but curiously did not include incest.

7. Subsequently she categorically denied that Byron had engaged in improper relations with Augusta.

So much for Lady Caroline and her role in the fall of Byron. The salient point around which any fabrication could develop was that Augusta found herself pregnant shortly after her sojourn in London, June–July 1813. There does not appear to be any reason to doubt the pregnancy or that it resulted in the birth of a baby which was baptized as recorded. Concerning that birth, several points emerge from the evidence.

1. The birth date was probably some days earlier than the recorded date of 15 April 1814.

2. Correspondence in the preceding July and August seems to support the time of conception as having been during Augusta's London season or immediately after it.

3. The earlier date of conception casts considerable doubt on paternity, because: (*a*) Augusta was a guest in a London house, possibly the Duke of Rutland's. (*b*) There is no record at all as to Leigh's activities, and while he could have appeared in London or wherever else Augusta may have been by the middle of July, there seems to be no reason to suppose that he did. (*c*) Upon Augusta's departure from London there is no certainty that she returned to Six Mile Bottom and some slight occasion to believe she may have gone to a house in the country.

4. That Medora was illegitimate is suggested by Augusta's sudden decision to take flight with Byron at about the time it became clear she was pregnant.

5. For what it is worth, Georgiana, the eldest Leigh daughter, and her husband told Medora—according to that unreliable lady's testimony—that Leigh was not her father (see page 227, below).

In spite of these circumstances, Colonel Leigh acknowledged paternity at the time of baptism, and Augusta's relatives, including Byron, stood as her sponsors. If the child was not born in wedlock the family had decided to put an exceedingly proper face on the situation. Obviously, on the assumption of illegitimacy, some other man than the Colonel accounted for it. Byron, since the time of Harriet Beecher Stowe, has been the nominee; proper procedure should require, first, demonstration of negative evidence, and then display of evidence that may involve some other man.

In the chapters, "The Time and Place of Conception" and "Augusta's London Season" several points contrary to the *Astarte* thesis were presented.

1. Augusta's season in London did not provide very good opportunity for sexual relations with Byron: (*a*) She was a house guest, possibly at the Duke of Rutland's or at Lady Gertrude Sloane's. (*b*) Except for afternoon visits, the two are known to have attended parties together only three times out of a possible fifteen or more evenings. (*c*) Augusta almost certainly went to a number of gatherings at houses where Byron would have been entirely unwelcome. (*d*) Byron engaged in a number of activities that in no way concerned his half sister and attended at least three known dinners at which she was not present.

2. The letters with respect to a possible duel imply that Byron may have been involved with some entirely different lady.

3. Those individuals who had most direct association with Byron and Augusta and who were obviously best informed—

Hobhouse, Hodgson, Lady Shelley, Mrs. Villiers for a time, the
first Lord Lovelace, and even Colonel Leigh—attached no credence to the charge of incest.

4. Acquaintances who were most familiar with the town gossip and who suspected Byron was pursuing a surreptitious romance arrived at quite different and variable suppositions—Lady
Jersey, Lady Holland, Lady Caroline herself, and even Lady
Melbourne.

5. Byron, as Marchand very cogently argued, never showed any
unusual interest in Medora, contrary to his usual concern for his
natural children.[1]

6. Despite various ambiguous statements, Lady Byron never
seemed to have extracted from Augusta an admission of incest.

7. Some of the more incriminating letters from Byron to Lady
Melbourne and to Augusta came under suspicion for authenticity.

8. Byron's use of the word "love" is such as to leave his meaning with respect to a specific physical act quite uncertain.

9. The open association of Byron and Augusta on a number of
occasions subsequent to the midsummer of 1813 can only be interpreted as a public proclamation of their innocence of incest or
as the most brazen effrontery.

Reasons that some of the most incriminating letters come under suspicion of forgery have been presented in detail. In recapitulation, the following points appear significant.

1. References and comments that seem to imply incestuous
relations with Augusta occur sporadically and in groups.

2. The use of "X" to denote Augusta occurs, except for two
atypical instances, only in the letters of October 1814 and amidst
a set of comments that would be particularly offensive to Lady
Byron, his engagement to whom had just been announced. Furthermore the context demands that the reader identify "X" as

Augusta, and only Augusta, and hence completely destroys any possibility of concealment, which could have been the only motive for the use of a new symbol.

3. The signature or symbol "X," as Byron and Augusta understood it, in reality was a cross or plus sign; its appearance as an X may well represent a forger's error.

4. Neither Byron nor Augusta showed any anxiety about this correspondence, and in 1822 the poet attempted to turn all these letters over to Moore for publication.

5. Lady Caroline Lamb apparently could have gained access to the letters at any time during a period of nine years, and had the skill, motive, and opportunity to make such alterations or additions as would serve to support the charge of incest.

6. Numerous forgeries of Byron's script are known, and hence it is not essential that Lady Caroline participated alone.

Impeachment of the authenticity of letters to Lady Melbourne —or of other letters—however logical, demands verification. Only a most painstaking comparison by an expert familiar with Byronic script and with other script of the period would be adequate, since Lady Caroline forged or procured the forgery of a note sufficiently skillful to deceive Murray, who had seen scores of pages of the poet's handwriting. Many other excellent forgeries are known to exist, some of them on display at Newstead.

Byron's letters to Augusta, most of which apparently exist in the form of copies, provide an even more complicated problem. In many instances the originals have not survived. The provenience of most of these derives from a set of rules Lady Byron imposed upon Augusta: she was to send to Annabella every letter she received from her brother. Lady Byron then made copies and presumably returned the originals.[2] The opportunity for errors in transcription would have been considerable, quite aside from any bias that could result unintentionally from efforts to set straight the poet's miserable punctuation. The looseness of such three-way correspondence, if it was known to a potential mischief-maker, would allow for the insertion of almost any kind of unverified and unverifiable material.

Very much to this point are two letters, published for the first time in *Astarte*.[3] One of them, with a date of 17 May 1819, bears no name or signature, though Lord Lovelace presented it as authentically Byronian and regarded it as addressed to Augusta. The theme of the letter is similar to that of some of Byron's most empurpled billets to Lady Caroline. If Byron wrote the letter it is the first time he had used X since his supposed letter to Lady Melbourne in 1815. Still more perplexing is that in context the X's seem to symbolize the name Mary. Just as suddenly as his ardor flamed up, it subsided; his next letters to Augusta are matter-of-fact and humorous. Again in a single letter of 1820 flaming ardor expressed in puerilities breaks out, accompanied by a profusion of X's. No other letter addressed to Augusta after Byron's departure from England contains any type of concealment; no other letter, though some of those in 1816 immediately after his departure are tender, expresses such amorousness as these. These two letters accord with nothing we know about the Byron of 1819–1820 and unless they are confirmed beyond any doubt, their existence among Lady Byron's documents reinforces the suspicion that someone inserted spurious material into the Byron-Augusta-Annabella-Augusta mail circuit.

As for the poetry, the argument that the hint of incest in *The Bride of Abydos* constituted a literary stratagem has appeared. An alternate explanation of *Manfred,* compatible with Byron's attitude toward the Milbanke faction and with his emotions at the time of its composition, has been offered. The hypothesis is logical, given that Byron's mind might function in such a manner. The ambiguity that surrounds Byron's varying definitions of love is such that one may regard some of the shorter poems as billets doux or as expressing an entirely different variety of love, in accordance with the interpreter's preconceptions.

If doubts of authenticity of some of the most damning letters are justified, the behavior of the principals—if they were guilty of incest—displays total sangfroid. They associated openly and on several occasions in 1813–14. While Byron may have been capable of challenging England and the world, nothing in Augusta's conduct at any time suggests that she had any interest in flaunting rebellion. It will be recalled that when it seemed likely that she would accompany Byron to Italy in 1813, a chaperon had been among her chief concerns, even if one no more adequate than one of her children. Was this the woman with whom Byron had carried on in July 1813 and of whose "abandon" Lady Melbourne wrote, implying that she was indeed passionate? It is safe to assume that Byron was reasonably lusty himself. That two such ardent and highly combustible spirits might hole up for a month at Newstead Abbey is understandable, but not that they would advertise it or that the husband of one of them would readily acquiesce. And if, as some biographers state, Byron all this while suffered the tortures of remorse, it seems inconceivable he could so far have tempted himself by these repeated associations.

If Medora was illegitimate and if there is some acceptable evidence against Byron's paternity, the question, of course, is who was her father? Throughout the presentation of evidence bits of information have accumulated. In sum, they consist of the following points.

1. The Leighs apparently enjoyed a temporary respite from their creditors from sometime in early September 1813 until the following spring. Byron could probably not have provided any assistance earlier than October or November.

2. When the poet did receive an access of funds, there is no certainty he provided any to the Leighs until June 1814.

3. The best explanation for acknowledgment and republications of "Lines to a Lady Weeping" is that Augusta had received certain promises from the Prince Regent which he had not fulfilled.

4. The selection of names for the child born in April 1814 points clearly toward some special obligation to the Duchess of Rutland.

5. The Rutlands alone among Augusta's connections appear to have had any power and influence with the Hanoverian princes.

6. As the Duchess was approaching confinement, the Duke may have suffered an enforced continence.

7. More than casual relationship with the Rutlands is evident much later, when the Duke adjourned a hunting party upon learning of the death of Byron and subsequently sent his carriage to join the funeral cortege. (Neither Lord Cawdor nor Mr. William Sloane Stanley sent his, though the degree of kinship was identical.)

8. The seal depicted on the title page of *Astarte,* if its interpretation is approximately correct, points either toward the Hanoverian princes or toward someone who enjoyed great influence with them.

9. In spite of the defamation she had undergone, Augusta was able to occupy her apartment at St. James's Palace and to take over her duties in the Household at a time when scandal was at its height, evidence that someone in very high position either totally disbelieved the rumors or had contradictory information.

It is clear that without some undiscovered acknowledgment of paternity it will never be possible to know the identity of the man who sired Medora. But it looks as if he is to be found among three gentlemen of the period: the Prince Regent, the Duke of York, or the Duke of Rutland. At all events, Byron seems to be entitled to the old Scottish verdict of "not proven."

❧ 27 ❦

SEQUELAE

After Byron's departure Augusta returned with Leigh to Six Mile Bottom, but their stay was rather brief. By midsummer, according to a letter from Mrs. Villiers to Annabella, Augusta had taken over her "grace and favour" apartment at St. James's Palace, and after the sale of Six Mile Bottom in 1818 the apartment became the Leighs' principal residence for the remainder of their lives. Presumably Colonel Leigh continued his usual activities and Mrs. Villiers suspected that the Leigh marriage was in difficulty. "Nothing can be more tiresome and impracticable than Colonel L. of which, alas! she seems more than ever aware." [1] But Byron wrote from Diodati in August with respect to Augusta's coming to Europe, "The great obstacle would be that you are so admirably yoked—and necessary as a housekeeper—and a letter writer—and a place-hunter to that very helpless gentleman your Cousin. . . ." [2] Mrs. Villiers continued in her letter to Lady Byron that Augusta had induced her half brother the Duke of Leeds to attempt to secure from Lord Liverpool some kind of sinecure for the Colonel. The effort failed and during much of the next ten years Augusta was estranged from the Leeds-Chichester part of her family. Whether or not she was frequently with the Carlisle daughters has not developed. All of the kin would have been in town at intervals and there is no evidence to point toward a rift. Relations with Mrs. Villiers continued friendly, and Augusta maintained rather regular correspondence with Hodgson. In 1817 or 1818 she received a curious caller, Lady Frances Wedderburn Webster.[3] One can be pretty certain that Lady Frances knew the nature of the gossip, and perceived that the accusations bore a close temporal connection with her own adventure. She certainly would have recalled her invitation to Augusta in the autumn of 1813. Her visit to a reputed rival in Byron's affections and a woman involved in a heinous offense is thus more than a little strange. It leads one to suspect that Lady Frances may have possessed quite contradictory information.

Byron, recovering finally from the furies that plagued him during his first ten months abroad, settled himself in Venice and devoted his time to uninhibited enjoyment of a succession of luscious and vivacious Venetian ladies. While the period is about equally often glossed over or described in detail, in spite of whatever debauchery went on, it was also a time of great literary productivity. Toward the end of the period he formed his alliance with the Countess Guiccioli and took up the regular and semidomestic role of *cavalier servente*.

Meantime Augusta continued to send up signals of financial distress. From Venice he replied, "I can battle my way through better than your exquisite piece of helplessness G. L. or that other poor creature George Byron, . . . I wish well to your George, who is the best of the two a devilish deal. . . ."[4] But no sums Byron may have remitted really aided the problems of the Leighs. Deaths, disappointments, and persistent "impecuniosity" dogged their remaining days. In 1819, the author of *The Diary of a Lady-in-Waiting* may have referred to Augusta in the following note:

Poor Mrs. G. L(—)e [the name was often misspelled "Lee"] how she has changed! Her fair freshness gone and all the fair freshness of her youth prematurely withered. Still there is something fine in her full rich lip; and it is some praise to be beaten down with sorrow. I fear she has had her share.[5]

If the entry is not a description of Augusta, it surely could apply to her as well as to Mrs. G. L(—)e. In that year her second-born daughter died. She and the Colonel were frequently at odds with respect to financial affairs and perhaps with the example he set for their children. In July 1819, after Augusta had written of a pain in her side, Byron replied, ". . . would a warm climate do you good? If so say the word and I will provide you and your whole family (including that precious luggage your husband) with the means of making an agreeable journey." [6]

But nothing came of all this. Colonel Leigh apparently persisted in his ways, and the financial situation in the grace and favor apartment grew steadily worse. In answer to an appeal, Byron wrote in August 1820:

And if I did *not* so love you—still I would not persecute or oppress anyone wittingly—especially for debts, of which I know the *agony by experience*. Of Colonel Leigh's bond, I really have forgotten all particulars, except that it was *not* of my *wishing*. . . . I would *not take the money if he had it*. You may judge if I would dun him having it not.

Whatever measure I can take for his extrication will be taken. Only tell me how—for I am ignorant and far away.[7]

In October, he writes again with respect to the situation that had caused Augusta so much anxiety. "I suppose by this time you will be out of your fidget, and that the dilatory Hanson will have set Colonel L[eigh] at rest upon the subject of the bond, etc." [8]

It is not out of order to remark at this point that during the whole of Byron's eight years on the Continent he seems to have sent no money to the Leighs; or if he did, Doris Langley Moore has not established such a fact in her detailed *Accounts Rendered*. Not all of Byron's letters to Augusta have survived, and only very few of hers to him. But if their relationship had been so fervent and if his love for her had persisted, as his letters would argue, it seems most remarkable that during his later years of relative affluence he made no remittances. And if there was any probability that Medora was his child, in the light of his provision for and care of his other natural children it can only be incredible that Byron would not have provided some continuing support for her.

During the time Colonel Leigh was at Byron's place in Piccadilly early in 1816, he had apparently tried to obtain an audience with the Prince Regent with respect to some available appointment, but either was refused an audience or fobbed off. Nothing came of it. In 1824 Leigh was one of the few attendants at Byron's funeral, perhaps out of a true affection and regard for Augusta. There is a glimpse of Augusta in the middle 1820s attempting once more through her other family connections to find some kind of place for the Colonel. Once more she had no success, but in 1830 Leigh finally received a pension of £300 per year.

Byron's affair with La Guiccioli continued, for the most part with very slight friction. He joined the Hunts and Percy Shelleys at Pisa, rode regularly, practiced with his pistols, and wrote the bulk of *Don Juan*. But in the course of time his quiet domestic existence began to bore him. Perhaps he grew weary of the Countess but lacked the will or the callousness to separate by any other means, or perhaps the old immature imaginings of the

Oriental Tales would not let him rest. By 1823 he had resolved upon joining the independence movements of the Greeks and by the end of the year had landed there. The rest of the story is familiar. In Missolonghi, after a series of events described in detail in the appendix, he died on 20 April 1824, at the age of thirty-six.

After a long sea voyage, immersed in a cask of spirits Byron's body reached England. There followed suitable public commotion and the usual interest in trying to see his body or touch his coffin. Hasty efforts to obtain permission to bury him in Westminster Abbey had come to nothing, and after some uncertainty his friends and Augusta decided he should be buried in the Byron vault in the church at Hucknall and the cortege set out, with the unoccupied carriages of a good many peers in train. At the edge of London the crested vehicles turned back. Only Colonel Leigh, Sidney Smith, Hobhouse, Burdett, and a few others remained with Byron to the bitterest of ends. After the funeral, arose the question of the disposition of his unpublished journal which was in the hands of Moore. The episode, a rather ugly one, reopened some old wounds, reembittered some ancient opponents, and created some new animosities. What it achieved was the destruction of Byron's own comments on the separation.

Not long after this, the oldest Leigh daughter, Georgiana, married a cousin, John Trevanion. If the Leighs had been somewhat estranged, they came to a sharp difference with regard to this marriage which Augusta strongly supported and the Colonel stoutly opposed.

The next ten years were not more pleasant. Lady Chichester stated that though Augusta had about £800 per year, she deprived herself of the necessities in order to assist in the support of Georgiana's children and to pay the debts of "her own worthless sons." [9] There is no indication that the Colonel contributed much except querulousness and irascibility.

Meanwhile Medora was growing up into precocious and evidently enticing young womanhood. Though whatever she writes has to be viewed with some skepticism, she claims that when she was about thirteen, Georgiana and her husband Trevanion told her she was illegitimate.[10] Not very long after this, on the occasion of one of Georgiana's pregnancies, Trevanion decided Medora was much to his liking and seduced her. For a time Medora lived in concealment, and one of the last glimpses of Colonel Leigh is his riding about London in a coach attempting to locate the girl. By this time he must have been in his middle fifties, a thoroughly disheartened and failed man. He fades out, and Somerset House has no record of a will that might be his. Fifty years later, according to Elwin, Augusta's nephew, the third Earl of Chichester, told Lord Lovelace that Leigh "abominated Byron, but absolutely totally denied and disbelieved in Mrs. Leigh's guilt." [11]

Though the Leighs recovered Medora and temporarily kept her in hiding, in due course Trevanion discovered her and took her away with him. The second elopement was more successful, for Trevanion and Medora went off to France where they lived for a time as M. and Mme. Aubin. After some years, as Medora might have anticipated, Trevanion deserted her and she then lived for a while under the "protection" of first one and then another. In 1841, when she returned to England in an effort to obtain all of a small fund that had been established for her, she learned—so she states—from Lady Byron that she was in reality the daughter of the poet.

After Trevanion's desertion, responsibility for the care and support of Georgiana and her children was added to the financial woes of the Leighs. Augusta by this time was middle-aged; if she had been "dowdy" in 1814 one can imagine she had become no picture of fashion in the interval. Medora, no very reliable witness, described her mother in the 1840s as the very picture of evil.[12] And Lady Wilmot Horton, she who had walked in beauty, wrote retrospectively to Lord Lovelace that "the state of abject poverty to which she was reduced—with *no* expensive habits" must have meant that she was being blackmailed.[13] This was a rather vicious insinuation, and quite gratuitous.

But the picture was not invariably dismal. Now and then there was a little kindness. In 1833 Mrs. Edward Bulwer, who had been a kind of protégée of Lady Caroline Lamb, wrote Mrs. Greene: "When you see dear Mrs. Leigh, tell her I have got a little bit of marble for her that Thorwaldsen gave me out of her brother's statue . . . and give her my best love." [14] It was a kindly—if inexpensive—gesture, and, contrary to Lady Wilmot Horton, it suggests that Augusta's reputation had undergone a certain degree of rehabilitation.

Most of the rest is obscure. Augusta retained apartments at St. James's, since at her death she is described as being a resident there. George Leigh died 3 May 1850. The following year Lady Byron, hearing that Augusta had been ill, sent for her and held the last interview, described in chapter 23, above. After the unsatisfactory meeting Augusta replied by letter that she had never implied she had anything new to reveal.[15] Like so many other letters and statements in the history of Byron, it leaves nothing settled.

Augusta died, shortly after the interview and the letter, on 12 October 1851, aged sixty-six. Whatever her relationships had been, she was not buried in the Byron family vault at Hucknall. That position was reserved for Byron's daughter, Ada, first Countess of Lovelace, who died the following year. Augusta left

a will that appears in proper section at Somerset House, under
date of 30 July 1858:

> The Will of the Honourable Augusta Leigh, late of Flag
> Court, St. James' Palace in the county of Middlesex, widow
> deceased, who died 12 October 1851 at Flag Court aforesaid,
> was proved at the Principal Registry by the oath of Amelia
> Mariana Leigh of Ryde in the Isle of Wight, Apwater and
> the daughter and sole executrix. The Letters of Administra-
> tion by the Prorogative Court of Canterbury, February 1852,
> having been revoked.

On the margin in a printed hand appears the notation, "Effects
under £200." And in script appears another notation, "Resworn
at the Stamp Office August 1859 under £8000." This is quite a
discrepancy, and one wonders why there was so much difference
in the figures for 1852 and 1859.

Meantime Lady Caroline Lamb's career became one of gradual
disintegration of body and mind. Sometime in the early 1820s,
Lady Charlotte Bury encountered her on several occasions. Both
eccentricity and irresponsibility had increased. Sometimes she
routed out her guests in the early morning hours to listen while
she played the organ with interminable improvisations of her
own creation. At other times she was less demanding:

> Lady C. L[amb] is certainly, I should say, a little mad—not
> sufficiently so to require restraint personally; certainly she
> ought to have a sensible person about her. . . . She spoke to
> me the other day of Lord B[yron] and endeavored to make
> believe she had never been in love with him, . . . she only
> said, with a sigh, "He is certainly a most unfortunate person
> to have been married to Lady B[yro]n." Then she added
> with great truth, "It was exceedingly unwise in her to

marry him, after having refused him. That is an affront no man ever forgave a woman." [16]

On a somewhat later occasion Lady Caroline invited Lady Charlotte to a formal dinner.

I dined at Lady C. L[amb]'s. She had collected a strange party of artists and literati, and one or two fine folks, who were very ill associated with the rest of the company. . . . I was much amused by observing this curious assemblage of *blues* and *pinks,* and still more so with Lady C[aroline] L[amb]'s remarks, which she whispered every now and then into my ear. Her criticisms were frequently very clever, and many of them were very true, but so impudent, it was difficult to understand how anybody in their senses could hazard such opinions aloud, or relate such stories. [17]

On yet another occasion Lady Caroline invited Lady Charlotte to an intimate dinner.

I dined tete-a-tete with Lady C. L[amb]. She is very amusing but her mind is in a sad state of bewilderment, and I fear it is likely to grow worse instead of better. . . . She appears to have a strong affection for her husband, but, as he is careless of her, her disposition, which is naturally *aimant,* leads her to attach herself to others. [18]

It was the sort of story a very sharp woman might concoct, or a rather sentimental one believe, but it probably didn't completely take in Lady Charlotte.

During much of the time from 1820 onward, the Melbournes contrived to keep Lady Caroline at Brocket, where at least she was out of the way. If she perpetrated any unsually outrageous folly, news of it would be slow to reach London, though it might well be exaggerated in the transmission. On one occasion she planned a great party and invited the gentry from the country all around, but so well known by this time was her eccentricity that no one attended the dinner, set for sixty.

In spite of her reputation and in spite of the seclusion provided for her, Lady Caroline managed to find some amusement. At one point, probably around 1824, she somehow met Edward Bulwer, then a young man who had just attained literary notoriety. Perhaps because he was young and literary and ambitious, he found the attention of Lady Caroline quite flattering. Perhaps for her it was a second-class replay of her great affair. But Bulwer was smitten for the time.

> Lady Caroline Lamb was then between thirty and forty, but looked much younger than she was, thanks, perhaps, to a slight, rounded figure and a childlike mode of wearing her hair (which was of a pale golden colour) in close curls. She had large hazel eyes . . . exceedingly good teeth, a pleasant laugh, and a musical intonation of voice [despite the Devonshire House drawl]. Apart from these gifts she might be considered plain. But she had, to a surpassing degree, the attribute of charm. . . .
>
> She interested me chiefly, however, by her recollections and graphic descriptions of Byron. . . . Of the hideous calumny concerning himself and Mrs. Leigh (indeed, of all calumnies involving the charge of crime) she certainly acquitted him. . . . I am bound to add that, in his letters to her, there was no trace of the selfish and heartless libertine; rather a desire to save her . . . from herself, and a consideration for her happiness. . . . I cannot think him the seducing party; and, certainly from her own confession, he was not the betraying one.[19]

The duration of the liaison with Bulwer seems to have been rather short, perhaps as long as he wished it and as long as Lady Caroline could remain concentrated on anything. It was only a short time before Bulwer added the following note.

> . . . I had wit enough to see that Lady Caroline and this gentleman [Mr. Russell, natural son of the Duke of Bedford] were captivated with each other. . . . He wore a ring. It was the one which Lord Byron had given Lady Caroline, one which was worn only by those she loved. I had often worn it myself.[20]

These were apparently among the last expressions of Lady Caroline's "aimant" character. Her health was failing, and though now and again she dressed and rode wildly and recklessly about the Brocket fields, deterioration moved apace. She became careless of her person and her rooms began to take on an appearance of utter disorder. Descriptions of remnants of food secreted in drawers, pieces of clothing left lying about, a total confusion of papers of every description, point toward something like schizophrenic collapse. Yet in the midst of such dilapidation, she could write in 1826 that she was "Happy, healthy, quiet, contented; I get up at half-past four, ride about with Haggard . . . read a few old books, see no one, hear from no one, and occasionally play at chess with Dr. Goddard. . . ."[21] In 1828 she died, unregretted by anybody unless it was William Lamb.

APPENDIX

BYRON'S DISEASE AND THE
CAUSE OF HIS DEATH

The diagnosis of a disease depends not only on the final out-
come but on the entire history of the victim, if the disease seems
to have been one of long duration. In Byron's case there was at
least one congenital anomaly—the deformation of his foot—and
possibly a second, involving the prominence of his left eye. One
of the conditions that may account for the prominence of an eye is
a vascular anomaly of the brain that consists of a meshwork of
small, interconnecting blood vessels. Lesions of this type are
frequently located at the base of the brain, not far back of the
eye socket. Since the vessels are abnormal in their origin and
development, small hemorrhages occur from time to time. The
usual symptoms of such events are headache, signs suggestive of
mild meningitis or irritation of the brain and its covering, and
occasional changes in personality.

The evidence of prominence of Byron's left eye is thoroughly
authenticated at many different times by many different ob-
servers, who include Augusta, Hobhouse, Lady Blessington, and
Medwin.[1] There also appear to be periods when leakage from the
meshwork may have occurred. In his journal late in 1813 when

Byron had been emotionally very unstable and had been dieting fiercely, he wrote, "My head, I think it was given me to ache with."[2] The complaint is that associated with increased pressure within the skull, but of course there is no proof that such was the cause of his pain.

By April 1814 he had largely resumed his ordinary occupations and activities and seemed to feel very well for perhaps about eighteen months. In late November and December 1815, when he again came under considerable psychological stress, his personality underwent a striking change, as Augusta perceived it. There followed the birth of his daughter Ada and the departure from London of Lady Byron.

Augusta described him in early January as looking very ill, "his face swelled. . . . His memory has failed him to such a degree he exclaimed at it himself. . . ."[3] Later in January, writing again to Lady Byron, Augusta says, ". . . ye pain in his head . . . It seems now just over one eye, then over ye other, then between and over the nose and at times spasmodic."[4] While it is possible Augusta was exaggerating, Hobhouse also observed a significant change in Byron's appearance. He wrote the illness had already affected his eyes, "made one seem smaller than the other and made him squint."[5]

Augusta wrote even more explicitly of what she thought (and perhaps what Byron thought) had taken place. "I talked to him of the lameness of the hip. He . . . says it is quite possible *that side* may have received a shock, tho not absolutely palsy, and that may account for ye small eye now looking so much smaller."[6] Apparently both Byron and his sister had noticed both a difference in his eye and an increased difficulty in the use of his right leg and foot. It is the only time any reference to lameness occurs. Naturally, each of them may have been attempting to adduce evidence of physical disease in extenuation of his recent conduct.

Since neither Augusta nor Hobhouse could be expected to understand the significance of these observations, it assumes importance that they corroborate each other. If one eye appears smaller than the other, loss of weight may cause the small eye to be less prominent, or a rise in pressure behind the prominent eye would cause it to appear larger. In consideration of the possibilities, Hobhouse's use of the word "squint" is very important. Squint may imply partial closure of the lid, a type of sidelong look, or an actual deviation of the eye from its normal position. Squinting, as partial closure of the lid, results from weakness of the muscles that raise the lid, or a voluntary or involuntary contraction of the muscles around the eye. Squint, as a deviation of the eyeball from the midline in forward gaze, or as a lid lowered from weakness of the muscle, signifies a neurological disorder. An individual who has difficulty in focusing for stereoscopic vision—certainly a difficulty to be expected if one eye had changed prominence with respect to the other—might partially close a lid in an effort to see more distinctly or to avoid double vision.

Whatever Hobhouse meant by "squint," in association with the pain Augusta described there is strong implication of some type of neurological disease. There does not appear to have been a permanent crossing of the eyes or deviation of the eyeball, and one is therefore justified in regarding the signs and complaints as not indicative of irreversible damage. Since there was no evidence of weakness of other parts of the face, the disease does not appear to have been acute facial paralysis (Bell's palsy), nor does it seem likely to have been so-called tic douloureux, since pain was inconstant in position. Viewed solely as a problem in neurology, the recorded abnormalities would lead one to think of some type of inflammation of the meninges at the base of the brain, with transitory weakness or palsy of the nerves to the eye. A very likely cause for a condition of this sort is a limited hemorrhage into the meninges and brain.

His Death

The cause of Byron's death has been a subject of speculation. About 1950, Professor Marchand showed the autopsy record and described the circumstances of Byron's death to the late Dr. Nolan D. C. Lewis, an eminent neuropsychiatrist of Washington, D.C. It was Dr. Lewis's guess that Byron probably died of uremia as a result of chronic renal failure.[7] Sir Ronald Ross, a noted malariologist, having been given an account of Byron's death, speculated that the cerebral form of malaria may have developed.[8] And Dr. P. M. Dale, in a book published in 1952, repeated the conclusion that Byron died of cerebral malaria.[9] It is hardly necessary to point out that the exact answer will not ever be known. The autopsy was so poorly performed and the description is so imprecise that they provide no reliable evidence. Byron's physicians were as inadequate after as before his death. Only one observation seems valid; and, in the face of all the other errors, even the seemingly valid one comes under suspicion.

To deal with uremia first, this disease results from some kind of chronic destructive disease of the kidney. The development of any of these diseases is usually quite slow and protracted. All of them produce anemia, all disturb the metabolism so that the affected individual loses strength, weight, and appetite. It is impossible in the terminal two months for people in this state to be functionally effective. The terminal condition is progressive, and the onset of unconsciousness is not followed by a period of partial recovery. The only evidence that Byron had any type of kidney disease is his account of having passed a stone on one occasion and his reporting, apparently twice, that some woman had "clapt" him.[10] In the absence of a course suggesting prolonged infection of the kidney, these established incidents are insufficient for a diagnosis of pyelonephritis. There is no evidence for any other type of renal disease.

Cerebral malaria seems, on the whole, a poor diagnosis. Byron stated that he had had what he called "malaria" during his first trip to the Near East. He probably was correct. He may also have had malaria during some period of his residence in Italy from 1816 to 1824.[11] The disease was fairly familiar to European physicians, and during Byron's life it was treated with quinine. So far as appears, Byron recovered from his attacks without difficulty, and the probability seems good that the variety of disease he had had was ordinary "tertian" malaria, which responds to quinine well and produces no serious complication.

The organism that produces the more serious forms of malaria, including cerebral, may have been present in Greece during Byron's stay, but February and March would have been quite the wrong season for the onset of the disease. Moreover, when this organism affects the brain, the process is totally prostrating and results in death within two or three days of the onset of manifestations pointing to the nervous system. Accordingly, malaria appears a possibility so unlikely as to be unacceptable, even though suggested by so eminent an expert in tropical disease as Sir Ronald Ross.

Nor could Byron's illness have been any kind of inflammatory disease of the brain or meninges, such as meningitis or encephalitis. No variety would have produced an onset distinguished by convulsions and unconsciousness without having been relentlessly progressive.

If one can exclude inflammations that result from generalized disease or direct infections, he is left with disease of the vessels of the brain. One possibility in a man of thirty-six years is hemorrhage into a tumor. In such a condition there would have been an initial bleeding with convulsion and unconsciousness. If the bleeding stopped and the patient survived, there could have been a second episode a few weeks later that could have been fatal. Such a tumor, since before the episode and after recovery from it Byron demonstrated no paralysis, loss of vision, loss of hearing, falling to one side, or any other localizing evidence would have had to be a "silent" tumor. Tumors of this type exist, and it is impossible to prove that Byron did not die of a tumor of the brain. Other possibilities rank higher simply because they are more common.

The first of these is meningo-vascular syphilis, which may have an onset and a termination remotely resembling Byron's. If he had had a primary lesion, the chances are it might have been inconspicuous. Secondary syphilis, with evident rash, was less common and obvious by Byron's period than in Shakespeare's, when it was the familiar Spanish, Italian, or French pox. Byron's activities, of course, would have entitled him to acquire syphilis, along with gonorrhea, which he acknowledged. Syphilis is fairly readily transmitted and one might expect evidence of it among either his *amies* or his offspring.

Naturally, the same difficulty applies to recognition of the disease in women as in men. However, a very regular feature of syphilis in women, especially when infection is recent, is first a miscarriage and, later, stillbirths. Only after such a sequence is a live child with congenital syphilis the result of impregnation. One point is certain: of some three infants known to be Byron's, none showed recognizable disease. On the other hand, Lady Oxford may have had a miscarriage. At one point Byron and she feared she was pregnant and very soon she was ill with what the poet described as a "hemorrhage" without specifying the site of the bleeding.[12]

Subsequent to this event Lady Byron became pregnant and bore a normal infant. There followed these births the Venetian sojourn, when, if he had failed to acquire syphilis before, the opportunities seem to have been numerous. The child Allegra was born to Claire Clairmont before this Venetian interlude, and Allegra seems to have been quite a healthy child, though she died young. No children are known to have resulted from any subsequent attachment.

The remaining test case is that of Teresa Guiccioli. She did not have a child, but she did have a miscarriage.[13] After that event she apparently did not become pregnant again. This bit of established fact could point to Byron's having syphilis and having transmitted it to his mistress. It is not conclusive since, of course, there are many other causes of miscarriage.

If any assumption from known facts is possible, it would be that if Byron had syphilis he probably acquired it between 1816 and 1818. In that case the interval between his first infection and the development of vascular disease of the brain would have been six to eight years, a somewhat shorter interval than is usual. In summary, cerebro-vascular syphilis remains a definite possibility, though the evidence in support of it is indecisive. Furthermore, if it had been highly probable, a physician with the knowledge of vascular syphilis of Dr. Nolan D. C. Lewis would certainly not have overlooked it.

One could speculate on the possibility of ordinary hypertension. Death from this condition in early adult life results usually either from heart failure or kidney damage. In either of these situations or even in the much rarer fatal stroke, there is characteristically a period of loss or impairment of vision, shortness of breath (often with angina), and eventually edema. But the people around Byron during the last weeks of his life were detailed in their accounts and none of them mentions any of these manifestations.[14] On the whole, hypertension with stroke seems the least likely of the possible diseases of the vessels of the brain.

This leaves for consideration some type of vascular malformation. One of these is the congenital "berry" aneurysm, a common cause of death from cerebral hemorrhage in relatively young individuals. The other is an arterio-venous fistula, in effect a meshwork of small vessels which shunt blood from an arterial trunk to a large venous channel. Of the two, the more likely seems to be the arterio-venous fistula, since intermittent bleeding from some of the dilated venules or capillaries may occur, while hemorrhage from a berry aneurysm is usually violent and proves either to be immediately fatal or to leave residual palsy.

The clinical course of Byron's last illness is also understandable in terms of a preliminary hemorrhage, followed by temporary clotting, and then by fatal bleeding. Byron's illness began in February when, after a period of increasing exasperation and annoyance, he experienced a convulsion. From this he recovered rather slowly, but by early April he was again on his feet and ready to take exercise. Having gone out for a ride, he and his retinue were caught in a thunderstorm and returned soaked. On 9 and 10 April (this is Pietro Gamba's account),[15] he had shivering spells and complained of pains throughout his entire body. By 13 April the fever was lower, but he continued to have pains at various places in his body. The following day he seemed much calmer and his fever was still less, but he was weak and continued to have pain in his head. There followed very restless nights, sometimes marked by delirium. On 19 April around noon, Byron was sufficiently clear mentally to translate a letter from French into English and a second one from modern Greek into English—a feat rather difficult since Byron's basic knowledge was of classical Greek. Nevertheless, before laying it aside he completed this difficult mental task. By late afternoon of the

same day, according to Gamba, Byron could hardly recognize
anyone and began to doze. "About half-past five he awoke. . . .
I sent Parry. My Lord knew him. He tried to express his wishes
but could not. About six o'clock he fell into sleep." [16] This lasted
until six o'clock the following morning, when Byron ceased
breathing.

Only in the past ten or fifteen years has the clinical picture of
hemorrhage from vascular malformation become generally recognizable and well defined. When it seemed logical that such a
condition might adequately explain the events that preceded
Byron's death, the logical step was to obtain a consultation. Upon
receiving a careful narrative of events from January to April, a
neurosurgeon concurred fully with the diagnosis and advised
that the patient should be admitted to hospital immediately. On
another occasion when Byron's case was presented as a clinical-
pathological conference to a group of internists, most of whom
held academic appointment, fifty-eight of the sixty agreed the
problem was that of a congenital malformation, either a berry
aneurysm or hemangioma. One favored cerebro-vascular syphilis
and one refused to attempt a decision. None of them suggested
uremia or cerebral malaria, except to exclude those possibilities.
A few said they considered some type of tumor of the brain, but
regarded a vascular anomaly as more probable.

In summary, it seems that the best diagnosis of Byron's condition is a congenital hemangioma of the brain, for the following reasons:

1. One congenital defect is often associated with others, and
the deformity of the foot is on record and sufficiently attested.

2. There appear to have been several episodes of vascular leakage—possibly in 1813; almost certainly in 1816, when he had
pains in the head, squint, and a complaint of difficulty in one

side of his body; again in February 1824, when he had a convulsion and lay unconscious for a time; and finally in April of the
same year.

3. The prominence of one eye, which seems to be well supported, signifies a difference in pressure in the tissues that lie
back of the eyeball. In some individuals, actual pulsation of the
prominent eye has been observed. A study of the easel portraits,
most of which are profile or three-quarters, is not of much assistance, but the full-face miniature by Holmes clearly shows
that the left eye is more prominent than the right. Certainly, if
the defect in the right foot and leg were of neurological origin,
the lesion should lie in the left side of the brain.

4. Byron's ability to carry out a difficult mental process, the
translation of the letters, excludes the possibility that he had any
deterioration of mental faculties—which should certainly have
been evident if his condition was the result of malaria, encephalitis, meningitis, uremia, or syphilis.

5. So far as the autopsy is concerned, it seems to support best
a vascular lesion, but it is of so poor a quality—even for the time
and place—as to be almost worthless. Such as it is, it is appended
(as taken from Medwin).

(1). On opening the body of Lord Byron, the bones of the
head were found extremely hard, exhibiting no appearance
of suture, like the cranium of an octogenarian, so that the
skull had the appearance of one uniform bone; there seemed
to be no diploe, and the *sinus frontalis* was wanting.

(2). The *dura mater* was so firmly attached to the internal
parieties of the cranium, that the reiterated attempts of two
strong men were insufficient to detach it, and the vessels of
that membrane were completely injected with blood. It was
united from point to point by membranous bridles to the
pia mater.

(3). Between the *pia mater* and the convolutions of the brain were found many globules of air, with exudations of lymph and numerous adhesions.

(4). The great *falx* of the *dura mater* was firmly attached to both hemispheres by membranous bridles; and its vessels were turgid with blood.

(5). On dividing the medullary substance of the brain, the exudation of blood from the minute vessels produced specks of a bright red colour. An extravasation of about 2 oz. of bloody serum was found beneath the *pons varoli,* at the base of the hemispheres; and in the two superior, or lateral ventricles, a similar extravasation was discovered at the base of the cerebellum, and the usual effects of inflamation were observable throughout the cerebrum.

(6). The medullary substance was in more than usual proportion to the corticle [*sic*], and of the usual consistency. The *cerebrum* and the *cerebellum,* without the membranes, weighed 6 lbs. (*mediche*).

(7). The channels or sulci of the blood vessels on the internal surface of the cranium, were more numerous than usual, but small.[17]

In nontechnical language, this report indicates that blood was found in the meningeal space and in the ventricles of the brain. Adhesions (if they were present) suggest that earlier mild meningeal inflammation, such as might have resulted from repeated previous hemorrhages, had taken place. Possibly also the examination suggests a long-standing abnormality of the circulation of the brain. The weight of the brain, as reported, is impossible.

NOTES

The biographies, memoirs, and letters that are listed in the first section of the References are cited here by author's or editor's name alone.

Chapter 1

1 Maurois, p. 245.
2 Henry Blyth, *Caro,* pp. 125–30 passim.
3 Drinkwater, p. 210; Murray, 1 : 100.
4 Elwin (pp. 417–26 passim) assumes all the earlier rumors dealt with homosexuality and points to Hobhouse's comment of 29 February as evidence that he had not heard the issue of incest raised before. However, Annabella had come up to London on 22 February, and on 26 February Mrs. Villiers sent her a letter dealing with the specific problem of incest.
5 Elwin, pp. 465–71 passim. See also p. 352.
6 Mayne, p. 446; Elwin, p. 183.
7 Of the biographers after 1921, the first and most important was Ethel Colburn Mayne, whose 1924 work became and remained for a time the definitive study of the poet's life. The consensus that Miss Mayne's book established incest beyond the shadow of a doubt was strengthened in the following year when Sir John Fox published an assessment of the available information, concluding that the weight of the evidence and of reasonable probability rendered tenable the charge of incest. Fox's analysis, detailed and careful, added the weight of a legal opinion to the more impressionistic view of Miss Mayne. The trade biographies by André Maurois and John Drinkwater followed not long after, Maurois accepting the *Astarte* theme, the other differing.

Nor was Drinkwater entirely alone in his dissatisfaction with the evidence. In an introduction to a collection of Byron's letters, Jacques Barzun indicated that he was not impressed by the case Lord Lovelace and his successors had made, and felt their evidence was inconclusive.

In 1953 Leslie Marchand published what is recognized as the definitive biography in terms of scholarship and thoroughness. As a consequence of his extensive investigation he concluded that although by its very nature incest does not allow of proof in the fullest legal sense, if Byron's letters to Lady Melbourne had any meaning at all, he could hardly see how they referred to anything other than an affair with Augusta (*Byron*, 1 : 404*n*). Against his dispassionate, reasoned, and exhaustive scholarship succeeding biographers have made but slight impression.

Since the publication of Marchand's book, some hitherto unavailable material has become accessible. In consequence, during the past decade both Malcolm Elwin and Doris Langley Moore have published biographies that challenge the accepted view. Their arguments derive from more complete information than was available to Marchand in 1953 about Lady Byron and her modes of thought and emotional make-up, as well as about some of the means she employed to obtain material from Augusta. Each author concludes—though not quite in so many words—that Lady Byron constructed an elaborate paranoidal system on generally weak premises. Elwin's arguments, however, appear to go rather to the system and its fabrication than to the premises themselves, while Mrs. Moore's work comprises an extensive analysis of correspondence.

The studies by G. Wilson Knight take a somewhat different tack. John Cordy Jeaffreson, who wrote in the very middle of the Victorian period, had suggested that Byron's numerous affairs with ladies were mostly Platonic (p. 164). Knight finds much that is credible in this point of view and, perhaps partly to offset the poet's generally unfavorable publicity, undertakes to celebrate Byron's Christian virtues—and indeed the poet had a few. Platonism, however, seemed not to be a sufficient answer, and to explain what he regarded as Byron's indifference to women Knight elaborated a hypothesis that the poet in 1813 engaged in a reckless homosexual attachment to some unnamed partner. (See *Christian Virtues*, pp. 208–32 passim, 262–63; *Byron's Marriage*, pp. 247–57 passim.)

The problem lies in the fact that everything, including his own admissions, indicates Byron found himself in a very serious scrape. If the scrape did not involve incest or homosexuality, what was it all about? Only Richard Edgcumbe, in his discussion in *Byron: The Last Phase,* seriously has suggested that some other woman than Augusta might have been the source of trouble. For the lack of any obvious lady he postulated a resumption of the poet's love affair with Mary Chaworth, a view Mayne peremptorily attacked in one of her appendices.

8   Barzun, pp. 56–57.

Chapter 2

1   M. W. Patterson, *Sir Francis Burdett and His Times,* p. 392. Lord Eldon's memorandum of 1 April 1823 informed King George IV that he owed Coutts £45,000. A. Aspinall, *The Letters of King George IV,* 1 : 483.

2   Chew, pp. 258–59; John Drinkwater, *Charles James Fox,* pp. 308–09.

3   E. Keble Chatterton, *England's Greatest Statesman: A Life of William Pitt, 1759–1806,* pp. 267–68; Jasper Ridley, *Lord Palmerston,* pp. 74–75.

4   Marchand, 2 : 529, 3 : 1127.

5   Chew, pp. 258–59; Jeaffreson, p. 227.

6   Peter Gunn, *My Dearest Augusta,* pp. 32–34 passim.

7   Lady Charlotte Bury, *The Diary of a Lady-in-Waiting,* 2 : 325, cf. also p. 359.

8   Marchand, 1 : 347, 352, 384; Thomas Creevey, *The Creevey Papers,* p. 259.

9   Earl of Albemarle, *Fifty Years of My Life,* p. 71.

10 T. Moore, p. 157, Journal entry, 1 December 1813.

11 Patterson, *Burdett,* 2 : 481; cf. also Evelyn Ashley, *The Life and Correspondence of . . . Lord Palmerston,* 1 : 87.

12 John Wilson Croker, *The Correspondence and Diaries . . . ,* 1 : 194.

13 Chew, pp. 258–59; Jeaffreson, p. 227.

14 Chew, p. 16.

15 Earl of Bessborough, *Lady Bessborough and Her Family Circle,* p. 360.

16 Marchand, 2 : 515. ". . . deeply ingrained in his unconscious mind a gloomy Calvinism made him feel that the majority of men and him-

self in particular had the mark of Cain on them and were slated
for damnation."

17 Prothero, 2 : 401, and Appendix, pp. 463–92.
18 Murray, 1 : 253, to Lady Melbourne, 29 April 1813.

Chapter 3

1 *Authentic Records of the Court of England for the Last Seventy
Years,* p. 67. Cf. Lytton Strachey, *Queen Victoria* (London: Chatto
and Windus, 1921), pp. 7–12 passim.
2 D. L. Moore, *Accounts,* p. 101.
3 *The Complete Peerage of England, Scotland, Ireland, Great Britain,
and the United Kingdom.* 13 vols. (London: The St. Catherine Press,
1912–   ), s.v. "Rancliffe."
4 Bury, *Diary,* pp. 4, 22, 69–70.
5 Harriette Wilson, *Harriette Wilson's Memoirs of Herself and Others,*
pp. vi–ix passim.
6 Lord David Cecil, *Lord Melbourne,* pp. 86–90 passim, 120–21.
7 Murray, 1 : 160. When Lord Oxford protested the persistent presence
of Byron and expostulated with his lady, Lady Oxford replied that
she might install the poet permanently and, as Byron wrote, his lordship "quietly ate his own words."
8 Ibid., pp. 181–212 passim.
9 D. L. Moore, *Accounts,* appendix 6, pp. 480–81.
10 Marchand, 2 : 606, 627.
11 Origo, Introduction, pp. xii–xv passim.

Chapter 4

1 Marchand, 1 : 25, 54–55; D. L. Moore, *Accounts,* p. 194n.
2 D. L. Moore, *Accounts,* p. 194n.
3 Lord John Russell, *Memoirs, Journals, and Correspondence of
Thomas Moore,* p. 265; T. Moore, p. 20.
4 Medwin, p. 3; Blessington, p. 5; Elwin, p. 407, quoting Hobhouse.
5 Mayne, pp. 20–21.
6 T. Moore, pp. 7, 151.
7 D. L. Moore, *Accounts,* p. 77.
8 Mayne, pp. 18–19.
9 T. Moore, pp. 19–20.

10 Ibid., p. 20.

11 Ibid., pp. 19–22 passim.

12 Medwin, p. 8: "an admirable horseman."

13 T. Moore, p. 11.

14 Elwin, p. 127. For a comprehensive account of Byron's sexuality see D. L. Moore, *Accounts,* appendix 2. A psychiatrist's appraisal, which differs from hers in no important respect, is to be found in *British Med. Journal* 2 (1974): 714–16. Dr. H. R. Rollin classifies Byron's make-up as a "polymorph-perversity." Dr. Rollin's discussion of psychological mechanisms does not depart significantly from the usual attributions—poor family history and a rather traumatic childhood.

15 Marchand, 1 : 125.

16 Quennell, 1 : 252.

17 T. Moore, p. 173.

18 Marchand, 2 : 497.

19 Scattered references to his teeth occur throughout letters and journals. Many of his letters from Italy specify types of tooth powder he wishes sent over from England.

20 For example, the Iron Duke, who comes down to us in heroic proportions, was five feet, nine inches tall, just a half-inch or so taller than Byron. Elizabeth Longford, *Wellington: The Years of the Sword* (New York: Harper and Row, 1970), p. 100.

21 Murray, 1 : 257.

22 Knight, *Byron's Marriage,* p. 56.

23 Ibid., pp. 247–57; D. L. Moore, *Accounts,* p. 89, and appendix 2, pp. 437–59.

24 D. L. Moore, *Accounts,* p. 77.

25 T. Moore, p. 151, Journal entry of 17 November 1813: "I wish I were in the country, to take exercise,—instead of being obliged to *cool* by abstinence. . . ." Byron's sexual prowess has probably received undue attention. Although he may have been at times rather indulgent, vigorous young bachelors rarely undertake to scotch legends of their virility. But at the time of this entry, which continues, Byron seems to have been struggling for celibacy: "But the worst is, the devil always came with it ["a little accession of flesh"],—till I starved him out,—and I will *not* be the slave of *any* appetite."

26 Quennell, 1 : ix; Maurois, p. 287.

27 Lord Lovelace refers to it as "a ruinous education." *Astarte,* p. 132.

28 T. Moore, p. 153; Prothero, 2 : 340.

29 Mayne, pp. 194–95, and note.
30 Ibid., p. 151.
31 Bury, *Diary,* 1 : 399, 2 : 293.
32 Murray, 1 : 226.
33 Prothero, 2 : 405.
34 T. Moore, pp. 118, 152, 153 ("aut Caesar, aut nihil"), 154 ("actions—actions, I say and not writing"), 157 ("I cannot stimulate myself to a speech").

Chapter 5

 1 Mayne, p. 244.
 2 Gunn, *My Dearest Augusta,* pp. 32–34.
 3 Ibid., p. 43.
 4 Ibid., pp. 37–42 passim.
 5 Quennell, 1 : 11, to Augusta, 25 October 1804.
 6 Elwin, p. 130n.
 7 Aspinall, *Correspondence of George, Prince of Wales,* 6 : 361, 3 February 1809.
 8 Mayne, p. 453.
 9 Prothero, 2 : 199, to Augusta, 26 March 1813.
10 Ibid., pp. 10–11 and note, to Augusta, 30 August 1811.
11 Quennell, 1 : 161–62.
12 Fox, p. 80n.
13 Murray, 1 : 161; Prothero, 2 : 226–27.
14 Prothero, 2 : 407n.
15 Marchand, 1 : 395–96.
16 Ibid., p. 395.
17 Elwin, pp. 161, 167.
18 Marchand, 1 : 404; see also Mayne, p. 245, quoting Lord Lovelace, "Her moral ideas were much confused."
19 Lovelace, p. 25.
20 Blessington, pp. 19, 155–56.

Chapter 6

 1 Aspinall, *Correspondence, P of W,* 3 : 404n.
 2 *Memoirs of the 10th Royal Hussars,* p. 507.

3   C. M. Franzero, *Beau Brummell*, p. 28.

4   Ibid., p. 29.

5   *10th Hussars*, p. 98.

6   Aspinall, *Correspondence, P of W*, 3 : 404.

7   *10th Hussars*, pp. 81–82, 89.

8   Ibid., pp. 91–94 passim.

9   Ibid., p. 96.

10 Aspinall, *Correspondence, P of W*, 4 : 78.

11 *Authentic Records*, p. 93; cf. Creevey, *Papers*, p. 113.

12 Aspinall, *Correspondence, P of W*, 4 : 84.

13 Ibid., p. 119.

14 Ibid., 3 : 252.

15 Ibid., 5 : 100–01.

16 Quennell, 1 : 7, 11.

17 Aspinall, *Correspondence, P of W*, 5 : 414.

18 Elwin, p. 171.

19 Fox, pp. 79–80, Byron to Lady Melbourne, 1 May 1815, though it is not certain that the allusion is to Leigh and Augusta.

20 Gunn, *My Dearest Augusta*, p. 40.

21 Elwin, p. 171.

22 Aspinall, *Correspondence, P of W*, 6 : 210, Augusta to McMahon, 7 September 1807.

23 Ibid., p. 296, Prince to Duke of York, 4 August 1808.

24 Ibid., p. 361, Prince to McMahon, 3 February 1809.

25 D. L. Moore, *Accounts*, pp. 46, 122–23. Moore states that indeed Leigh faced court-martial as a result of various peculations.

26 Prothero, 2 : 10–11, note 1.

27 Marchand, 1 : 299.

28 Murray, 162; cf. Elwin, p. 171.

Chapter 7

1   Countess of Airlie, *In Whig Society*, p. 88; Cecil, *Melbourne*, p. 56.

2   Airlie, *Whig Society*, p. 90.

3   Bessborough, *Lady Bessborough*, p. 130.

4   Ibid., pp. 130–31.

5   Cecil, *Melbourne*, pp. 86–87.

6   Airlie, *Whig Society*, p. 91.

7 First Earl of Minto, *Life and Letters of Sir Gilbert Elliott, First Earl of Minto,* 3 : 361.
8 Harriette Wilson, *Memoirs,* p. 306.
9 Airlie, *Whig Society,* p. 117.
10 Ibid., p. 119.
11 Ibid., p. 146.
12 Bessborough, *Lady Bessborough,* p. 232.
13 Drinkwater, p. 210; Murray, 1 : 100 ("Have I not complied with her [Lady Bessborough's] own professed wish?"); Blyth, *Caro,* pp. 125–30 passim.
14 Marchand, 1 : 331.
15 Jeaffreson, p. 150.
16 Airlie, *Whig Society,* p. 143.
17 Murray, 1 : 71. "*They* are safely deposited in Ireland."
18 Ibid., p. 129.
19 Barzun, pp. 56–57.

Chapter 8

1 Elwin, pp. 131–33 passim; D. L. Moore, *Accounts,* p. 101*n.*
2 Lovell, quoting Hobhouse, p. 63.
3 Murray, 1 : 189.
4 Elwin, p. 147.
5 Cecil, *Melbourne,* p. 106.
6 Marchand, 1 : 472–74 passim.
7 Prothero, 3 : 86–87, to Moore, 31 May 1814.
8 Marchand, 1 : 439.
9 Murray, 1 : 203, to Lady Melbourne, 17 October 1813.
10 Harriette Wilson, *Memoirs,* pp. 594–95.
11 Lovell, pp. 90–93.
12 Ibid., pp. 135–36.

Chapter 9

1 Mayne, p. 453; Marchand, 1 : 446.
2 Elwin, p. 130*n.*
3 Ibid.
4 Murray, 1 : 249.
5 Marchand, 1 : 443–44.

6 Mayne, p. 453; Elwin, p. 165.

7 Lord Glenbervie, *The Diaries of Sylvester Douglas, Lord Glenbervie,*
   3 : 112-13.

8 Charles Mackay, *Medora Leigh,* p. 127.

9 Elwin, p. 311.

10 Hobhouse, *Recollections,* 1 : 105.

11 Murray, 1 : 251.

12 Marchand, 1 : 169, 455. Webster's note on "She Walks in Beauty" had
    the apparent advantage of first-hand observation. However, his
    memory of the event may not be accurate; and since he was neither
    notoriously intelligent nor excessively sober, one has to weigh his
    recollection against that of Isaac Nathan, who thought there was some
    kind of understanding between Byron and Augusta regarding the
    lady to whom the poem was addressed. Nathan thought it was for
    Augusta, but obviously there was no reason for her to be in mourn-
    ing. There were, of course, two Mrs. Wilmots, the first the wife of
    Robert John Wilmot, cousin of Byron, the other a writer who sub-
    sequently became Lady Dacre. It was the second Mrs. Wilmot, the
    minor writer and the author of a failed play, of whom Byron wrote
    that "she is a Swan."

Chapter 10

1 The last date on which one can be certain that Augusta was in London can be derived from Byron's letter to Moore, 8 July 1813, in
   which he remarks that her presence is a great comfort to him
   (T. Moore, p. 140). She probably did not leave immediately, but only
   speculation exists as to how much longer she remained.

2 It is not at all certain that some kind of communication from Augusta
   to Byron occurred, but see the discussion in chapter 11.

3 Murray, 1 : 168.

4 T. Moore, pp. 143, 144.

Chapter 11

1 Prothero, 2 : 226, 307*n*.

2 Although married to William Sloane Stanley, this lady was referred
   to as "Lady Gertrude Sloane" by her contemporaries.

3 Prothero, 1 : 65.

4   Ibid., 2 : 226–27.
5   Murray, 1 : 161.
6   Ibid., p. 162.
7   Ibid.
8   Hobhouse, *Recollections,* 1 : 345.
9   Airlie, *Whig Society,* p. 156.
10 Lovell, p. 70, account of Sir Robert Ainslie.
11 T. Moore, p. 140.
12 Ibid., p. 141.
13 Ibid.
14 D. L. Moore, *Accounts,* pp. 199–200.

Chapter 12

1   D. L. Moore, *Accounts,* pp. 199–200.
2   T. Moore, p. 141.
3   D. L. Moore, *Accounts,* pp. 201–02. Mrs. Moore reports that Byron
    made purchases on 24 July, the day before he wrote the letter to
    Tom Moore. If this is correct and a tradesman did not mistake the
    day, Byron's dash into the country was even shorter than described.
    If it comes to what is known rather than inferred, the exact informa-
    tion is only that Byron traveled by night and came or went through
    Epping Forest, which lies along the road to Six Mile Bottom—and
    several other places.
4   Murray, 1 : 167.
5   Ibid., p. 168.
6   Prothero, 2 : 244–45.
7   Ibid., 3 : 99–100.
8   Murray, 1 : 168. While in his correspondence with Lady Melbourne
    Byron used "Lady C." to refer to Lady Caroline Lamb, it strains the
    imagination to conceive that Augusta was proposing to take Caro
    along as a chaperon. On the other hand no other "Lady C." occurs
    to one as being likely, and if there was even a whiff of suspicion that
    Lady Caroline was about to go with Byron and Augusta Lady Mel-
    bourne's vigorous objections would have been thoroughly under-
    standable. However low her regard for Caroline, Lady Melbourne's
    great anxiety would have been for the protection of her son William
    and the prevention of any scandal in any fashion related to him. If

Lady C. was not Caroline Lamb the implication can be only that
Byron was involved with some other lady whom the initial designated.

9   Elwin, p. 438, quoting Augusta to Hobhouse.

Chapter 13

1   Marchand, 1 : 398.
2   Ibid., p. 399.
3   T. Moore, p. 140.
4   Marchand, 1 : 398–99. Cf. D. L. Moore, *Accounts,* p. 205.
5   Murray, 1 : 168.
6   Ibid., p. 172.
7   Prothero, 2 : 327*n*.
8   Medwin, p. 152.
9   Murray, 1 : 169, 175.
10 Ibid., p. 179.
11 T. Moore, p. 150, Journal entry, 17 November 1813.
12 Murray, 1 : 179.
13 Prothero, 2 : 264–65.
14 Marchand, 1 : 144–45; Marchand records the exchange with a Mr.
    Twiddie, a most unlikely name for a brawler. Russell's *Memoirs of
    T. Moore,* 2 : 229, relates that Davies acted as second in an aborted
    duel with Harry Greville; the nature of the disagreement is not re-
    corded. Davies also participated in Byron's earlier challenge to Moore
    himself.
15 Murray, 1 : 218.
16 Ibid., p. 175.
17 Ibid., p. 182.
18 J. S. Fletcher, *The History of the St. Leger Stakes,* p. 107.
19 Murray, 1 : 185.
20 Ibid., pp. 197–98.
21 Ibid., p. 210.
22 Prothero, 2 : 269.
23 Murray, 2 : 197.
24 Quennell, 1 : 280, "that wide word," love.
25 Prothero, 2 : 362.
26 T. Moore, pp. 159, 161, Journal entries, 17 December 1813.
27 Murray, 1 : 223, 224, 227.

28 Ibid., p. 223.
29 Lady Frances Shelley, *The Diary of Lady Frances Shelley,* 1 : 52.
30 Ibid., p. 53.
31 Ibid., pp. 53, 82, 81.
32 Prothero, 3 : 12.
33 Ibid., p. 275; Rev. James T. Hodgson, *Memoir of the Rev. Francis Hodgson,* 1 : 272–74 passim; D. L. Moore, *Accounts,* p. 202. Moore asserts the sum advanced to Hodgson was in reality £1,240.
34 T. Moore, p. 177.
35 Prothero, 3 : 21–27, 33, 35, letters to Murray on 4, 5, and 7 February.
36 T. Moore, p. 182, Byron to Moore, 12 March 1814.
37 Lovell, pp. 55–56.
38 Prothero, 3 : 99–100. Byron refers to a transfer of this sum. However, D. L. Moore, who has studied his disbursements minutely, states that he had transferred funds to Augusta as early as the preceding autumn, though she does not furnish a specific date or cite the nature of her evidence. At some date, she writes, the poet had provided Augusta with £1,000, and by the spring of 1814 the total had reached £3,000. However, none of Byron's published letters refers to an earlier transaction, while his letter of 9 May makes it appear that the transfer of funds had taken place very recently. His subsequent letter of 24 June reinforces this interpretation.
39 Murray, 1 : 241.
40 Marchand, 2 : 590; also Murray, 1 : 244.
41 Marchand, 1 : 437.
42 Prothero, 3 : 55.
43 Murray, 1 : 273.
44 Prothero, 3 : 67.
45 T. Moore, p. 175.
46 Murray, 1 : 251.
47 While the text questions the exact meaning of the "Ape" letter, Byron's letters of 13 and 16 January 1814 to Lady Melbourne (Quennell, 1 : 261–66 passim) as well as that of 10 June (ibid., p. 288) imply that he may have been accepting responsibility for the pregnancy: e.g., "You *have* done everything in your power . . . to make me act rationally; but there is an old saying . . . 'Whom the gods wish to destroy they first madden.' "
48 Murray, 1 : 254.

Chapter 14

1   T. Moore, p. 191.
2   Ibid., pp. 411–12. On 14 June 1814, Byron had written to Moore, "Keep the Journal, I care not what becomes of it."
3   Ibid., p. 143, 22 August 1813, p. 176.
4   Ibid., Journal, p. 151.
5   Ibid., p. 160.
6   Murray, 1 : 215.
7   Earl of Malmesbury, *Memoirs of an Ex-Minister,* 1 : 24.
8   Murray, 1 : 215.
9   Ibid., p. 164.
10 *Complete Peerage,* note under subject "Tankerville." Ossulstone was the junior or courtesy title of heirs apparent to the earldom of Tankerville.
11 Murray, 1 : 216.
12 Ibid., pp. 254–55.
13 Ibid., p. 264.
14 Ibid., pp. 218, 245, 256.
15 Ibid., pp. 257, 261, 264.
16 Ibid., p. 217.
17 Ibid., p. 256. The PS. *ad.* is quite a long one, and is the second appended to Byron's letter of 1 May:
    "It, indeed, puzzles me to account for ——: it is true she married a fool, but she *would* have him; they agreed, and agree very well, and I never heard a complaint, but many vindications of him. As for me, brought up as I was, and sent into the world as I was, both physically and morally, nothing better would be expected, and it is odd that I always had a foreboding and I remember when a child reading the history about a *marriage* I will tell you of when we meet, asking ma mère why I should not marry X.
    "Since writing this I have received yᵉ enclosed. I will not trouble you with another, but *this* will, I think, enable you to appreciate *her* better. She seems very triste, and I need hardly add that the reflection does not enliven me."
18 Prothero, 2 : 272–85 passim.
19 Ibid., p. 300.

20 Murray, 1 : 268–72 and 287–91 passim.
21 Two other instances of Byron's use of the "cross" or "plus" symbol
    appear in his correspondence with Augusta. One letter was in 1819,
    the other in 1820, and both of them are incredibly amorous, with
    expressions of undying love and all that sort of thing. Both before and
    after these two exceptional instances his other letters to Augusta are
    simple, straightforward, and kindly. Further reference to them appears
    in chapter 26. It may be mentioned here that the dates of the "X"
    letters correspond to a time when the poet's attachment to Teresa
    Guiccioli was comparatively fresh and that he was using similar sym-
    bols in his correspondence with her.
22 Mayne, p. 236. See also the illustration facing p. 176 in Gunn, *My
    Dearest Augusta.*
23 Quennell, 2 : 362.
24 T. Moore, pp. 198–99 passim.
25 On one occasion Lady Caroline stated that Byron showed her letters
    and revealed things that were unmentionable (Marchand, 1 : 460*n.*).
    Since this took place before the surreptitious interview with Anna-
    bella, one may be sure that nothing Byron told her would have suf-
    fered diminution as Caro transmitted the story. On the occasion of
    the unmentionable revelations the poet was doing his best to break
    off the relationship with Lady Caroline.
26 Marchand, 2 : 581–85 passim.

Chapter 15

1 Murray, 1 : 162.
2 Quennell, 1 : 282–83.
3 Phillips's sittings book, entries for the year 1813–14. The portraits
   present an almost impenetrable tangle. In just less than a year Thomas
   Phillips seems to have produced six portraits of Byron, two sets of
   three each. The first seems to have been *The Portrait of a Nobleman
   in Albanian Dress,* about which Byron wrote Lady Melbourne in early
   July. This portrait depicts him with mustache and Albanian or Suliot
   or Arnaut costume, and except for an early painting Phillips's set of
   "Albanian Dress" is the only portraiture in standing position. They
   are three-quarter length and two are large, one in the National

Portrait Gallery, the other at the British Embassy at Athens. A much smaller version is at the publishing house of Murray.

The other set, apparently also three versions of the same pose and costume, depicts the poet seated. The costume consists of an open shirt with flaring collar, what seems to be an embroidered or studded jacket that is just visible, all covered by a dark (maroon?) cloak. Since they were all painted within a few months of each other, obviously the question of which is the original is almost academic. One of these belongs to Colonel Byron, bears Phillips's monogram and the date 1813. This painting apparently is the one entered in the sittings book as #372, later exhibited with the number 172 in the exhibition of the Royal Academy in April 1814, and subsequently in the possession of Augusta Leigh and then of the successive Lords Byron. One almost identical and of the same dimensions hangs in Newstead Abbey, and another is in the possession of Mr. John Murray—a version D. L. Moore regards as the "original." It is possible there may have been yet other versions.

4   Royal Academy of Art, Catalogue of Exhibition, April 1814.

Chapter 16

1   Murray, 1 : 214, to Lady Melbourne, 22 November 1813.
2   T. Moore, p. 155, Journal entry, 26 November 1813.
3   Murray, 1 : 175, to Lady Melbourne, 21 August 1813.
4   National Portrait Gallery Catalogue. Westall's portrait is described as being 36¼ x 28 inches. Phillips's sittings book lists the dimensions of all the portraits of 1813–14 (except for the one or more "in Albanian Dress") as 36 x 28 inches.
5   T. Moore, p. 383.
6   Ibid., p. 133, Byron to Murray, 21 April 1813.
7   Archives, Nottingham Public Library, Byron to T. Asham, Cornhill, 14 December 1813.
8   Prothero, 3 : 575, Byron to Murray, 16 February 1816: "Have you got your picture from Phillips?"
9   Murray, 1 : 217, to Lady Melbourne, 25 November 1813.
10 Ibid., p. 224, to Lady Melbourne, 8 January 1814.
11 Ibid., p. 217, Byron to Murray, 25 November 1813.

Chapter 17

1 T. Moore, p. 149.
2 For example, the simple seal on the letter of 24 March (?) 1813, to Murray. Archives, Nottingham Public Libraries.
3 Roe-Byron Collection at Newstead Abbey. G-25, a letter from Byron, bears a seal that seems to reveal quarterings on the shield.
4 Seals on letters in the British Museum, B 2623 (Cat. XI-16), 4729 (XI-234), and 4752 (f-10), resemble the simple seal cited in note 2 above where any of the wax is preserved. Color of the wax varies, but usually is red.
5 Prothero, 3 : 7, note 2.
6 Ibid.
7 Murray, 1 : 223–28 passim.
8 Lovelace, p. 37.
9 Aspinall, *Letters, George IV,* 2 : 664, addressed to the Duke of Rutland at Chevely Park. There are many others in the same period.
10 A. M. W. Stirling, *Coke of Norfolk and His Friends,* p. 498.

Chapter 18

1 Prothero, 3 : 8, Byron to Murray, 7 January 1814.
2 *Complete Peerage,* note under subject "Rutland."
3 It may be noted, however, that Lady Gertrude Sloane had been one of the sponsors of Augusta's second daughter, and since Augusta apparently was keeping sponsorship within the family it may not occasion remark that the Duchess of Rutland was Medora's sponsor. This point, however, does not cloud the issue of the selection of the names, Elizabeth and Medora.
4 Lovell, pp. 87–88, quoting Lord Lovelace, "from a Lady 'not in all respects trustworthy.'"

Chapter 19

1 Glenbervie, *Diaries,* 2 : 72. Lady Glenbervie described the duties of a Woman of the Bed Chamber as being to "sit in the worst place at the

table, talk to the most disagreeable person and make everybody do what they don't like."

2 Archives, Windsor Palace (letter to the author, November 1973).

3 Howarth, pp. 236–37, 21 September 1818.

4 Aspinall, *Correspondence, P of W,* 3 : 262n.

5 Aspinall, *Letters, George IV,* p. 460n.

6 Lady Jerningham, *The Jerningham Letters,* 1 : 229.

Chapter 20

1 Quennell, 1 : 293.

2 Murray, 1 : 224.

3 Quennell, 1 : 280, to Lady Melbourne, 30 April 1814.

4 Maurois, p. 245.

5 Murray, 1 : 225, 8 January 1814.

6 T. Moore, p. 190.

7 Murray, 1 : 260, 21 June 1814: "What shall I do about Ph. and her epistles?"

8 Lovell, pp. 82–95 passim.

9 Marchand, 1 : 171; Prothero, 3 : 107.

10 T. Moore, p. 194, 3 August 1814.

11 Prothero, 3 : 132, to Murray, 7 September 1814.

12 Quennell, 1 : 290–92.

13 Ibid., pp. 306–07, to Lady Melbourne, 4 November 1814.

14 T. Moore, p. 197.

15 Marchand, 2 : 503.

16 Marchand, 1 : 187, 2 : 502.

17 Elwin, p. 247.

18 Hobhouse, *Recollections,* 1 : 197.

19 Marchand, 2 : 532, 549–50.

20 Lovelace, p. 163. Augusta is reported to have returned to London 15 November.

21 Elwin, p. 357.

22 Ibid., p. 307.

23 R. H. Gronow, *Reminiscences and Recollections of Captain Gronow,* p. 121.

24 Marchand, 2 : 545. The first bailiff seems to have arrived about the first week in November.

25   Elwin, pp. 352–72 passim; Lovelace, pp. 197–262 passim.
26   Hobhouse, *Recollections,* 2 : 245: "A determination to be wicked."
27   Elwin, pp. 358, 378.
28   Marchand, 1 : 229.
29   Elwin (p. 460) states that Lady Byron broke off relations with
     Augusta within two days after the interview with Lady Caroline.
30   Elwin, p. 461.
31   Elwin, pp. 425–26; Lovelace, pp. 5–8.
32   Hobhouse, *Recollections,* 2 : 349.
33   Elwin, p. 428.
34   Ibid., pp. 439–40.
35   Marchand, 2 : 590, quoting Hobhouse MS of 22 March 1816, in Berg
     MS Collection, New York Public Library.
36   Elwin, p. 387.
37   Ibid., p. 404.
38   Murray, 1 : 307.
39   Ibid., p. 308.
40   Marchand, 2 : 589.
41   Hobhouse, *Recollections,* 1 : 325.
42   Ibid., p. 337, 27 April 1816.
43   Marchand, 2 : 590.
44   Hobhouse, *Recollections,* 2 : 340.
45   Fox, pp. 147–52 passim.
46   Elwin, pp. 424–25; Lovelace, p. 217, also letter of Mrs. Clermont,
     p. 324, note 4.
47   Marchand, 2 : 598.
48   Jeaffreson, pp. 227–30 passim; Chew, pp. 258–59.

Chapter 21

1   Barzun, pp. 56–57.
2   Fox, p. 119.
3   Elwin, p. 144.
4   Mayne, *Lady Byron,* p. 223; Murray, 2 : 453–54.
5   Airlie, *Whig Society,* p. 172.
6   Ibid., pp. 177–78.
7   Earl of Lytton, *Life of Edward Bulwer, First Lord Lytton,* p. 120.
8   It should be noted that this discussion of Lady Caroline's attitudes

and motives corresponds quite closely with Doris Langley Moore's view of her activity (*The Late Lord Byron,* pp. 230–50 passim). In the light of what the lady said and did, no more charitable interpretation is possible.

Chapter 22

1 Mayne, pp. 226–27, 235.
2 Elizabeth Longford, *Queen Victoria: Born to Succeed* (New York: Harper and Row, 1965), p. 17.
3 Longford, *Wellington,* p. 170; Cecil Woodham-Smith, *Queen Victoria* (New York: Knopf, 1972), pp. 18, 112.
4 Robert Southey, *New Letters of Robert Southey,* ed. Kenneth Curry (New York: Columbia University Press, 1965), 2 : 327.
5 T. Moore, p. 388.
6 Ibid., p. 182. "I neither have nor shall take the least *public* notice, nor permit anyone else to do so." *"Silence* is the only answer. . . . I care little for attacks, but will not submit to defense."
7 Mayne, p. 235.

Chapter 23

1 Marchand, 2 : 589.
2 Mayne, *Lady Byron,* pp. 234–41 passim.
3 Ibid., p. 239.
4 Lovelace, pp. 229–45 passim.
5 Ibid., p. 229.
6 Ibid., p. 231.
7 Ibid., p. 236.
8 Ibid., pp. 235–37.
9 Ibid.
10 Mayne, *Lady Byron,* p. 253.
11 Lovelace, p. 21*n*.
12 Ibid.
13 Mayne, *Lady Byron,* p. 506.
14 Ibid. Maurois (p. 547) furnishes a short version of the meeting, while Gunn's account (*My Dearest Augusta,* pp. 257–63) is the fullest available.

15 See reference to Gunn in note 14. See also Jeaffreson, p. 493. Elwin
    treats Lady Byron rather harshly: "she never in her life neglected an
    opportunity to assert the infallibility of her own opinions" (p. 190).
    He writes also of "her subsequent relentlessness in building up her
    case against Augusta" (p. 238).

16 The two excerpts appear in Jeaffreson, p. 493, Annabella's to Augusta
    from Brighton, 12 April 1851, and Augusta's reply from St. James's
    Palace, 26 April.

Chapter 24

1   Marchand, 1 : 404*n*.
2   T. Moore, pp. 411–12.
3   Elwin, p. 413.
4   Theodore G. Ehrsam, *Major Byron*, pp. 167–76 passim.
5   Byron refers to a considerable number of forgeries prepared by "a man
    named Johnson" (T. Moore, p. 250). See also D. L. Moore, *Accounts*,
    pp. 121*n* and 129*n*.
6   Knight, *Byron's Marriage*, pp. 159–97 passim.
7   Hobhouse, *Recollections*, 3 : 173; 4 March 1827 is the date of Hob-
    house's entry and while he does not state precisely the reason Lady
    Cowper showed him the letters, it was a time when he was quite up-
    set about both published and projected biographies of his friend.
8   Murray, 1 : 129.
9   Ibid., p. 136.
10 Lovelace, p. 106.
11 Lovell, p. 353.

Chapter 25

1   T. Moore, p. 160, Journal entry: "Mine is drawn much from *existence*
    also."
2   Ibid., p. 154, Journal entry: "the mighty stir about scribbling and
    scribes."
3   Quennell, 1 : 204. Byron to E. D. Clarke, 15 December 1813.
4   Ibid., p. 280.
5   Murray, 1 : 255.
6   Ibid., p. 254.

7   Ibid., p. 300.

8   *The Poetical Works of Lord Byron,* A New Edition, 6 Volumes (London: John Murray, 1856). See *Manfred,* Act III, sc. iv, note 6, where Murray quotes a letter from Byron in which the poet refers to Lewis's reading of *Faust.*

9   Ibid.

10   Quennell, 1 : 351.

11   T. Moore, p. 258.

12   Prothero, 4 : 80, to Moore, 25 March 1817.

13   T. Moore, pp. 249, 260, 273.

14   Mayne, *Lady Byron,* p. 271.

15   Quennell, 1 : 357, Journal entry, 29 September 1816. The journal of his trip through the Alps was designed primarily for Augusta's benefit.

16   Prothero, 4 : 5, 33, letters to Hanson on 11 November and 26 December 1816. In the second he admonishes his attorney: ". . . pray take all proper and legal measures without delay . . ." to prevent Lady Byron's bringing Ada to the continent.

17   Quennell, 2 : 363.

18   Ibid., pp. 368–69.

19   Ibid., pp. 376–77.

20   T. Moore, p. 253.

21   Ibid.

Chapter 26

1   Marchand, 1 : 446*n.*

2   Lovelace, p. 134.

3   Quennell, 2 : 451–52, to Augusta, 17 May 1819. Fox (p. 143) states that this is a copy Lady Byron made of a letter presumably from Byron to Augusta. All letters from the poet to his sister, according to this authority, are taken from *Astarte.*

Chapter 27

1   Lovelace, p. 240.

2   Fox, p. 80*n.*

3   Mayne, *Lady Byron,* p. 280.

4   Howarth, pp. 204–05, 3 June 1817.

5   Bury, *Diary,* 2 : 189–90.
6   Barzun, pp. 154–56.
7   Lovelace, p. 300.
8   Ibid., p. 302.
9   Mayne, *Lady Byron,* p. 351.
10 Mackay, *Medora Leigh,* p. 127.
11 Archives, Nottingham Public Library. Earl of Chichester to A. Hayward, 21 January 1870: "All the statements in E. M. Leigh's supposed biography as far as they affect her mother are utterly false. . . ."
12 Catherine Turney, *Byron's Daughter,* pp. 194–95.
13 Mayne, *Lady Byron,* p. 309.
14 Lytton, *Bulwer,* 1 : 271, Mrs. Bulwer to Miss Mary Greene, 23 November 1833.
15 Gunn, *My Dearest Augusta,* p. 262.
16 Bury, *Diary,* 2 : 206–07.
17 Ibid., p. 213.
18 Ibid., pp. 242–43.
19 Lytton, *Bulwer,* 1 : 119.
20 Ibid., p. 124.
21 Lytton, *Bulwer,* 1 : 164.

Appendix

1   Medwin, p. 3; Lady Blessington, p. 5.
2   Quennell, 1 : 213.
3   Elwin, p. 236.
4   Ibid., p. 370.
5   Ibid., p. 407.
6   Ibid., p. 356.
7   Marchand, 1 : xvij.
8   Philip M. Dale, *Medical Biographies* (University of Oklahoma Press, 1952), p. 182.
9   Ibid., pp. 182–83.
10 Marchand, 1 : 270, Byron to Hobhouse, 15 May 1811: "we were all clapped."
11 Marchand (1 : 239, 258n, and 260) refers to chills and fever during Byron's first trip to the east. While Byron was in Italy, 1816–1823, there were several episodes of febrile illness about which one cannot

NOTES TO PAGES 237-43

be certain, but almost surely one or more represented either a new
infection or a recurrence of the earlier ones. The first report of fever
during the second Mediterranean residence appears in a letter to
Moore, 10 March 1817 (Quennell, 2 : 397), and thereafter there are
repeated references that differ little.

12 Marchand, 1 : 386. Byron reported in some detail to Lady Melbourne
on the subsequent hemorrhage (Murray, 1 : 155).

13 See Lovell, pp. 226-27, for Fanny Silvestrini's account. Byron's report
appears in a letter to Augusta in Quennell, 2 : 465.

14 Detailed individual accounts appear in Lovell, pp. 560-95. Marchand
summarizes and weighs critically the reports of different witnesses
(3 : 1203-27).

15 Pietro Gamba's summary of the last weeks appears in Hobhouse,
Recollections, 3 : 365-74.

16 The description of Byron's death as his long-time valet, William
Fletcher, recounted it in a letter to Hobhouse does not differ in any
important detail from the Gamba account. For Fletcher's version, con-
sult Lovell, pp. 590, 594-95.

17 Medwin, pp. 287-89.

REFERENCES

Biographies, Memoirs, and Letters of Byron

Barzun, Jacques, ed. *The Selected Letters of Lord Byron.* New York: Farrar, Straus & Young, 1953.

Bigland, Eileen. *Passion for Excitement.* New York: Coward-McCann, 1956.

Blessington, Countess of. *Conversations of Lord Byron with the Countess of Blessington.* Philadelphia: E. L. Carey & A. Hart, 1836.

Brecknock, Albert. *Byron—A Study of the Poet in the Light of New Discoveries.* London: Cecil Palmer, 1926.

Chew, Samuel. *Byron in England: His Fame and After-Fame.* New York: Charles Scribner's Sons, 1924.

Cline, C. L. *Byron, Shelley, and Their Pisan Circle.* Cambridge: Harvard University Press, 1952.

Dallas, Robert Charles. *Recollections of the Life of Lord Byron.* London, 1824.

Drinkwater, John. *The Pilgrim of Eternity.* New York: George H. Doran, 1925.

Edgcumbe, Richard. *Byron: The Last Phase.* New York: Haskell House, 1972. Reprint of 1910 edition.

Elwin, Malcolm. *Lord Byron's Wife.* New York: Harcourt, Brace & World, 1963.

Fox, Sir John C. *The Byron Mystery.* London: Grant Richards, 1924.

Galt, John. *The Life of Lord Byron.* London: J. J. Harper, 1931.

Howarth, R. G., ed. *Letters of George Gordon, Sixth Lord Byron.* New York: E. P. Dutton, 1953.

Jeaffreson, John Cordy. *The Real Lord Byron.* New York: New Amsterdam Book Co., 1898.

Knight, G. Wilson. *Lord Byron: Christian Virtues.* New York: Oxford University Press, 1953.

Knight, G. Wilson. *Lord Byron's Marriage*. New York: Macmillan, 1957.

Lovelace, Mary, Countess of, ed. *Astarte*. London: Christopher's, 1921.

Lovell, Ernest J., Jr. *His Very Self and Voice*. New York: Macmillan, 1954.

Marchand, Leslie A. *Byron: A Biography*. 3 vols. New York: Alfred A. Knopf, 1957.

Maurois, André. *Byron*. New York: D. Appleton, 1930.

Mayne, Ethel Colburn. *Byron*. New York: Charles Scribner's Sons, 1924.

Medwin, Thomas. *Journal of the Conversations of Lord Byron*. New York: Wilder & Campbell, 1824.

Moore, Doris Langley. *The Late Lord Byron*. Philadelphia: Lippincott, 1961.

———. *Lord Byron: Accounts Rendered*. New York: Harper and Row, 1974.

Moore, Thomas. *The Life and Letters of Lord Byron*. New York: Leavitt and Allen, 1857.

Murray, John, ed. *Lord Byron's Correspondence*. 2 vols. London: John Murray, 1922.

Origo, Iris. *Le dernier Amour de Byron*. Paris: Librairie Plon, 1957.

Paston, George, and Quennell, Peter. *To Lord Byron*. London: John Murray, 1939.

Prothero, Rowland E. (Lord Ernle). *The Works of Lord Byron: Letters and Journals*. 6 vols. New York: Octagon Books, 1966.

Quennell, Peter. *Byron: A Self-Portrait*. 2 vols. New York: Charles Scribner's Sons, 1950.

Trelawney, Edward John. *Recollections of the Last Days of Shelley and Byron*. New York: Philosophical Library, 1952.

Related Material

Airlie, Mabell, Countess of. *In Whig Society*. London: Hodder & Stoughton, 1921.

Albemarle, Earl of (George Thomas Keppel). *Fifty Years of My Life*. New York: Henry Holt, 1876.

Ashley, Evelyn. *The Life and Correspondence of Henry John Temple, Lord Palmerston*. 2 vols. London: Richard Bentley & Son, 1879.

Aspinall, A. *The Correspondence of George, Prince of Wales, 1770–1812*. 8 vols. New York: Oxford University Press, 1968.

———. *The Letters of King George IV*. 3 vols. London: Cambridge University Press, 1938.

Authentic Records of the Court of England for the Last Seventy Years. London: J. Phillips, 1832.

Berry, Mary. *Extracts of the Letters and Correspondence of Miss Berry, from the year 1783 to 1852.* Edited by Lady Theresa Lewis. London, 1865.

Bessborough, Earl of, ed., with Aspinall, A. *Lady Bessborough and Her Family Circle.* London: John Murray, 1940.

Blyth, Henry. *Caro: The Fatal Passion.* New York: Coward, McCann & Geoghegan, 1972.

Bury, Lady Charlotte. *The Diary of a Lady-in-Waiting.* Edited by A. Francis Steuart. 2 vols. London: John Lane, The Bodley Head, 1908.

Cecil, Lord David. *Lord Melbourne.* Charter Books. Indianapolis: Bobbs-Merrill, 1962.

Chatterton, E. Keble. *England's Greatest Statesman: A Life of William Pitt, 1759–1806.* Indianapolis: Bobbs-Merrill, 1950.

Creevey, Thomas. *The Creevey Papers: A Selection from the Correspondence and Diaries of the Late Thomas Creevey, M.P., 1798–1838.* Edited by Sir Herbert Maxwell. London: John Murray, 1906.

Croker, John Wilson. *The Correspondence and Diaries of the Late Right Honourable John Wilson Croker, L.L.D., F.R.S.* Edited by Louis J. Jennings. Second edition. London: John Murray, 1885.

Drinkwater, John. *Charles James Fox.* New York: Cosmopolitan Book Corporation, 1928.

Dyce, Alexander. *Recollections of the Table-Talk of Samuel Rogers.* New Southgate, 1887.

Ehrsam, Theodore G. *Major Byron: The Incredible Career of a Literary Forger.* London: John Murray, 1951.

Fletcher, J. S. *The History of the St. Leger Stakes.* London: Hutchinson, n.d.

Ford, Richard. *The Letters of Richard Ford.* Edited by R. E. Prothero. London: John Murray, 1905.

Franzero, Carlo Maria. *Beau Brummell: His Life and Times.* New York: John Day, 1958.

Glenbervie, Lord. *The Diaries of Sylvester Douglas, Lord Glenbervie.* Edited by Francis Bickley. 2 vols. Boston and New York: Houghton-Mifflin, 1928.

Granville, Castalia, Countess of, ed. *Lord Granville Leveson Gower, Private Correspondence, 1781–1821.* New York: E. P. Dutton, 1916.

Gronow, R. H. *The Reminiscences and Recollections of Captain Gronow.*

Abridged and with an introduction by John Raymond. New York: Viking, 1964.

Gunn, Peter. *My Dearest Augusta*. London: The Bodley Head, 1968.

Hobhouse, John Cam (Lord Broughton). *Recollections of a Long Life*. Edited by his daughter, Lady Dorchester. 6 vols. London: John Murray, 1910.

Hodgson, Rev. James T. *Memoir of the Rev. Francis Hodgson*. London: Macmillan, 1878.

Jerningham, Lady. *The Jerningham Letters*. Edited by Egerton Castle. London, 1896.

Lamb, Lady Caroline. *Glenarvon*. Gainesville, Fla.: Scholars' Facsimiles & Reprints, 1972.

Lieven, Princess. *The Unpublished Diary and Political Sketches of Princess Lieven*. Edited by Harold Temperly. London: Jonathan Cape, 1925.

Lytton, Earl of. *The Life of Edward Bulwer, First Lord Lytton*. 2 vols. London: Macmillan, 1913.

Mackay, Charles. *Medora Leigh: A History and Autobiography*. London: Richard Bentley, 1869.

Malmesbury, Earl of. *Memoirs of an Ex-Minister: An Autobiography*. 3 vols. Leipzig: Bernhard Tauchnitz, 1885.

Mayne, Ethel Colburn. *Life and Letters of Anna Isabella, Lady Noel Byron*. New York: Charles Scribner's Sons, 1929.

Memoirs of the 10th Royal Hussars. N.p., n.d. Copy in the Historical Section of the War Office, London.

Minto, Earl of. *Life and Letters of Sir Gilbert Elliott, First Earl of Minto, from 1751 to 1806*. London: Longmans, Green, 1874.

Morgan, Lady. *Lady Morgan's Memoirs*. London: William H. Allen, 1862.

Nathan, Isaac, *Fugitive Pieces and Reminiscences of Lord Byron*. London, 1829.

Patterson, M. W. *Sir Francis Burdett and His Times, 1770–1844*. 2 vols. London: Macmillan, 1931.

Ridley, Jasper. *Lord Palmerston*. London: Panther Books, 1972.

Russell, Lord John, ed. *Memoirs, Journals, and Correspondence of Thomas Moore*. 8 vols. Boston: Little, Brown, 1853.

————. *The Early Correspondence of Lord John Russell*. Edited by Rollo Russell. 2 vols. London: T. Fisher Unwin, 1913.

Shelley, Lady Frances. *The Diary of Lady Frances Shelley*. Edited by Richard Edgcumbe. 2 vols. London: John Murray, 1912.

Stanhope, Lady Hester. *Memoirs of the Lady Hester Stanhope.* London: Henry Colburn, 1845.

Stirling, A. M. W. *Coke of Norfolk and His Friends.* London: John Lane, The Bodley Head, 1912.

Turney, Catherine. *Byron's Daughter: A Biography of Elizabeth Medora Leigh.* New York: Charles Scribner's Sons, 1972.

Wilson, Harriette. *Harriette Wilson's Memoirs of Herself and Others.* New York: Minton, Balch, 1929.

INDEX

Rutland, Duchess of (*cont.*)
Medora, 148; influence at Court, 152; characterized, 153
Rutland, Duke of, xv, 21, 146, 260; owner of filly, Medora, 146; character, 153; respect for Byron, 153

Sanders, Thomas, 134
Scott, Sir Walter, 161
Seymour, Major H.: attacks George Leigh, 45–47
Shelley, Lady Frances, xvi; describes Augusta, 106; dislikes Lady Byron, 107
Shelley, Sir John, xvi; visits Six Mile Bottom, 106; old friend of Leigh, 107; interest in racing, 148
Shelley, Percy Bysshe, 179
Sheridan, R. B., 11, 29
Sloane, Lady Gertrude, xvi, 148, 152, 253; favorite cousin of Augusta, 36; her country house possibly Augusta's refuge, 79, 80, 89
Smith, Sidney, 226
Spencer, Lady Henrietta, 53
Stafford, Marquess and Marchioness of, 121
Stanhope, Lady Hester, 9
Stanley, Lady Gertrude. *See* Sloane, Lady Gertrude
Stowe, Harriet Beecher, 3, 216

Thorwaldsen: statue of Byron, 228
Tooke, Horne, 11
Trelawney, Edward John, 3
Trevanion, John: marries Georgiana Leigh, 226; seduces Medora, elopes, 227

Vaughn, Susan, 63
Villiers, Lady Elizabeth, 53
Villiers, Mrs. Theresa, xvi, 205; hostess to Augusta, 105; reports rumors of incest, 163; joins forces with Lady

Byron, 164, 185–89 passim; possible double role, 186–87, 189

Wales, Caroline, Princess of, xii, 12, 116; political position, 11; Byron at her parties, 29
Wales, Prince of (later George IV), xiii, 36, 84, 146, 221, 225; in politics, 11; gives Leigh Six Mile Bottom, 35; honorary colonel of 10th Hussars, 41; patronage of General Leigh, 41, 49; insists on George Leigh's promotion, 43; appoints George Leigh to Household, 44; dismisses George Leigh, 49, 50; grants stipend to Augusta, 151; high regard for Duke of Rutland, 152; confidence in Miss Elphinstone, 183
Walpole, Horace, 8
Webster, Lady Frances, xvi, 16, 99, 122, 155, 174, 175; moral uncertainty, 10; hostess to Byron, 100; invitation to Augusta, 103; personality and appearance, 103–04; departs for Grampian Hills, 104; ready to elope with Byron, 127; surreptitious correspondence with Byron, 127, 261; identified as "**," 139–40; pseudonym in sonnets, 148
Webster, James Wedderburn, xvi; at Aston, 100; jealousy, 102, 124
Wellington, Duke of, 249
Westall, Richard, 137–38
Wilmot, Robert John, xvi; acquainted with rumors of incest, 163; sides with Lady Byron, 165
Wilmot, Mrs. Robert John (later Lady Wilmot-Horton), xvi, xvii, 83, 228, 253; Medora's sponsor, 72
Wilmot, Mrs. *See* Dacre, Lady
Wilson, Harriette: meets Byron, 65

York, Duke of, 41, 49, 84, 146, 221; trade in commissions, 43–44; love affair with Duchess of Rutland, 152